Praise for

Read 'Em and Weep:
A Bedside Poker Companion

"A can't-put-it-down collection . . . a sociopolitical look at poker through the eyes of an eclectic pot of interesting writers. . . . Read 'em."
—*Arkansas Democrat-Gazette*

"Varied and well balanced."
—*Library Journal*

"A straight flush. . . . Literary card sharks from David Mamet to Mark Twain all show their hands in this one, and we're betting you'll love it."
—*Maxim*

Dava Stravinsky

About the Editor

JOHN STRAVINSKY is the author of five books and has written on sports for a number of publications, including the *New York Times Magazine*, the *Village Voice*, the *Wall Street Journal*, *Billiards Digest*, and *Men's Journal*. He lives on Long Island, New York.

READ 'EM and WEEP

A BEDSIDE POKER COMPANION

EDITED BY
JOHN STRAVINSKY

Perennial
An Imprint of HarperCollinsPublishers

To Dava, my Queen of Hearts

HarperCollins books may be purchased for educational, business, or sales promotional use. For information please write: Special Markets Department, Harper-Collins Publishers Inc., 10 East 53rd Street, New York, NY 10022.

First Perennial edition published 2005.

Designed by Elliott Beard

The Library of Congress has catalogued the hardcover as follows:

Read 'em and weep: a bedside poker companion / edited by John Stravinsky.—1st ed.

    p.   cm.
   ISBN 0-06-055958-6
   1. Poker—Literary collections. 2. American literature. 3. English literature.
I. Title: Read 'em and weep. II. Stravinsky, John.
PS509.P62R43   2004
810.8'0357—dc22   2003060800

ISBN 0-06-055959-4 (pbk.)

05 06 07 08 09 ❖/RRD 10 9 8 7 6 5 4 3 2

ACKNOWLEDGMENTS

I owe special thanks to my editor, Marjorie Braman, at HarperCollins for her long-standing support and enthusiasm; to Chris Calhoun for his sterling agentry; to Peter Alson, Billy Collins, David Hayano, Anthony Holden, and Jim McManus for their kind generosity; to Bob Byrne, Tom Farber, Bob Goldberger, Jay Helfert, Jeff Z. Klein, Leonard Schneir, Doug Simmons, Al Silverman, and Mike Tronnes, for assorted tips and research assistance along the way; to Faith Barbato and Kelly Bare at HarperCollins, Dorianne Steele at Crown, Elaine Smyth at the LSU Carriere Collection, Nan Bunce and Judy Kerstetter of the South Country Library, and Howard Schwarz of The Gambler's Bookshop, for all the time and help; and lastly, to Fred "Permdude" Courtright for his invaluable expertise at charting the often-troubled waters of rights and permissions.

CONTENTS

PREFACE

In the course of compiling this superb collection of writings, I've often felt like the curator of a broad retrospective, or a house dj at a very jumpin' scene. The process is, of course, ultraselective—what to choose, what to leave out. It's a question of taste (mine) and what I hope works best for readers of—if not exactly the same taste, then at least—like sensibilities. And I am betting that there are a lot of reader/poker players out there who will feel the same way I do about this material.

It's not just that I love poker and anything written about the game; it's a feeling that jumps from page to gut and tells me *this is the nuts*. Like when Martin Amis opens with, "A man can find out a lot about himself playing poker. Is he brave? Is he cool? Does he have any money left?" Or when A. Alvarez closes with a line from a savvy high roller: "The guy who invented gambling was bright, but the guy who invented the chip was a genius." The former leads to an amusing, self-deprecating account of a losing session; the latter caps off a heady appraisal of the color of money in the game's stratosphere. Knockouts both. When Clark Clifford recounts a Truman aide pleading (re Winston Churchill's poker failings), "But, Boss, *this guy's a pigeon*," the call, in but a few words, captures the gist of the excerpt. Or how about Pete Dexter's "This [drink] is lost its bouquet," a seemingly innocuous plaint from Wild Bill Hickok moments before his death. Too perfect.

James McManus pays me a compliment when he refers to "numerous gems . . . unearthed" in his introduction. Unearthing is one of the true pleasures of editing a book of this nature. While I am thankful for the suggestions from friends and works gleaned from related anthologies, the most gratifying finds were those dug up from periodical guides, short-story indexes, and arcane bibliographies. But these weren't necessarily deep excavations. There's no shortage out there of fine literature dealing with poker. Rest assured that the very best of the best has found its way to these pages.

Another note on personal taste. I have tried to keep my selections short in length, which I feel in this case promotes readability. Anthologies are generally read randomly, not straight through, and the jump-back-and-forth mode seems most accessible if the entries are not too ponderously long. Also, entries excerpted from larger works were chosen here in part for their ability to stand on their own as (unchopped) set pieces. Again, readability.

If there's one single thread of continuity—other than subject—that runs throughout this entire book, it's the strong sense of confidence that accompanies all of the writing. Some of the works may be eclectic, some may deal with the frailties of human psyches, but each in its own way is remarkably self-assured, unequivocal. This may be no mere coincidence, since the most skilled of poker players are themselves a generally fearless bunch. In a collective sense, so too are these writers intrepidly grounded as they embrace the hard-edged aura that surrounds the colorful game. Enjoy them. Read 'em and laugh. Read 'em and weep.

—*John Stravinsky*
FALL 2003

INTRODUCTION

BY

JAMES MCMANUS

As the thirty-nine selections in this omnibus amply suggest, the case could be made for poker having supplanted baseball as our national pastime. What used to be called "the cheater's game" is now, for better or worse, at the heart of America's romance with market democracy. Witness poker's usefulness in game theory, in formulating business and battle plans, not to mention the way that the game's terminology has infected American English. "Call the bluff," "up the ante," "stacked deck," "ace in the hole," and "poker face" are but a handful of the commonest idioms. In poker, "the buck stops here" originally referred to the dealer's button; later, it would become poker-playing President Harry Truman's way of saying that he accepted full responsibility on his watch.

It's also fair to say that more than in politics, warfare, business, or physical sports, poker has become the arena in which the sexes and races compete on the most equal footing. First legalized in California in the late nineteenth century (and in several more states in the mid-1980s), the game has recently evolved from its good-old-boy roots into a stronghold of multicultural opportunity. No other pastime now attracts such a diversity of ages, physiques, nationalities, genders, incomes, and levels of education—or inspires more notable writing.

One of the numerous gems John Stravinsky unearths for us here is Leonard Kriegel's "Poker's Promise," a memoir of how, as part of the immigrant's rite of passage during the 1950s, poker, like baseball, "eased us into American aspirations, suggesting how each of us might bankroll his sense of belonging." Kriegel recalls listening as a boy to middle-aged furriers, garment workers, and taxi drivers "vehemently discussing in Yiddish the trials and tribulations of their weekly poker game. I can still hear the echo of those voices dripping with derision as a player's efforts were dismissed with the contemptuous, *'Er spelt vee ah greener.'* ('He plays like an immigrant.') No condemnation could have been more formidable, no dismissal more damning. For to play like an immigrant was to deny the very entitlements America offered. . . . Even in the golden land, one listened carefully to opportunity's knock." Young Leonard gradually realizes that, "Along with the intricacies of baseball, poker was a cultural bridge that helped you cross over into a wider world."

Approximately 80 million of us play poker these days, making it the *first* great national pastime: first to make its appearance, first in the number of participants. Is it a coincidence, then, that the rhythms of poker and baseball are so much alike? Both games are contested in groups, yet place a huge premium on individual success. The tactics of both are dominated by probability. Managers deploy pinch-hitters, shifts, lefty-righty matchups, and alter rotations and batting orders; pokerists factor in pot odds, randomize bluffs, fold when their hand is a statistical underdog, raise when they're getting the best of it. In both contests position, aggression, decoys, and stealing are critical, but patience is what turns out to be the most necessary virtue. Baseball players and poker players spend most of their time picking up signs and working the count, but at least once every nine chances or so they really do have to come through. And more than in most competitions, luck becomes pivotal. A batter makes more solid contact with a nasty cut fastball when he flies out to the centerfield warning track than when he bloops a bases-clearing double to the opposite field, yet the weak hit is what gets the job done—just as weak Texas Hold'em hands like A-7 suited routinely crush pocket cowboys.

And poker, like baseball, is highly susceptible to literary treatment, mainly because of the unhurried pace of both games. Even bookish hoopsters like Woody Allen or John Edgar Wideman are unlikely to choose a fine prose account of an NBA playoff match-up over watching the game from a courtside seat. Too much of basketball's color, its jazzy rhythms and explosive physicality, goes missing on the page, even in the most superb writing, whereas precious little poker action is lost in translation to prose. In fact, much is gained. Railbirds or even other players at the table surely failed to notice all the factors in play when Jack Straus trapped Jesse Alto for $40,000 during a side game at Binion's Horseshoe during the 1981 World Series of Poker. But reading A. Alvarez's famous account of this hand, we experience the game as it's played at the highest level in something akin to real time. "Alto did not move, but his erect back seemed to curve infinitesimally, as if under the pressure of a great weight. He sat considering the alternatives while Puggy Pearson lit a giant cigar. Did Straus have a king and an ace in the hole, or even two pairs, like Alto himself?" The passage continues for another 650 words of lapidary English that correspond perfectly to the five or six minutes it took Straus and Alto to play out the actual hand.

Along with Alvarez, *Read 'Em and Weep* includes other names in poker's literary pantheon—Twain, Yardley, Mamet, Holden—as well as several you might not expect: Bertolt Brecht, Billy Collins, Martin Amis, Clark Clifford, Somerset Maugham, Barbara Tuchman. Each of them fruitfully cultivates a patch of the garden of poker delights without ignoring for a second the game's more terrifying dimensions.

And then there are names that you might not have heard of at all. George Devol, for example. Mignon McLaughlin. Katy Lederer. This last, it turns out, is a young New York poet who compares the steel-trap memories of her famous poker-playing siblings, Howard and Annie, to her own "more visceral way of remembering." This has much to do, happily, with why Katy became a writer instead of a rounder. "I was able to 'read' people, but it proved problematic. I would sit at my table, look around at my opponents, and try my best to assess them by their postures and expressions, but it would be strangely painful. Or, not painful. It would make me feel *dirty*. . . . We would sit there, growing filthy together, handling our cards and the dirty plastic chips, trying not to bite our nails for fear of what had lodged itself beneath them."

Poker's "dirty" intimacy and fiduciary hazards aren't for everyone, certainly. Perhaps this is why its outlaw cachet continues to linger, even when today's game is played mostly in air-conditioned card rooms by mostly well-behaved women and men of all classes sipping mineral water. *Liquor Up Front, Poker in the Rear?* Crooked Nose McCall gunning down Wild Bill Hickok? Not anymore. An ornery Marlboro Man raising you big bucks from behind mirrored shades? Mirrored shades maybe, but smoking is banned at all major tournaments now, as are cursing and loutish behavior. What remains just as cool, maybe more so, is that this great American game is alive and well in Paris, France, and Paris, Texas, San Jose, California, and San Jose, Costa Rica, not to mention in the pages that follow.

READ 'EM AND WEEP

FROM

THE MAN WITH THE GOLDEN ARM

BY

NELSON ALGREN

Surrounded by a group of luckless losers, Frankie Machine, the author's drug-addled anti-hero, finds respite in the magic of his talents as a card dealer. The passage is pure Algren at his hard-core, late-40s hipster best, the prose juxtaposing Frankie's reverie with the rhythmic routine of his calling.

Algren himself played high and low stakes poker with little success; according to biographer Bettina Drew, he would routinely pass off his losses at low-life dives to "gathering research." The slumming paid off in literary backdrop—*The Man with the Golden Arm* won the first National Book Award (1950)—and may well have inspired Algren's classic adage: "Never play cards with a man named Doc (and never eat at a place called Mom's)."

Each night he slipped singles and fives and deuces into the green silk bag. Frankie dealt the fastest game in the Near Northwest Side when he was right, and he was more right now with every night; at moments it seemed to him he was faster and steadier than he had ever been. At any second, through all the hours, he knew to a nickel how the pot stood and controlled the players like the deck. They too were aces and deuces, they too were at his fingertips once more.

For like the deuces and aces they all came home to him toward closing time. Turned face up at last, their night-long secret bluffing was exposed at last: the fat florid kings, the lean and menacing black jacks and those sneaky little gray deuces, all betrayed the sucker by morning.

In the early light Schwiefka, with his fry-cook's complexion, called "Change it up!" to the steerer for the last time. And went south with the bundle.

There had been only one serious argument at Schwiefka's while Frankie was in the slot, for Frankie had the knack of anticipating funny business. He sensed the sort of desperation which would tempt a man to slip a single exposed ace around the hole card, flashing it so fast it gave the impression of a pair. It had been that one pulled, for the sake of caution, on the slow-witted umbrella man, in which Frankie had trapped Louie cold.

Everyone knew immediately what had happened—everyone but Umbrellas. All Umbrellas knew was that Louie had said "bullets" and reached for the pot. Frankie had flipped Louie's cards open before the fixer had had time to get them back into the deck.

"I *swear* I seen bullets," Louie had pretended casually, and nobody told him he lied. But Umbrellas had gotten the pot and Louie had never quite forgiven the dealer for exposing him. "You'd think it was comin' out of his own pocket," he complained later of Frankie.

Since that time there came a moment every night, before the first suckers started knocking, when Frankie would look uneasily at Louie and say, "I call the hands. What I say goes. That's how it's always been 'n that's how it's gonna stay 'n nobody's gonna change it." He told Louie that exactly as some sergeant had once told it to him when he'd questioned an order. It had worked on Private Majcinek. So ex-Private Majcinek assumed it had an effect on the fixer's narrow head.

And studied each fresh sucker with a practiced eye. Schwiefka sent occasional stooges into the game to keep his dealer straight—usually one wearing a loudly flowered tie and sideburns; with a habit of finding the dealer's toe under the table to indicate that a bit of co-operation with that deck wouldn't go unappreciated. Good-time Charlies with the usual whisky glass in the middle of the forehead and that certain faraway look which never troubled to count a winning pot to see whether it was right. "*We* trust each other, Dealer," was the implication of that look.

The dealer trusted no man on the other side of the slot. He had outlasted forty such touts. They didn't call him Machine just because he was fast. They called him Machine because he was regular.

He couldn't risk being anything else; dealing was the sole skill he owned. "The day I get my musician's union card is the day I'll steal Schwiefka blind," he planned in his tough-skinned larcenous little heart. Until that day he would be as straight as one of Widow Wieczorek's ivory-tipped cues.

One by one Schwiefka's shills would give place, as the winter night wore on, the stakes would grow higher as the air grew heavier and the marks grew lighter; to be replaced, one by one, like so many sausages into the same sure grinder.

While at the door Sparrow urged losers and winners alike: "Tell 'em where you got it 'n how easy it was."

Till Frankie would sit back wearily, sick of seeing them come on begging to be hustled, wondering where in the world they all came from and how in the world they all earned it and what in the world they told their wives and what, especially, they told themselves and why in the world they always, always, always, always came back for more.

"More, more, I keep cryin' for more more—"

Some tattered walkathon tune of the early thirties went banging like a one-wheeled Good Humor cart of those same years through his head as the cards slipped mechanically about the board and his fingers went lightly dividing change in the middle, taking the house's percentage without making the winner too sharply aware of the cut. It was one thing for a player to understand he was bucking a percentage and quite another to see it taken before his eyes. To the mark it always seemed, vaguely, that the dealer might have overlooked the cut, just

this once, out of sportsmanship. For when the sucker held a hot hand
five per cent didn't trouble him—he'd be feeling too smug about having the case ace concealed while that chump across the board was
pitching in his last desperate dollar in the hope of hooking that same
ace. And when he wasn't involved in the pot the sucker didn't care if
the dealer took ninety per cent. It wasn't any skin off his hide then,
the sucker figured.

"I hope I break even tonight," was the sucker's philosophy, "I need
the money so bad."

And always the same tune clanging like a driverless trolley down
some darkened backstreet, past familiar yet nameless stops, through
the besieged city of the dealer's brain.

"More, more, I keep cryin' for more more more—"

A tune he'd heard some afternoon when he and Sophie were first
engaged and he'd liked taking her down Division because she dressed
so sharp and had that haughty, hard-to-get stride that had had everyone fooled but himself: he'd solved it before she'd had a chance to
develop adult defenses.

A stride somewhere between a henwalk shuffle and a Cuban grind,
one of the boys had once described it. A walk as provocative as a strip
teaser zipping down one black glove on the runway just to give the
boys an idea of how much there was to zip before taking it all away
again. And those silk-sheathed legs as proud-looking as a fawn's.

Once, when both were still in their teens, he'd ignored Sophie for a
month just to show her he didn't care one way or another. Until she'd
asked him straight out if they were still sleeping together on Saturday
nights or not.

He'd fished a nickel out of his pocket and slipped it into her palm.
"Here's a nickel, kid. Call me up when you're eighteen. Right now I
got to do some shoppin' around."

She'd gone off in such a high-heeled huff he'd thought that that
was surely the end of *that*. But two days later she'd slipped him a note
in front of the corner *apteka*. "I have to talk to you."

But in her own living room there really hadn't been anything to talk about after all. She'd come down off that high horse onto her knees. He'd brought her down till she'd never have her full height again. He'd broken her pride for keeps that afternoon.

Now for ten years she had held him in the hope of recovering that lost pride; till it had grown too late to loosen her grip up on him. If she let go of him now she let go of everything.

The old days, the old days, Frankie thought nostalgically. When every other door was a tavern and you had as much on the next guy as he had on you. When the worst thing the neighborhood bucks got pinched for was strongarming and no one fooled with anything deadlier than whisky. When there weren't any fixers strolling through the Safari with more dough tied up in a single brown drugstore bottle than in a case of the best bonded scotch behind the bar.

And the old days before the old days, when burlesque was still burlesque, Kenny Brenna was the funniest man in town and the streetcar men got salt out of the box down on Augusta Boulevard to melt the ice in the switches. Down on Augusta where they'd played the same games other children played in less crowded neighborhoods—but had played them with little vicious twists unknown to luckier stubs. They'd played Let Her Fly simply by wrapping up garbage from the nearest can and sneaking up on a privately selected opponent with it: one who never knew he was anyone's opponent at all until the garbage hit him in the teeth. For the game's single rule had been that the player at bat was anyone with garbage in his hand who had voice enough to call out, "Let her fly!" before pitching it. The kid who didn't duck fast enough lost right there.

Rules had been added and the game extended but you still had to be ready to duck every second. "Jacks check, the bullets say a buck," he intoned unemphatically, hearing his own voice going on and on like a voice belonging to someone else. "King sees, a buck to you Jacks, Jacks bump a buck, Big Ace sees 'n here we go, down 'n dirty, when you get a hunch, bet a bunch, nothin' to it if you know how to do it—turn 'em over when you're down—man with the hammer bumps a buck, Jacks call—one bucket of paint all red—a winner every hand, hooked it in

the dark he says well well, slip me a half 'n make me laugh, thank *you*,
the more you bet the more you get—"

"More, more, I keep cryin' for more more more—"

The old days, the old ways, before all the stoplights turned to red
and there was still time between deals for a laugh or two over a nickel
beer.

"He ain't even got his first papers 'n he got a City Hall job," somebody complained of somebody else and the night was long, so long,
and all night long the derisive little diamonds mocked the fat and
happy-looking hearts. And the sour spades, that had seen too much
of everything and had been disappointed in it all for so long, stood
aside with cynical indifference while the murderous black clubs
ambushed the hopeful four flushes and the foolishly faithful four-
card straights; while the little old gray deuces died, heartbroken, by
the way. Till the green silk bag was filled and emptied, half secretly,
half guiltily, as a thousand green silk bags had been filled and emptied
secretly before. And were always brought back for more more—

"I keep cryin' for more more
Give me more more more—"

As this night followed a thousand nights and these men followed a
thousand hopers who had sat there before them to go down to their
graves holding a four-card straight in one hand and would never be
remembered at all. Their mouths were stuffed with race-track dust;
and no one to remember at all.

Their sons had taken their places, passing the time, while waiting
for death to deal one from the bottom, by drawing to aces and eights.
Their hell was a full house that never won and their last hope of
heaven a royal flush.

"He got a loaf of bread under his arm 'n he's cryin'," somebody
said of somebody else. While the biggest sucker of them all sat in the
dealer's slot till morning, getting relieved fifteen minutes every two

hours, and thought and thought and thought. For every time he was relieved his newly recovered confidence slipped an inch. And the old regret, like the old wound fever, struggled in him to kindle fresh flames of guilt. Guilt that burned like so many small strange flowers putting out petals of fire in place of leaves. "I told her in the hospital I was gonna make it all up to her. I'm makin' it up to her awright. Just one flight down. Through a different door."

"What's it mean when a dealer's hand gets shaky?" Louie asked Schwiefka without looking at any dealer at all.

"That's the first sign of insanity," Schwiefka decided.

"Hell, it's the last sign," Frankie threw them both, out of sheer irritability. "I blew my stack a long time ago settin' right here watchin' tinhorn West Side gamblers tryin' to make a pair of bullets out of one little acey."

"Don't give *me* that old *kapustka*," Louie ordered him. "You ain't the guy to be rememberin' *anythin'*."

"Okay," Frankie conceded with his hand around the deck, "maybe it's time we both started forgettin', Louie."

Louie nodded and held his peace. "The price just went up on you, Dealer," he told himself confidently. "That stuff is gonna be awful hard to get around the middle of next week."

"Deal, deal," Schwiefka demanded uneasily, sensing something old, unspoken and violent in the air, and the players all began wheedling the dealer at once. "Give us somethin' to remember you by, Dealer—we're gettin' quartered to death here."

"Toward morning the farmer gets lucky," Frankie assured every farmer present. And the cards went around and around.

Thus in the narrowing hours of night the play became faster and steeper and an air of despair, like a sickroom odor where one lies who never can be well again, moved across the light green baize, touched each player ever so lightly and settled down in a tiny whiff of cigar smoke about the dealer's hands.

Now dealer and players alike united in an unspoken conspiracy to stave off morning forever. Each bet as if the loss of a hand meant death in prison or disease and when it was lost hurried the dealer on.

"*Cards, cards.*" For the cards kept the everlasting darkness off, the cards lent everlasting hope. The cards meant any man in the world might win back his long-lost life, gone somewhere far away.

"Don't take it hard, your life don't go with it," was the philosophy of the suckers' hour.

But each knew in his heart, when he said that, that he lied: each knew that his life was reshuffled here with every hand.

Till the last fat red ten had been dealt, the final black jack had fallen, the case deuce hadn't helped after all and the queen of spades had been hooked, by somebody, just one hand too late.

"If it hadn't been for me—if it hadn't been for me—"

And the last discouraged sucker had thrown in his cards to the biggest sucker of them all.

Chan Is Bluffing (We Think)

BY

Peter Alson

Harvard graduate Peter Alson is the author of *Confessions of an Ivy League Bookie*, an autobiographical novel. He's also a veteran chronicler of high-stakes poker, his gambling articles having appeared in *Details*, *Esquire*, and *Playboy*. In this 1989 profile (from *Esquire*) of world champion Johnny Chan, he discovers (and deals with) the enigmatic nature of one of the game's all-time greats. Since the article was written, Alson has himself battled through a number of tournaments, playing his way to a $22,000 second-place at a Foxwoods (Connecticut) event in 1999, as well as finishing in the money at the $3,000 No-Limit Hold 'Em division of the 2001 World Series of Poker in Las Vegas.

Just inside the front of Binion's Horseshoe casino in Las Vegas, it is business as usual: a tour group from Columbus, Ohio, is holding Dixie cups of quarters, slugging it out in a gridlock of slot machines. Behind them, in a zone free of clanging change and midwestern avarice, the real players, for whom a "nickel" means five hundred dollars, hold court at two emerald-topped poker tables. A coterie of world-class cardslingers—their gold Rolexes and fat diamond pinkie rings the accoutrements that distinguish them from the average casino denizen—these are the survivors of twelve withering days in the Hall of Fame Poker Tournament. The original field of ninety-seven is down to eighteen players in a five-thousand-dollar buy-in, no-limit, Texas hold 'em shoot-out. The crowd of tourists and cognoscenti is jostling and pressing at the black leatherette rail as Johnny Chan levels his cold-eyed stare across the green felt at Phil Hellmuth, a cocksure twenty-four-year-old on a devastating run.

Hellmuth has won four big hands in a row and is building a miniature stairway out of gray five-hundred-dollar chips. When he looks up again, over the top step, his mouth is twisted.

"C'mon, baby," he jaws at Chan. "Let's go. Just you and me, baby. Just you and me!"

Chan has heard this kind of talk before. His back-to-back triumphs in the World Series of Poker in 1987 and 1988—a feat akin to a jockey winning the Triple Crown two years in a row—have created a rep-making target. With all the vagaries of luck involved, it must seem to some poker pros that Chan has made a pact with God, the devil, or a casino dealer. Hellmuth, like every other player in town, would like to prove Chan human. To the delight of the crowd he lays out his challenge openly: "The buck stops here, baby."

If Chan is disturbed by the taunts or by the sight of Hellmuth's ever-escalating stairway, nothing in his calm, round face gives him away. He protects his cards with the fingers of his left hand, his eyes sweeping the table behind three-quarter-closed lids and lightly tinted Yves St. Laurent glasses.

At this level, all the players possess similar mathematical skills; all of them can tell you the odds in any situation and can recall every card that's been played. What defines them is their psychological makeup: the best are the ones who have the strongest self-control, the discipline to prevent a bad "beat" from "putting them on tilt" (coming unglued), or to prevent anger or frustration from clouding their reason. The best ones also possess a nearly supernatural insight into their opponents' intentions and are masters at disguising their own.

In all this, Johnny Chan is peerless; watching and listening to Hellmuth's attempts to draw him in, he employs a form of mental jujitsu that will take his opponent's energy and turn it against him. The other players at the table seem annoyed that Hellmuth, by focusing on Chan, is cold-shouldering them. A couple make big bets at Hellmuth as if to get his attention but by doing so they play right into his hands. Since this is no-limit, in which a player can bet all of his chips on any turn of the card, two of them get more of Hellmuth's attention than they could possibly want; one folds in the face of a big Hellmuth bet (chips equal power!); the other calls and is eliminated. The rush continues: Hellmuth's chip-step structure has climbed $110,000 high. Later on Chan will say, "With this kid you have to stop him or else he'll just keep on going." For now Chan does nothing. As tough as it must be to watch Hellmuth roll on unchecked, Chan merely sits there in his white-with-orange-fringe Fila warm-up suit. He presses together his thin lips, blinking deliberately, a cardsharking yogi slowing his heartbeat so that when all the air is sucked out of the room, he alone can breathe.

The funny thing is that Johnny Chan didn't even know they had poker in Vegas the first time he went. At sixteen, he already had a taste for the big bet, and he flew in on a junket with friends from his hometown of Houston. It had taken months, working in the family Chinese restaurant and playing poker against the boys from K.C. Air Conditioning and Repair, to build up a bankroll. In Vegas, it took him two days, betting five hundred dollars a pop at blackjack, to blow it. He went home dead broke.

Six months later he was back, but his luck was no better. In fact, Chan had to tap out a half dozen times before he had a vision of his future: "I was at the Golden Nugget," he says, "when I stumbled across the cardroom. I went, 'Poker games. Jesus!' Up until then I just hadn't *known*. I got two thousand on my American Express card and sat down in a pot-limit hold 'em game."

Three hours later Chan was wondering what the hell he'd been doing at the blackjack tables. He had twenty thousand revelatory dollars in front of him and a very different life. But revelation doesn't come easy. The next day, playing head on head with a drowsy-looking

Texan named E. W., the eighteen-year-old Chan got busted in a matter of hours. If it was hard to stomach the loss, it also got him thinking: there are levels to this, and then there are levels. One thing was sure, he'd been bitten.

In 1979 the twenty-one-year-old Chan dropped out of the University of Houston and moved to Vegas. "He was a wild player back then," recalls poker pro Bob Ciaffone, who finished third to Chan in the 1987 World Series. "He was just always shoving money into the pot, bluffing and moving around." He was also broke most of the time. "I took a job working as a fry cook at the Fremont Hotel," Chan remembers. There are people who talk about him in those days going straight from the kitchen to the cardroom at the end of a shift, still wearing the little white apron around his waist.

"C'mon baby, I'm running away with this thing," Hellmuth goads, after stealing an ante. It's the third straight he's snaked. His legs are bent under his chair; only the toes of his wriggling brown penny loafers touch the garish green carpet.

Chan sips some lemonade through a straw and shrugs. But in the very next hand, in position to steal the two-thousand-dollar ante himself, he makes a six-thousand-dollar bet. The players to Chan's left fold. It comes to Hellmuth. Leaning forward, his heels tapping restlessly, he peers at Chan's remaining chips. "How much you got in your stack, baby? Huh?"

Chan clears his throat. His chirpy tenor doesn't work right after hours of disuse. Hellmuth, smirking, dismantles forty thousand dollars of his stairway and pushes it into the pot, saying, "Let's go, baby!" Forty thousand is all Chan has left. The railbirds lean closer. Then, in one quick motion, Chan pushes all his chips into the center and flips his cards over. A pair of queens. Hellmuth swallows. His lips retract. He turns his cards, too: a pair of nines. The western-bow-tied dealer burns a card and flops three up in the middle, burns and turns another, then another. The only card that can rescue Hellmuth is a nine, but it doesn't come.

As Chan rakes in the monster pot, Hellmuth tries to hide his disappointment. "I thought you were trying to run me over, baby!" he blusters. "I learned better!"

"You don't miss a trick," Chan says, allowing himself the thinnest of smiles.

"I just missed a forty-thousand-dollar trick against you, baby," Hellmuth mutters. Underneath the table, his leg is vibrating like a tuning fork.

With his most dangerous foe on near-tilt, Chan takes command of the tournament. The next day, he blitzes over Hellmuth and the remaining players on the way to his third straight tournament win at Binion's, along with the $194,000 first prize. Chan will say later: "I let my ego get out of hand when I was younger, too. But Phil will be world champ someday. All he has to do is learn to tuck it in a bit."

Johnny Chan lives in Cerritos, California, in a perfect neighborhood for a man with a permanent poker face; the endless rows of neat, one-story stuccos give nothing away. He prefers this southern Los Angeles suburb to Vegas because of its proximity to the Bicycle Club poker room in Belle Gardens, scene of a lot of the heavier action these days. But there is something else: he is more anonymous in Los Angeles, less worried about people finding out where he lives and breaking in.

Still, even here, with a visitor he's been expecting, Chan does not put out the welcome mat. The afternoon I arrive, he greets me at his door, dressed in boxer shorts and a yellow T-shirt, wiping three hours of sleep from his eyes after an all-night session at the Bicycle. Rather than invite me in, he suggests I wait for him out in my car. When I do not retreat immediately, he shrugs and closes the door in my face, saying he will be out in a few minutes.

Suddenly, as I sit crouched in my rented car, taking notes, I become aware of someone standing outside the car window.

"What are you writing?" Chan asks, sliding in next to me.

"Just some notes," I say. "Nothing to worry about."

"I thought you were going to call before you came."

"I did. I left a message on your machine."

"Oh, so you just thought you'd take your chances, huh?"

"A gamble," I say. "Look, wouldn't it be more comfortable talking inside?"

"No, it's a mess," he says.

I persist, but so does Chan. I'm the first to fold. The rest of the interview takes place in the car. Chan plays his private life as close to the sweat shirt as he does his cards. He's like the master actor gone so deep into his role that even when he's offstage, he can't shed it. About his history before Vegas, Chan says that he was born in Canton, in the People's Republic of China, the eldest of three children, that he came to this country when he was nine with his parents, émigrés from the violence of the Cultural Revolution, and that he sees nothing ironic in his lifeline leading from the birthplace of Mao Tse-tung to the gambling capital of the world. Most of Chan's closest friends still live in the tight-knit Chinese community of Houston where he grew up. That's where his wife of ten years, Fay, is from, and where she is raising their two children, Jason, seven, and Jennifer, six. He phones his wife and kids nearly every day, but he is not often home with them.

Even in Vegas, Chan keeps to himself. He looks to the cardroom as his "office"; when he sits down to play he is "going to work." For a man looking to live between worlds, it is probably the ideal spot: no one has a history or cares about one, no explanations are ever necessary, and in the only language that means anything, Chan's eloquence is unmatched.

While tournaments have made poker respectable—players pay taxes on their winnings and get their pictures in the local sports section—the heavy games are played on the side, often while the big tournaments are in progress. In these side games, careful accounting is difficult, and the IRS generally comes up empty. Johnny Chan made $900,000 playing in tournaments in 1988. But by one player's estimate, he made another $1.5 million on the side.

During the first week of the Hall of Fame tournament, before playing in the main event, Chan got involved in a wildly expensive marathon game with a debonair French millionaire. The Frenchman, draped in a charcoal suit, bore a striking resemblance to Yves Montand. He had crossed the Atlantic to test his wits and mettle. In addition to Chan, the lineup included Chip Reese, seen by most as Chan's closest rival in these side games; Doyle "Texas Dolly" Brunson, a two-time world champion; and Roger Moore (not to be confused with the actor), who had a "license to kill" poker rep.

Because there is an element of luck involved, poker is one of those rare pursuits in which it is possible to compete with the best in the world and not look ridiculous. If broken down into percentages, it would probably come out luck, 10 percent; mathematics and discipline, 40 percent; psychology, 50 percent. In the case of the Frenchman (who insisted on anonymity, fearful that his weakness for gambling huge sums of money would be discovered by business associates and family), it was more than the adrenal rush; it was ego. He believed he could beat these men.

Since this was Vegas, where everyone lives by the golden rule—The man who has the gold makes the rules—the Frenchman set the stakes for the game, decided when it would start and when it would stop. And Chan and the other professionals submitted to his whims because they knew that when the gold dust had cleared, one or two of them would be shimmering with it.

During the first couple of days of what turned into a five-day marathon, the Frenchman's belief in his ability looked like more than hubris. Playing for stakes so high that at times there was nearly $1 million in cash and chips on the table, the Frenchman kept attacking and retreating at just the right times. The game went on practically round the clock, starting each day at noon, breaking at 8:00 P.M., resuming at midnight and continuing till dawn. And at noon of the third day, when Chan, Brunson, Reese, and Moore made for a far-off back corner table, away from the onlookers, and started unloading their racks of chips, as inconceivable as it seemed, the Frenchman was the big winner. He joined them a few minutes later, elegant as always in a pastel-green cashmere sweater and dark slacks, his features full of crinkles and cigarette smoke, his gray hair beautifully coiffed. He didn't even seem to mind when Chan greeted him with a friendly "How you doing, Frenchie?"

The tickets ran cold as the session began, and after tossing in his tenth hand in a row, Chan asked the dealer to put in a new deck. It is a remarkable thing, but even at this level of play, players have superstitions. They all know that luck will even out, that over time skill will triumph, but that doesn't stop them, if the cards are running badly, from making a move to change things. During the last two World Series, Johnny Chan kept an orange by his chips and would stroke it periodically. Of course, it was part con too: he wanted other players to think he was lucky. No one who was sitting at the table with the Frenchman bought into that, though, and this time Chan was orangeless.

During a lull in the action, Chan pointed out a well-scrubbed man in a three-piece green polyester suit distributing leaflets beyond the rail. "You oughta go talk to that guy," he said. "He used to be a player. He knows me."

Rick Hamil handed me a yellow leaflet that had two pictures on it. "They're both me," he said as I studied the two images. One said "Old Man" and showed a stubbly-faced, sleazy-looking guy in sunglasses and gold chains; the other said "New Man" and showed Hamil as he looked now, bright-eyed and midwestern wholesome. For more than ten years he'd lived the Vegas life of a big-stakes poker player, but then he'd been "saved." Now he was a born-again Christian minister come back to save others. He called the casino his "garden." He acknowledged that he knew Johnny from the old days, and added solemnly, "There are very few who don't pay a tremendous price from living this lifestyle. The hunger it produces, the need to have action, can become insatiable. But," he held up a finger, "Chan is one of the very few who approaches this life as discipline and work. He doesn't drink, doesn't do drugs or smoke. He's very centered and controlled."

It is true that unlike most poker pros, who tend toward physical sloth, Chan actually exercises in those Fila tracksuits, jogging several miles each day and working out at the gym. Often in the middle of a game he'll get up and run around the casino block to clear his head.

"But what do you think makes him such a control freak?" I asked Hamil.

He shook his head. He'd never had Chan's discipline to keep him from giving in to excess. Not with so many temptations around. Most of the top professionals, he explained, had a "leak," a weakness in their character that caused them to indulge in losing propositions—sports betting, craps, blackjack, booze, and drugs. Ultimately, most or all of the money they won was frittered away. "The thing about Chan," Hamil went on, "is that I don't think he's reached a point yet where he's asking if there's anything more to life than what he's doing. Which is what happened to me. What I thought was going to bring happiness was just an empty dream." Hamil nodded at Chan's table. "You see Doyle Brunson and Chip Reese? They've both found the Lord."

"And they're still playing?"

"They don't see any conflict. There are other players who trust in Jesus, too."

Back at the table, Chan's stack of chips had grown. A gray-haired Howard Cosell look-alike in a white jumpsuit was kneading Chan's shoulders and whispering in his ear. When he moved away, across the casino floor, I intercepted him. "I'm the guy who gives Johnny shoulder rubs during the big tournaments," he explained happily. "John Formica. They call me the Italian Stallion." He said he and Chan used to play together in small hold 'em games. But unlike Chan, he'd hit his level and couldn't go higher. He claimed he was Chan's best friend in the gambling world, but that Chan didn't open up to anybody. "Not even to his wife or kids." Last year during the World Series, Formica gave Chan a massage in the break before the final and Chan made him take a thousand bucks. "That's what kind of friend Johnny is," Formica said. "Very generous."

Chan looked bemused a few minutes later, hearing what Formica had said. He told me I should talk to a couple of his "real buddies": Dr. Jerry Buss, owner of the Los Angeles Lakers, and Gabe Kaplan, the actor. "Jerry Buss," he said admiringly, "has got all the money in the world. But he's like normal people. He wears blue jeans and cowboy boots. I try to be like him—well, I'm not even close, what can I say? But I'd like to be." Buss and Kaplan, both serious amateur players, happen to be sitting at tables nearby. "I don't want to talk about him," said Buss. Kaplan found it strange that Chan had mentioned him as a good friend. "The only contact we've had is at the poker table," said TV's onetime Mr. Kotter. "I don't know anything about him away from the table. And at the table I don't know much either. He's not into the male-bonding part, which most guys are, at least to some extent. And I don't think it's an accidental thing. He's just deeper into the game than anyone else."

By the end of the third day's session with the Frenchman, Chan was up to more than $100,000, and "Frenchie" had given back some of his earlier winnings. Chan appeared to have taken the measure of the Gallic millionaire. Afterward, Chan went to the room Binion's keeps on permanent reserve for him on the fifteenth floor. He apologized for the mess, though aside from a couple of balled-up black socks and a T-shirt on the floor, the room was bare. Tired and stiff, he tried to work the kinks out on one of the two double beds, while I sat at the edge of the other, watching. Hanging his head and shoulders off the foot of the bed, he twisted his neck one way, then the other, while letting his hands brush along the floor. Still in the same position, he rolled his shoulders, sighed, and then swung his body around, let his head sink into the pillow, and put a rolled white towel over his eyes. "What do you want to know?' he asked.

I said I was curious about a hand in which he had caught the Frenchman trying to bluff.

"A lot of players," he said, "want to bluff in their mind, but in their heart, they just can't push those chips out there. You have to convince yourself of what you're doing. If you don't really believe it, it shows. But a great player doesn't make his money catching someone bluffing. He makes it when he has a top pair with a kicker and figures someone else for a top pair with a smaller kicker. And he squeezes all the money he can out of him. A lot of times I just call when I sense someone is weak—even if I'm weak, too. I don't raise and try and steal the pot. Because when I call, my opponent doesn't know where I'm at. And on the next card I can get an extra bet from him and then push him out of the pot. But that's a play that's beyond poker, really." Chan laced his hands across his chest and thrust his elbows down into the bed before relaxing. "What else you want to know?"

I mentioned Rick Hamil and what he had said about the born-agains, Doyle and Chip.

Chan shrugged. He is a nonpracticing Chinese Baptist. "That's their lives," he said. "If it makes them happy, fine. I enjoy my life the way it is."

"So is it all about money, for you?"

"If it's not money, what are we playing for?" He lay still for a moment, then lifted the towel from his face and cocked an eye at me. "What I really want to do is win the World Series again this year. The third time in a row. No one's ever done it. If I can do that, they'll think I'm God."

He let the towel fall back across his eyes. I stared at him in the ensuing silence, mystified. I had always imagined that to reach his level of mastery in poker one would have to be like a great novelist, capable of enormous self-knowledge, able to understand the landscape and range of human emotions, able to feel great empathy. But if this was true of Chan it had, strangely, made him not a bigger person but a smaller one, one who knew himself because there was less to know. I asked him what it was that made him able to divine the intentions of the people facing him down across a patch of green felt. After a long pause and a shrug, he replied, "Instinct."

During the final session with the Frenchman, on the fifth day, Chan took his game to a higher level. Actually, his most advanced poker move may have come on the fourth day, when instead of playing, he stayed in his room and slept. Now with everyone else a little ragged, Chan came down looking frighteningly refreshed. Of the five players, the Frenchman seemed most in need of a blood change. Despite his reflexive elegance, he looked older, shrunken, ready to be taken. But the full spectacle of Vegas and its power to induce fever was now manifest: the Frenchman ordered the stakes raised from $800–$1,600 to $1,200–$2,500. This was the moment he'd come for, bust or bonanza, and he wanted it to happen fast.

Now Chan settled down to work, calmly folding a stick of Big Red gum in his mouth and pushing his tinted Yves St. Laurents back against the bridge of his nose. Chip Reese had told me that one of the things he admired about Chan was that "when he wins, he wins the table. He tries to get every last chip."

For a long time, the Frenchman had been catching perfect, but now things began to go against him. One hand in particular put him over the edge. It started with the Frenchman, showing a ten of diamonds, raising Doyle Brunson's jack. Chan showed a six but had a pair of kings (one of them a diamond) underneath; he re-raised, which forced out Brunson, then watched the Frenchman re-raise him. "He don't know what I'm raising on," Chan said, "so when he re-raises, I figure he's trying to sell me on his hand. Make me think he has trips or a pair of hidden aces. But I peg him for two high diamonds in the hole, ace and queen. I know by now he likes to raise on the come. I know if he's got trips, he just calls there to suck me in." On the next card, the Frenchman caught a ten of clubs, giving him a pair of tens showing; Chan picked up a four of hearts. When the Frenchman bet his pair of tens, Chan raised, then watched the Frenchman re-raise him again.

Almost anyone else would have taken the re-raise to mean the Frenchman now had trips or at least two pair and that it was time to fold. But to Chan it meant the opposite: "When he re-raised me," Chan said, "I knew for sure he's playing the two high diamonds in the hole. No way he re-raise me earlier on a pair of tens. And if he got aces with the tens, he don't re-raise me now because he gotta be scared I have trips the way I'm betting."

On fifth street, the Frenchman caught a seven of diamonds and Chan got a nine. Still with only a pair of kings, Chan re-raised again in the face of the Frenchman's bet, and this time got only a call. "I figure he still needs a card to make his hand, I gotta bet mine for value. Even though I know he's got four diamonds, he's still about a two-to-one dog against me."

After the sixth and seventh cards were dealt, Chan still hadn't improved. But when the Frenchman bet, Chan called the $38,000 pot with his lonely pair of kings. All that early raising and re-raising, and

Chan was certain the Frenchman had nothing in his hand but dreams. Sure enough, the Frenchman's last card—a nine of clubs—hadn't helped; his first two hole cards were the ace and queen of diamonds. Exactly as Chan had figured.

It was inevitable after that: the Frenchman and his money went separate ways and four hours later I accompanied Chan to the cashier's window and watched him cash out for more than $250,000, fifty banded packets of $5,000 each. This was what they'd been playing for: a quarter of a million dollars. But the money looked unreal, just like little green bricks, no more real than the chips it had been traded for. Chan requested his safe-deposit box—he keeps several around Vegas—and loaded the money in. All the money, that is, save for thirty thousand.

"What's that for?" I asked him.

"Just a little to walk around with until tomorrow. I'll probably lose it at the crap table."

Chan could not stop bluffing. In fact, he'd probably take a Jacuzzi, go to his room, rest up, and get ready to play again tomorrow.

"You don't give anything away, do you?"

His hooded black marble eyes fixed me. Irony was not a part of the poker lexicon. "Look, I'm just a normal person," he said. "I do things other people do." He shoved the thirty grand in his pocket, closing the argument.

As he took his leave of me, I noticed Rick Hamil over near the cocktail lounge, alone, thumbing through his Christian leaflets. Chan strode briskly past on the way to his room. He didn't nod and he didn't take a pamphlet. God could wait until Johnny Chan's luck ran out.

MONEY: THE LANGUAGE OF POKER

FROM *Poker: Bets, Bluffs, and Bad Beats*

BY

A. ALVAREZ

English poet Al Alvarez dealt action-loving literati a mortal lock when he wrote "The Biggest Game in Town" for the *New Yorker* in 1981. The two-part article survives in book form as the holy scripture of poker writing—a fascinating insider take on the world of high-dollar action. *Poker: Bets, Bluffs, and Bad Beats* (2001) makes liberal use of themes and stories from the earlier work, including here an anecdotal examination of the very stuff around which the game revolves. Alvarez explores the meaning of money at poker, how different players relate to it, and most importantly, how a blatant disregard of its value can serve the stronger players at the highest levels of the game.

In *My Little Chickadee*, someone asks W. C. Fields if poker is a game of chance. He answers, "Not the way I play it." He was speaking as a cardsharp, but he was also speaking the truth. Serious poker is no more about gambling than rock climbing is about taking risks. Both are risky activities, of course, and accidents sometimes happen to the canniest experts. Climbers misjudge the weather or the solidity of the rock or the difficulty of a move or the limits of their strength; and when they do the consequences may be painful—frostbite, a broken limb, a broken neck. Similarly, even the best poker players must endure terrible runs of cards when nothing goes right and every good hand is outdrawn: "In the long run there's no luck in poker," Rick Bennet wrote sourly, "but the short run is longer than most people know." But in poker, as in climbing, the point of the game is to develop enough skill to minimize the element of chance.

Repeat: minimize, not eliminate. Chess is a game of pure information, like poker with all the cards exposed; the better player will *always* win; that is why a computer can be programmed to play it so well. But the only way a computer could be made to play top-level poker would be by introducing a randomizing factor into the program that would correspond both to the element of bluff and to the random way the cards fall. The better player will usually win at poker, but because the cards are shuffled and dealt haphazardly the sucker occasionally gets lucky and beats the expert—occasionally though not for long. According to Terence Reece, a great cardplayer who played bridge for England, there is nothing to choose between bridge and poker in terms of skill. Yet that's not how the uninitiated—or the suckers—see it. For example, before the British Parliament passed the Gaming Act, in 1960, it was illegal to play poker in a card club, because whichever bureaucracy controlled these matters had officially classified it, along with bingo, craps, and roulette, as a game of chance. I suppose the civil servants were confused, as they often are, by the appearance of the game, rather than its reality. Poker looks like gambling—and at a low level it is gambling—because it has to be played for money.

Playing for money, however, means two different things, depending on whether the emphasis is on "playing" or "money." This, for example, is how David Sklansky begins the first chapter of his book *Poker Theory*, and the italics are his: "When we play, we must realize, before anything else, that we are *out to make money*." Sklansky is a Las Vegas–based expert, and his books are bibles for small-time hustlers who grind out a living in low-stakes games and reckon their success by their hourly earning rate: if they can come out a bet and a half ahead each hour—$30 in a $10–$20-limit game—then they are making a satisfactory living. This is subsistence poker and it is geared to what Sklansky calls "positive expectation": extracting the maximum return from the very few unbeatable hands a player might expect to get in any session.

This is a businessman's attitude to poker, the small-minded, remorseless style that Jack Straus dismissed when he said, "I wouldn't pay a ten-year-old kid a dime an hour to sit in a low stakes game and wait for the nuts." He called it, contemptuously, "a disciplined job," adding, "Anyone who wants to work out the mathematics can be a limit player and chisel out an existence. You just have to discipline yourself to sit there and wait." Mickey Appleman, another high roller, though not in Straus's league, put it more romantically: "Certain individuals come here just to make money," he said. "They grind, grind, grind in the small-stakes games, they make a living and they have no down side. But they have no gamble in them, either, so they will never know the enjoyment of the high roller, the romance of gambling. Poker playing is strictly a business to these small-stakes players, but to the high rollers it's a business and also a pleasure; it's fun, it's a game, it's gamesmanship. After all, what are we all here for at the Horseshoe? When you are playing for hundreds of thousands of dollars, it's not the money. I mean, how much do you need? It's the gamesmanship, the competition, the thrill of letting it all hang out. Poker for big money is a high-risk sport, like driving a racing car."

What Appleman is describing is a polar difference in temperament. Straus was an artist and an adventurer at the poker table, a man with a huge natural talent for the game who loved playing the finest of fine lines instead of waiting for those rare, unbeatable hands that gamblers call "the stone-cold nuts." Sklansky, in contrast, is a mathematician with a flair for statistics and probabilities and an unusual ability for analyzing the odds on the spot, as the cards turn. On one level both of them would have agreed: the art of playing well is to make the most out of your good cards and lose the least on the less good. Where they differed was in the mind-set which, in the course of the game, translates poker chips into real money, the kind you use to pay the rent, to buy food and drink, to lead a life. And that is something the top players never do.

According to Chip Reese, who is generally considered to be one of the best all-round players in the world, "Money really means nothing. If you really cared about it you wouldn't be able to sit down at a poker table and bluff off fifty thousand dollars. If I thought what that could buy me, I could not be a good player. Money is just the yardstick by which you measure your success. In Monopoly, you try to win all the cash by the end of the game. It's the same in poker: you treat chips like play money and don't think about it until it's all over." As it happens, Reese was speaking truer than he knew. I once played in an impromptu game in London. The stakes were serious, but we had no chips, so the host filched his son's Monopoly set and we used the bills at their face value.

This ability to immunize yourself from the real value of money, to treat the chips as what A. J. Meyers, another top player, called "just a bag of beans," explains the curious and—to the newcomer—disconcerting Las Vegas custom of dropping the zeroes from bets. The first time I played in a pot-limit hold 'em game in Vegas, I bet $50 after the flop and was disconcerted when the dealer said "A nickel to play." Two players called. A cowboy sitting across the table eyed me, eyed my stack, then, without seeming to count them, separated twelve green $25 chips from the pile in front of him and growled, "Raise it up a quarter." "A quarter to you," the dealer said. When I looked puzzled, he explained patiently, as though to a dumb child, "Two hundred and fifty dollars, sir."

This was my first lesson in the Las Vegas truth that chips have only a relative value; they are merely a convenient way of keeping score. According to the size of the game, a "nickel" is $5 or $50 or $500, a "dime" is $10 or $100 or $1,000, and when the whales bet a "big dime" in their giant games, they mean $10,000. If you ask them why they use this shorthand, they will usually answer, "It makes things simpler." But what they are really doing is expressing their indifference to money as the rest of the world sees it.

This is a universal procedure among high rollers, although they take it further in Las Vegas—the only town on earth, they say, which makes you think a $100 bill won't buy a loaf of bread. The pros wander around with great wads of those bills stuffed in their pockets—fifty bills to a wad and each wad casually held together with elastic bands— but few of them carry small change. Lesser bills seem below the level of their attention, mere trifles they use for tips, though sometimes, when the heat is really on, they even tip in hundreds. During one gigantic game at Binion's Horseshoe, Jimmy Chagra, a drug baron who was in town for a final fling while he unsuccessfully appealed against a thirty-year sentence in Leavenworth Penitentiary, tipped a cocktail waitress $10,000 when she brought him a complimentary bottle of Mountain Valley water. Similarly, when the photographer Ulvis Alberts was at the World Series in 1980, shooting the wonderfully atmospheric portraits of players which he published in his book *Poker Faces*, some of the contestants asked him for prints. He tried charging them $75, but "suddenly there was a problem," he told me. "Nobody had change. So I charged them $100 and everyone was happy."

The idea that poker is a game that has to be played for money, therefore, means two different things, according to temperament. For the "rocks," who bet only on certainties and treat the game as a source of steady income, money is always money. For the more creative players, who are not necessarily more reckless but know better how to calibrate the risks they take, money is a tool of their trade, like a wrench to a plumber, and chips are just a way of keeping score. According to Eric Drache, "The trick is to look on chips as units. It doesn't matter whether it costs you $500 a bet or $5, the odds remain the same."

Chips, however, have a third and more profound significance in poker: they combine with the cards to form the very language of the game. What you do with your chips—when and how you bet or check or raise—is a form of communication. You ask subtle questions with them and receive subtle answers. The questions and answers may be misleading—a big bet might be a sign of weakness, an attempt to drive the other players out of the pot because you do not have the hand you purport to have—but the combination of cards and money and position at the table creates a complex pattern of information (or illusion) that controls the flow of the game. In poker, betting and what is called "money management"—knowing when to call or raise or fold so that your bankroll is never fatally depleted—are as much an art as reading the cards and reckoning the odds.

This is true, above all, in no-limit hold 'em where a player can bet as much as he wants, regardless of the size of the pot. One of the masters of this game is Crandall Addington, an elegantly bearded Texan who used to set the sartorial standards for the World Series—a mink Stetson, silk shirts, suits of fine linen, and Dior ties he never loosened no matter how long he played. Addington is an amateur who made his millions in oil and real estate and doesn't play for the money, but he is a fearsome competitor. "Limit poker is a science, but no-limit is an art," he once said. "In limit, you are shooting at a target. In no-limit, the target comes alive and shoots back at you."

I began to understand what he meant by that when I heard him discussing a no-limit hold 'em hand with a friend. The friend had been dealt ace-ten of hearts and had called a raise from someone sitting in an early position. The flop was a black king and two low hearts, a six and a deuce; there was $2,000 in the pot. An early raise before the flop usually indicates that the player is holding an ace and a king. Sure enough, the man came out betting.

"How much?" Addington asked.

"The pot," said the friend. "Two thousand dollars."

"So what did you do?"

"I just flat called him."

"Wrong," said Addington. "You should have raised him fifteen thousand and let him think about it."

If he had been made to think about it, what deductions would the other player have drawn from the huge raise? Would he have been able to put Addington's friend on a drawing hand? What kind of four flusher would dare to bet so much? Wouldn't he rather have thought that the raiser had a pair in his hand—two deuces, two sixes, even two kings—cards that gave him a set (three of a kind) and thereby made his own ace-king worthless? When the target starts shooting back the marksman is in trouble.

Here is another example of the fierce but subtle language of poker that uses chips as a form of communication. I described this hand in *The Biggest Game in Town,* and it was played in what was, without any doubt, the biggest game in Las Vegas while I was there in 1981. It was a cash game strictly for the heavy hitters. Doyle Brunson, Jack Straus, Puggy Pearson, and Crandall Addington were sitting around the table, along with Jesse Alto, a car dealer from Houston famous for his stamina—he once played a whole week without taking a break. The atmosphere was mellow, but the stakes were high. The boys were playing a little poker together, wisecracking, needling, and outsmarting one another from behind mountains of chips and banded wads of $100 bills. No one had sat down with less than $50,000.

Before the flop, Alto raised the opening bet, then called when he was modestly re-raised by Straus. The other players folded. The flop came king, ten, eight, all of different suits. Alto, who had a king and eight of diamonds in the hole, checked to trap Straus. Straus paused, then bet $1,000—again, modestly by the standards of the game, but large enough for a bluff. This was what Alto had been hoping for; with his two pairs, kings and eights, he raised $5,000.

Straus slumped even further in his chair. He always sat hunched at the table, shoulders forward, curly gray head and curly gray beard sunk between them, as though denying his great height. As I mentioned earlier, away from the poker table as well as at it Straus was a big-game hunter and he had marksman's eyes: dark blue, slanting down from right to left, the left eye always slightly closed, like a man taking aim. He watched Alto in silence for a long time, but Alto did not stir. Then Straus cupped his hands around his cards and squeezed them slightly upward with his thumbs. Another pause. Then quickly, almost fretfully, he pushed several stacks of chips into the center.

The dealer counted them carefully and said, "Raise thirty thousand dollars."

The target had come alive and was shooting back.

Alto did not move, but his erect back seemed to curve infinitesimally, as if under the pressure of a great weight. He sat considering the alternatives while Puggy Pearson lit a giant cigar. Did Straus have a king and an ace in the hole, or even two pairs, like Alto himself? Or did he have a pair that gave him, with the flop, a set of kings or tens or eights? Or did he have a queen and a jack in the hole and was betting "on the come," hoping to complete a straight? Or, since this was Jack Straus, the master of the withering bluff and a man with a reputation for total fearlessness, was he simply bluffing?

For long, empty minutes, the two players faced each other across the table, unmoving and unspeaking, like figures in stone. Finally, Alto counted out his chips and pushed them gloomily forward. Straus's bet had set him in for all his money, so there would be no more betting. He turned over his king and eight. Straus nodded, and then, in a matter-of-fact way, turned over his hole cards: two tens. The ten in the center had given him a set of three, and only another king could save Alto. The dealer burned—discarded—the top card and dealt a seven, burned the next card and dealt a four. The three tens were good.

In hold 'em at this level, the target does not just shoot back, it also shifts about like a will-o'-the-wisp, maneuvering for position. In the previous hour, Straus had bet twice in precisely the same pattern, but with weaker cards; both times, Alto had called him and won. The only difference was that the sums involved had been much smaller—a couple of thousand rather than tens of thousands. I had watched those two earlier hands uncomprehending, for it seemed—even to an outsider and relative novice like me—that Straus was betting on losing cards. Yet I was also aware that if I knew it so did he, since one of the many gifts that separates the professionals from the amateurs is the ability to read their opponents' hands with uncanny accuracy from the tiniest clues: timing, position, the way their fingers move their chips or their eyes flicker, even the pulse beat in their neck. Like all the top professionals, Straus had that unnerving clairvoyance and had played for so long, and with such concentration, that nothing was new to him or unfamiliar or unfathomable. Yet there he was, apparently throwing away his money as carelessly as any tyro. I was wrong, of course. Straus had been setting Alto up for the kill, raising his confidence, lulling him into the belief that he, Straus, was playing loosely, so that when his moment came he could make the same ploy with a monster hand and Alto would call him. The two losing hands were investments that finally yielded a disproportionate return—$8,000 to make $40,000.

Twenty years ago $40,000 was enough to support an average family for a year in comfort. Granted, average wage earners don't play high-stakes poker. Of the millions of poker players in America, only a few thousand ever graduate to the games at Binion's and, of them, not more than a dozen or two would stand a chance in the really big games. Even so, the normal regard for money seems to be on hold in poker games, especially during tournaments, when amateurs from private games in the prosperous suburbs—businessmen, lawyers, rich doctors and orthodontists—flood into town for the action. They breeze into the bigger games, call every raise, play their half-decent hands too strongly, drop a couple of grand, then race back into the casino to try to recoup their losses at craps or blackjack. They are noisy, cheerful, and intermittently aggressive, but they seem not quite to know what is happening from one minute to the next. There is a bullish, head-down urgency about them, and their eyes are unfocused. All they want to do is cram as much action as they can into the time they have stolen from their routine lives and their families. They are men with a mission, running on adrenaline, pursuing some impossible mirage, and, for them, money is beside the point. What matters is the thrill of action. Their Western equivalents are the ranchers and wildcatters, the good ol' boys who roll into town to whoop it up a little and just loo-ove raising and reraising with second-best cards into those unbeatable hands that Sklansky and his friends wait all night for. All of them are grist to the professionals' mill, and they keep the poker economy running.

"This town hypnotizes people," Doyle Brunson told me. "Guys who won't bet $20 at home come out here and bet $500 or $1,000 without even thinking—particularly during the poker tournament. It's like being inside a pressure cooker. If you're not careful, you reach boiling point and explode. Then you just throw your money away. They keep hammering and hammering at you, until you lose touch with reality about everything." Poker in Las Vegas is like a speeded-up experiment in evolution. Players from all over the globe beat their local games, then come into town and lose their money to the local experts.

A few grand up and down means nothing much to the wealthy amateurs, though their wives might not agree. Indeed, even the wives of the top professionals sometimes find it hard to adjust to the insane world their husbands take for granted. Eric Drache told me that his wife, Jane, once called him in the middle of a game to say she'd been in a car accident. The conversation went like this:

ERIC: "Are you hurt?"
JANE: "No."
ERIC: "Is anyone else hurt?"
JANE: "No."
ERIC: "That's all right then."
JANE: "But I've done $1,500 damage to the side of the car."
ERIC: "Then call the insurance."
JANE: "But $1,500 damage to our beautiful Jaguar!"
ERIC: "Honey, I'm stuck four beautiful Jaguars at this moment. Call the insurance."

The wives are living in the real world of groceries and clothes and dentists' bills, whereas the husbands are temporarily in a dreamland where play's the thing and money isn't quite real. It doesn't even look real. Instead of a green treasury bill validated by a president's face, it's a colored disk stamped with a number and the name of a casino. Chips, in fact, are the currency of Las Vegas. When a gambler arranges a line of credit with a casino, he takes the money in chips. You tip with them, pay for meals and drinks and sex with them, and could probably buy goods with them in stores. The better adjusted to them you become, the further reality recedes. To eat a slap-up meal with all the trimmings and pay for it with a couple of battered green disks is no longer a business transaction, it is magic.

The poker chip is like a conjurer's sleight of hand that turns an egg into a billiard ball, a necessity of life into a plaything, reality into illusion. People who freeze up at the sight of a hundred-dollar bill, thinking it could buy them a week's food at the supermarket, will toss a black chip into the pot without even hesitating if the odds are right. "Chips don't have a home," said Jack Straus. "People will play much higher with chips than they will with cash. For some reason, it is harder for inferior players to turn loose of money, but give them chips and they get caught up, mesmerized by the game." A New York gambler who goes by the name of Big Julie put it best when he remarked sagely, "The guy who invented gambling was bright, but the guy who invented the chip was a genius."

POKER NIGHT

FROM *Visiting Mrs. Nabokov (and Other Excursions)*

BY

MARTIN AMIS

In 1990, *GQ* magazine asked Amis and four other writers—three of whose writings (A. Alvarez, Anthony Holden, and David Mamet) also appear on these pages—to spend an evening playing poker and then report back on the ordeal. The fee, 500 pounds, was paid in advance in chips (to be replenished out-of-pocket as necessary). Judging by Amis's clever appraisal of the session and his fellow players, the ensuing loss of house money doesn't appear to have been too devastating.

A man can find out a lot about himself, playing poker. Is he brave? Is he cool? Does he have any money left? I am obliged to say that I felt pretty hip and well-hung for much of the evening, in that little paradise of the private room, with its pro dealer, its full bar, its pleasant company, its complimentary poker chips—and the oncoming cards, from which hope unceasingly springs. By the end of the evening, I confess, I was feeling much less formidable: much less butch, and much less rich. But what an enthralling process. When can I go through it again?

From the start I sensed that I was the *rabbit* (the easy mark). This suspicion, along with all the free money, had a liberating effect on me. Unlike the scarred sharpers I faced, I wasn't bringing any rep to the table. I hadn't *sat down* for a decade, and had never played hold 'em. Originally, the fashionable poker variant was draw; then stud; then, during my brief heyday (in my late teens I played every night for three years), it was seven-card high-low. Now it's hold 'em, the purists' game, with its austere and subtle variations on the theme of the shared five cards.

When you sit down, you confront the force fields of opposed personalities. You shouldn't do this (it's a callow distraction), but you do. You look around for someone to bully, someone to be scared of. I found John Graham, the noted bridge player, to be easily the most emotional presence at the table: his operatic profile, tranced pauses, flustered raises. He is all joker, all wild card: he seems regularly astonished by his own unpredictability. As it happened, he lost; and was soon eagerly into a thousand pounds of his own money. But on another night you could imagine him cleaning you out with a jack high.

Al Alvarez I took to be an excellent percentage man, interspersing his play with the occasional and prohibitive bluffs that his accuracy earns him. Al's style is as metronomic as the wheezing of his pipe. He won't come in often; when he does, you can't wait to get out of the way. But it was Anthony Holden who appeared to me to possess the most dangerous mixture of froth and flair. Tony is toney; he has his Vegas mannerisms: the exaggerated slouch, the languidly scornful flickaway of the dead cards. When the pot gets high, the hour late, and you need to see what he has in the hole, then the lounge lizard melds into a loanshark. Like his mentor Al Alvarez, Holden writes whole books about hold 'em. He is the Imam of hold 'em. He is practically *called* Holdem.

David Mamet was the only stranger. The others were familiar presences (I have known Tony for twenty years, Al for thirty) but Mamet I had only glimpsed electronically—on the small screen. There, he struck me as someone who had been put together by an Atlantic City biochemist: a human construction called POKER 1. The opacity, the staring stillness, the transcendental inscrutability. In addition, Mamet is American, and what's more he wrote *House of Games*, that tour de force of manic hazardry and compound deceit. On top of all this he was only drinking *tea*. Son of a bitch . . . Men with a sheen of silence easily intimidate their fellows (these helpless prattlers); we imbue that silence with an unblinking censoriousness—or with our own self-doubt. Anyway, it's perfect for poker. Humanly, David Mamet opened up over the course of the evening. But his style remained impeccably closed. I felt very potent and twinkly when I called an early bluff of his, and was then reduced to a pale onlooker as he slowly bled me white.

Oh, we all talk tough at the table ("it's not about reality," "it's all ifs and buts," "you gotta speculate to accumulate") and then go home and sob in our wives' arms: tears of loss, tears of gorgeous relief. As you play, unfamiliar chemicals flood the body—money chemicals. In the color-coded diagram, you could portray them as poker chips, helixed and value-stamped. Money is the language of poker. A defeat at chess leaves you flattened, chastened, but not visibly poorer. In poker, defeat means submission to a more worldly power. It's tough out there. And it's tough in here. The winner's silence says to you: *That's* why I'm rock-hard. *That's* why I'm ice-cold. If I weren't, do you think I could get through this either?

Postscript: Anthony Holden was the big winner (well over a thousand pounds); David Mamet doubled his money; Al Alvarez lost, and John Graham lost heavily, as they say; I came out with £200 of the magazine's money. But then I had to write the piece. Holden, in effect, was paid £2 a word for his contribution; I was paid 25p.

TELLS

FROM *Poker Nation*

BY

ANDY BELLIN

At age twenty-two, Andy Bellin left his graduate school studies (*astrophysics!*) for the world of semi-pro poker. He spent the better part of the next ten years honing his game in casino card rooms and New York City's underground poker clubs. *Poker Nation*, his 2002 memoir/exposé, offers penetrating observations on a unique subculture, and at the same time covers the finer points of high-level play.

On the book's opening page, Bellin rates himself an "excellent" player, placing in a theoretical top one-thousandth percentile in the world, albeit with a significant caveat: out of 135 million who play the game, that would still leave 135,000 who play better than he does. But going by the wisdom found in the enclosed chapter, "Tells," he may be selling himself short.

> *A guy walks into a bar and notices three men and a dog playing poker. The dog is playing beautifully.*
>
> *"That's a very smart dog," the man says.*
>
> *"Not really," says one of the players. "Every time he gets a good hand he wags his tail."*

My close friend Steve and I spent the last week of August 1984 up in the Adirondack Mountains at my grandmother's place. Even at an awkward sixteen, Steve had a fantastic gift for finding women to date, no matter where he was. He had a girlfriend at the time to whom he was supposed to be faithful, but for as long as I've known him, that sort of nominal monogamous commitment has been inconsequential. On this summer trip he managed to conjure up a female companion out of the limited population of Paul Smith, New York, and proceeded to spend most of his six-day vacation with her. The night we got home, Steve and I met some friends at a restaurant, one of them being his girlfriend. He walked up to the table and kissed her passionately. She looked him dead in the eye and said, "I can't believe you cheated on me again."

After the obligatory exchange of accusations and denials, Steve finally confessed to his infidelity and groveled for forgiveness. A few hours later she accepted his apology (wasn't high school great?) and they went on to another glorious three weeks of being together. After receiving absolution that night, Steve asked his girlfriend how she figured out his indiscretion so quickly.

"Easy," she said. "First, you didn't look at me while you were walking over to the table. You were staring at the ground the whole time. Second, you kissed me like you were some porn star. And to top it all off, once I accused you of cheating on me, all you did was smile and blink." I looked over at Steve while she was saying this, and sure enough, he was smiling and blinking like crazy. Steve had, as it's known in poker, a tell.

Pop psychologists theorize that tells are unintended actions birthed in the subconscious. At an early age most people are taught a number of rules meant to govern their actions throughout their lives. Parents and teachers, and even the Bible, preach to us that nothing bad can happen if we tell the truth. That rigorous education settles in the subconscious and becomes the foundation for the character we display as we grow into adults. Tells are simply a result of a conflict between the notion of morality implanted by authority figures during our childhoods and our intention to deceive.

We give our little secrets away every day, even though we don't want to. It's said that only the guilty sleep well in jail. The theory goes that if you're guilty and get caught, you figure that you are where you belong and might as well get some sleep. An innocent man tosses and turns, trying to figure out how to resolve his situation.

We are riddled with these tics and twitches. They are everywhere and in everything we do. Those of us who have not been trained to deceive have a tendency to cover our mouths or avoid eye contact when telling lies. That's why I've never dated an actress. While normal people are studying the market economy of the original thirteen colonies or trigonometry, actors are learning how to look you dead in the eye and issue an absolute fabrication.

Our innate desire to tell the truth is most counterproductive at a card table. Having a poker tell can be disastrous. When I was just learning the game, I bought a book called *The Body Language of Poker: Mike Caro's Book of Tells.* I actually never got around to reading it until the night after I got knocked out of the 2000 World Series. Caro described a tell in which a player, thinking about whether to call a bet, suddenly asks the dealer or another player how much it costs to raise. Caro's point was that anybody playing in a decent-size game knows how much it costs to bump a bet. Somebody taking a lot of time and then asking that question has got to be trying to seem stupid or desperate. When I read that, I thought, Caro's got to be making that one up. No one's that dumb.

The next day I went to watch the final table of the tournament I'd just gotten knocked out of. When I arrived, there were only three players left, all great talents. At one point Melissa Hayden bet into Men Nguyen—a three-time champion—and he just sat there looking confused. After a while Men looked at his cards and then asked an official how much it cost to raise. The guy told him, and then Men raised. Melissa called, and Men turned over a full house, laughing as he collected the pot. I guess even the great players have tells.

Overcoming a tell is as difficult as changing any habitual aspect of your personality. I knew a cardplayer who videotaped his regular card game every week for a year. He would watch the tape for hours and take notes about his mannerisms and reactions to make sure that his body language wasn't giving away anything about his hand. He found that even after playing the game for thirty years, he still had, by his estimate, about ten noticeable tells.

I asked him if he thought that any of these were severe enough for other players to notice. Without a thought he said, "I don't know, you tell me. I smile when I have good cards and pout when I don't. Think somebody was gonna pick that one up eventually?" He had a good point there.

If you think about it logically, anyone playing poker is trying to deceive his opponents. It's essential to the game. Therefore, most tells become common sense. In Texas Hold'em, if somebody hits the flop huge, what is he going to do? Well, common sense dictates that since he is trying to deceive, he'll act as if the flop missed him completely. And sure enough, a lot of players do just that. It's a huge tell. They feign disinterest in the hand. They will look away, watch TV, talk to the other players, anything but look directly at the cards on the table. Somebody who stares at the flop for a long time almost certainly missed it. It's like he is examining it in the hope that he will suddenly notice something new.

Now I'm going to do something extremely stupid. For the benefit of my readers, I am going to open up my book of tells that has taken me almost twenty years to create, and let everybody I've ever played with know what their little tic is. I suspect it's going to cost me in the long run, but hey, nothing is as important to me as the happiness of those who have taken the time to peruse this work.

I'll start with my brother. I mentioned before that he's a sturdy player. In fact, he's such a sturdy player that he remains completely calm when he's bluffing. His hands are steady as a rock when he's betting out with garbage. But, and this took me a long time to figure out, when he's got the nuts, and he's got a player trapped, he gets so excited that his hands shake. They tremble when he's got the winning hand.

There are some other classic tells in my Tuesday-night game. Johnny California, a man with the worst posture in the history of primates, sits up straight as a board when he's got good cards. Tom Lemme has a chip-stacking giveaway. When he bets and stacks the chips neatly while putting them in the pot, he usually expects to be getting the chips back. When he throws them into the pot aggressively, he's usually trying to pull off a bluff. And when he tosses them in sloppily, he's usually making a very reluctant call.

I feel like a heel admitting this, but the kind math professor who mentored me through my developmental years of poker in graduate school had a tell. I never told him that I picked it up. I guess I should have, but we used to play together a lot, and keeping it to myself saved me a lot of money. I know that's no excuse. My good friend the professor had a tendency to quickly look at his chips when he hit a good card. It was far from a casual glance. As soon as the good card came up, his eyes shot to his stack of chips. It's like he wanted to make sure that his money was still there to bet with. If, for example, we were playing Texas Hold'em and he had a pair of nines after the flop, and the turn card came up a nine, giving him three nines, he'd stare at his chips and then look away into the distance. I knew what that meant. I folded a lot of top pairs after the turn was dealt when he looked at his chips like that. Sorry, Doc. A better man would have told you sooner.

He is a perfect example why a player should never look at the flop as it's being dealt. Most people gets so fixated on what cards are about to come that they often give something away by their reaction. Don't watch the cards while they are being dealt; watch the faces of the players watching the cards being dealt. You can check your hand later. It's not going anywhere. Just see if anybody flinches or blinks or even looks away when the flop hits the table. It'll certainly tell you something about what's going on around you. This is also the very reason why dealers flip all three cards in flop games at the same time. That way, nobody can clock a player's reaction to each individual card as it comes out.

There are two great tells in my big Monday-night Wall Street Hold'em game. Andrew Megget has this weird way of looking at his cards. He picks them up so only one card is visible, then puts them back down on the table, slides one over the other, and then lifts them again so he can see the second card. He does this the same way every time. Well, almost every time. Occasionally, Andrew takes a second look at the first card. It took me the better part of a year to figure out why this happened. When the first card is inconsequential, like a 5 of clubs, he quickly looks at the second. But if the second card is an ace, he's got to flip back to the first one to see if the suits match because he didn't pay much attention the first time. In every instance that he examined his cards a third time and then called the bet, he's played an ace and a small card of the same suit. Knowing this, of course, is a huge help.

The other great tell in that game is Chris Wigmore. He was, for a long time, a very conservative player; but sometime in the mid 1990s he took a job at an Internet company and made a fortune. Chris started playing very loose after cashing in on those stock options. He's now got a very aggressive game. But even though his checkbook has allowed him to be so carefree at the table that it seems like money means nothing to him, his subconscious is stuck back in 1991, when he was a lowly ad exec, hoping not to lose so much in a $5–$10 game that he couldn't pay his rent. Whenever he makes a big bet in my direction, I just kind of sit there and wait. He probably thinks that I'm calculating pot odds or something like that, but I'm not. I'm just waiting for him to get uncomfortable. When he's got a great hand, Chris is dead serious. He waits me out without saying a word. When he's bluffing, he *tries* to act like he's waiting me out, and strikes up nonchalant conversations with people at the table. That's when I call him.

Chris also has a funny tendency to separate his winnings from his buy-in. This doesn't make much difference in limit games, but in no-limit, that can be a huge disadvantage. A player who stacks his chips this way is obviously very concerned with his outcome. He likes to know that he's up. So whenever we're playing no-limit, if Chris has the $300 stacked separately from his two grand buy-in, I know that—unless he's got a huge hand—any raise over that $300 will usually knock him out, because he wouldn't want to end with less money than he started with.

While I was at Wesleyan I used to play with a guy we called Stoner. He was, as his nickname implies, a full-on dope fiend. Stoner was peppered with practical tells. It's not that he wasn't smart enough to figure them out and make corrections, it's just that he didn't really care enough to change. If the flop was three cards of the same suit, and Stoner didn't look at his pocket cards and did bet, I always knew he had a flush. But if after a suited flop he looked at his pocket cards right away, then I knew he was too high to remember what suits they were and had to check them before figuring out what to do. If, after checking his cards, he called any bets, then I knew he didn't have the flush yet, but one of his pocket cards definitely matched the suit on the board, and therefore he needed one of the two cards left to make the flush. He'd do the same thing in seven-card stud. If he got his third of one suit on fifth street and had to pick up his down cards to check them out, then I knew that he didn't have the flush just yet.

Stoner also was one of those players that never bet an incomplete hand in five-card draw. If he was dealt a four flush or straight, he always checked or called and then drew one card. But if he bet or raised and then took one card, that meant he had two pair. Also, the way he looked at the drawn card was always a huge giveaway. When he was on a flush draw, he'd shuffle the drawn card into his hand and then squeeze it out slowly.

He'd do the same thing in seven-card stud. When he was dealt the river card, if he shuffled it into the rest of his down cards, then he was always on a draw. If he just picked it up and looked at it, then he always had a made hand before the river.

The last hand Stoner and I ever played together was a heads-up game of pot-limit five-card draw. He dealt me the ace and king of hearts, the three and eight of spades, and the nine of clubs. I had been losing all day, so I opened the betting with $3. Stoner called. I threw the 3, 8, and 9 away and drew three cards. He drew one. After dealing himself the card, he picked it up and looked at it. I miraculously drew a ten, jack, and a queen, ended up making an ace-high straight (known as "Broadway"), and bet the maximum. He raised me back the amount of the pot. That was a scary raise. Against any other player, I would have been terrified that they had made a full house or a flush. But not Stoner. Since he had just called my original bet, and then taken one card, I knew he didn't have two pair, so a full house was out of the question. And then after he dealt himself the one card, he picked it up and looked at it—he didn't shuffle it into his hand and squeeze it out like he does when he's looking for a flush. So I knew he had a straight. Since I had the highest straight possible, the worst I could do was chop the pot with him, so I raised him back the value of the pot. We each raised once more, then he finally called and flipped over his king-high straight. He lost over $200 in one hand of a heads-up game with a dollar ante. And that's hard to do.

He actually accused me of cheating after that hand because my last raise was, in his eyes, suspicious. He wanted to know how I didn't put him on a flush or a full house and therefore just call him. Well, buddy, here's your answer.

That hand that I played with Stoner was a perfect example of the deductive reasoning necessary to becoming a winning poker player. Each observation alone didn't help me all that much. But when I put them all together, it became extremely useful information.

Obviously, the more familiar you are with a player, the longer you play against them, the easier they are to read. Over time, you make notes about their play, and eventually you will be able to predict their actions. There are, however, certain universal truths about human nature that transfer directly to the card table. Take any cliché about the human psyche, and you will find something that applies to poker players.

Somebody much smarter than me once said, "The vigor of youth gives birth to the misconceptions of immortality." It's a little flowery for my taste, but has a fantastic application at the poker table. Younger players have not yet become jaded by years of improbable beats. They feel virile at a table. For the most part, the younger the player, the looser they are, and the more likely it is that they will bluff. Older players tend to be wiser, more in control of their emotions, and play a much more straight-up game. The older a player is, the less likely it is that he will represent cards that he doesn't have.

The things players do and say unrelated to poker often open a revealing window into their psyche. Drunks bluff more. People betting on sports or the horse races while playing poker only participate in hands when they have premium cards because their attention is being diverted elsewhere and they're not concentrating enough to bluff with any savvy. Same is true for people eating at the table. Individuals who dress up for the game in fedora hats or fancy sunglasses often play a complicated game. They'll bluff or semi-bluff and slow play a lot more than the average player.

A few nights after I got knocked out of last year's World Series, I played a medium-size pot-limit Texas Hold'em game at Binion's. There was one hand in which I found myself heads-up with a gentleman who looked exactly like Uncle Fester from the Addams family. After many raises and reraises, the river was dealt. By the last card I had exactly what I started with, a pair of jacks. There was no possible flush on the board, no easily playable straight, and the only card that was higher than my jacks was a queen that came on the river. I had ended each round of betting before the river, meaning that I had either bet or raised and Fester had called me. But as soon as the river was dealt, Fester bet the pot—about $500. Now, I had never met this man before in my whole life. I had no real thought about him before that hand other than to picture him with a lightbulb in his mouth. I had no way to figure out whether he was bluffing or not. I decided to try an old standby move; I faked like I was going to call his bet by motioning toward my chips while watching to see if he had any reaction to my move. Most of time a player will react to a called bet. If he slumps in his chair, he's got nothing. If he jumps toward his cards to flip them over, he usually has a huge hand. Well, Fester didn't do anything. He just sat and watched me. He did, however, get steamed that I tried such a sophomoric move on him. So he started to coffee-house me. "What the hell was that, you trying to steal the money, kid? What you gonna do with it anyway, buy some Rogaine?"

I had managed to piss off a total stranger, which I didn't feel so good about. But then I began to think about his insult. Now, I do have a receding hairline, that is an undeniable fact, but I still have a good deal of hair on my head. So what was this gentleman trying to say? If some guy with a full head of Fabio hair levied that volley at me, I would have thought that he was trying to piss me off and therefore make me call with a losing hand, so I'd fold. But this man was full-blown, Telly Savalas bald. I'm not even sure he had eyebrows. Some guys can get away with that sort of look, but it wasn't particularly flattering on him. So what's up with the pot calling the kettle puce? Why is he talking to me about Rogaine? I saw it for the desperate insult that it was, so I called. Fester turned over his pocket tens, I turned over my jacks, and the dealer pushed me the $1,000 pot.

My read on Fester could have been completely wrong. He could have predicted my reasoning and insulted me, hoping that I'd call. That's why a lot of players actually have fake tells. They are, after all, trying to deceive you. But one thing is certain—the more you pay attention to the body language of your opponents, the less money you'll leave on the table when you walk away.

FRAUDS IN PLAYING AND POKER SHARPS

FROM *The Complete Poker Player*

BY

JOHN BLACKBRIDGE

John Blackbridge, a late-nineteenth century New York City attorney, was one of poker's earliest literary proponents. "So many cultivated men love this game," he wrote in the preface to his 1880 *Practical Guide-Book*, "that it is impossible for me to do otherwise than respect it." Blackbridge goes on to defend the relatively new pastime against those who opposed it on moral grounds: "The child, who tries to win a prize at school by diligent mental culture, is a fair example of the honorable cardplayer who tries to win agreed-upon stakes, from associate players, by superior calculation of chances, or superior mental force."

In these selected pages, however, we find Blackbridge alerting readers to potential treachery at the hands of the *dis*-honorable. By every indication Blackbridge was a conservative player who didn't book too many losers, a man who must have steered clear of the sharpers he warned about. Still, one can only imagine what a minefield the game was in its infancy. "Undetected roguery" indeed.

The visible boil upon the surface of the human body proves that there is invisible corruption within, and the occasional discovery of frauds at cards practiced by men who up to that time had been regarded as honorable, proves the existence of much undetected roguery.

Now and then card-playing circles are shocked by unexpected disclosures, but it is very seldom that men are suspected until the moment when they are found out. But the detections must be very rare in proportion to the offenses; being either the result of accidents, or carelessness on the part of the operator, or of long-continued watchfulness on the part of some one observer; all of which are less likely to happen than the offense itself, which is the carefully matured fruit of deep design and laborious education.

If card-sharpers exist, and they certainly do, because now and then they are detected, under what circumstances shall we find them? Not playing against Faro Banks, because the banks handle the cards. Not playing among poor people in the beer houses, because poor people have no money to lose. But we shall find them among people of means, playing a game that admits of card manipulation, and that is played for money. The game of Poker exactly satisfies these conditions and as it is played more than any other gambling game at cards, so the chances are greater that this particular game is infested by sharpers.

I had for years deduced these conclusions, but had never verified them, although I had not failed to be impressed with facts in connection with the play of certain players. But in the summer of 1874, I obtained the confidence of a card-sharper who explained to me the manipulations that can be, and are, practiced at Poker-playing; with full permission to disclose them, provided always no mention were made of his name. For although I informed this man that I should probably publish his revelations, he evidently did not think I would take the trouble to do so; and even if such should be the case, he did not feel that he should be the loser by it. His name not being made known, the chances of injury to him are indeed infinitesimal.

This man visited my office by appointment, after usual business hours, and the sixty minutes which he passed with me were as full of instruction to me as any twenty-fourth part of a day of my life. He was a very good-looking man of about forty years of age, having the appearance of one who had been leading a temperate and thoughtful life. There was not the slightest affectation of conscience about him, and feeling safe with me, and being absolutely alone, there was no reserve in his communications.

His first step was to prove to me that it was quite possible to hold two cards in the left hand while dealing, which two cards could be previously eliminated from the pack in the process of shuffling, and would be, of course, two aces. As he did this quite as often as I asked him to, in the broad light of day, under close circumspection, I could not doubt the almost perfect safety with which an expert could perform the same act by gaslight amid careless company. It was thus entirely evident that a skillful dealer can hold a pair of aces, or three, whenever he likes, which would be often, but not too often.

He then showed me that he could deal a card or several cards from the bottom of the pack without my knowledge. He dealt four hands around on my desk six or eight times, giving himself each time the card from the bottom of the pack and naming it, and I could not see that it was so dealt. This he told me was one of the easiest tricks, and the one most practiced by so called "gentlemen" card players, of whom he has had several under his tuition.

In most cases, he said, the dealer can find means to catch a glimpse of the bottom card. But if he cannot, he may cultivate his sense of feeling so as to distinguish an *ace* or *court-card* by the tips of the fingers. This of itself affords a large percentage, for if the dealer goes in on a pair of aces, and has an ace on the bottom of the pack, he is then sure of *three*, and *may* get four; and if he goes in on a pair of kings, he has one chance in three of a king if he feels a court card above his fingertips, besides the chance of a king in the other two cards on the top, or the bottom of the pack.

If the dealer should happen to have a four flush, or four straight, and knows the bottom card to be the proper card to fill, he has an opportunity to raise the other players, and on the whole, the general advantages of this one accomplishment, he assured me, would enable a player to withstand almost any run of ill-luck and to win largely with average good fortune.

"Poker players often make this use of these accomplishments," said this man, "they play into the hands of their friends and divide afterwards, as I will now show you." Thereupon after some little shuffling which I carefully watched, he dealt four hands, and requested me to take up a certain hand in which I should find three aces. I did so, and sure enough the three aces were there. In the next round he dealt four aces with equal facility, for where one can deal cards at will, there is no more trouble in dealing four aces than three.

This last maneuver, this man informed me, was not to be baffled by cutting, because under skillful manipulation the cards take such shape that a person cutting them carelessly, cuts them precisely as the sharper wishes; and furthermore the cut amounts to nothing anyhow, if the sharper does not wish to recognize it, as he can usually replace the two parts of the pack *as they were*, and no one shall be the wiser for it. In the usual excitement of the game, such details are not closely watched.

This man stated to me, and indeed it is very obvious, that a manipulator does not need to manipulate all the time, in order to win. He need only do it at critical periods, as for instance when the luck is running against him; or when he has a four flush, or four straight; or two pairs, "aces up," in which latter instance the knowledge of the bottom card affords a "dead sure thing," for a raise. "A card sharper," he said, "must not be over greedy, and must not overdo the business."

Much as this man told me, I am satisfied there was much he did not tell me. But if the reader will accept these statements of mine as true, and there is certainly no reason why I should make untrue statements in regard to such an interview, enough has been disclosed to make honest card players very wary of the society of *any man who habitually wins.* This is the only way of punishing the card sharper; as for exposing him, it is almost impossible. Suppose you see a dealer giving himself a card from the bottom of the pack, you cannot speak of the occurrence until it has occurred. By the time it has taken place the card is his, and the pack is on the table. You affirm; he denies. In such a case there can be no umpire and your position is a false one, because you assert what, from the nature of the case, you cannot prove. The chances are indeed infinitesimal that two or three of the players should see the act together. The card sharper chooses a time when he sees the players occupied, so that while a person who undertakes to play with six cards *may* be taken "red-handed," another, who confines himself to dealing from the bottom of the pack, and to holding two cards till the final deal to himself, can only be exposed by a species of miracle.

Now to return to the main argument, in a small game the honest player will lose much less by the card sharper and what is of more consequence to him, he will rarely meet with this bird of ill-omen in a small game. For no man of average *assumed* respectability will care to practice fraud where the stakes are so small as to be played for amusement only. This I take to be the chief reason why gentlemen should play Draw-Poker for the recognized *minimum* of the game, that is, two dollars and a half.

Another argument in favor of playing the limited game is, that it can be played with a contented mind. The game of Poker should be intellectual and not emotional; and it is impossible to exclude the emotions from it, if the stakes are so high that the question of loss and gain penetrates to the *feelings*. No man can play his game well if he feels that on the turn of a card depends his solvency, or the comforts of his family, or the payment of his bills, or if in short the losses may amount to a sum which he cannot afford. I allude, of course, only to the case of honorable men who intend to pay at once whatever they lose.

All Poker-players will agree with the writer, that as soon as the feeling of anxiety as to the amount of their losses enters into their game, their play is ruined. In this respect the Poker-sharp has a great advantage over the gentleman player. The sharp never has any anxiety as to the future, no matter how large the stakes are, because he has such extra percentages in his favor that no vicissitudes can permanently injure him.

As soon as this feeling of anxiety besets a player, it makes itself manifest, and tells on his entire game. He usually begins to try to "force" the game, and of all games Poker is the last to be successfully forced. The more he forces, the more he loses; the more he loses the more he forces, in order to win. When a player is in bad luck and play-ing beyond his depth—circumstances which often depend on one another and accompany each other—he backs his luck, usually, very much beyond the dictates of experience and common sense. He is therefore engaged in a direct warfare against the laws of averages, and in this unequal battle nothing but extraordinary luck will save him. But by the hypothesis he is already in bad luck, and is backing it up fiercely, hoping for the turn. Under such circumstances his losses are only limited by the amount of the stakes, by his credit, and by the compassion of his antagonists.

I was once playing in a $25.00 game in which luck was running against me. I filled a Jack full, and meeting with some resistance on the part of another player, I called at the second raise, winning a pool of about $150. Another player who was sitting in worse luck under-took to criticize my play, and said that *he* would not have called at anything like so early a period. I patiently accepted the criticism. In a few moments *he* drew a good hand and also met with resistance on the opposite side of the table. Raise followed raise until he himself had invested $250, there being $600 in the pool. At this period, seeing no signs of weakening on the part of his antagonist, he called, with a Queen full in his own hand, finding four of a kind out against him. This ill event, added to his previous bad luck, made an end of him, for the loss was beyond his ready means, and his play during the remain-der of the evening was frozen down to a mere negation.

Baron Rothschild's maxim is in this connection a golden one for Poker-players—"cut short your losses; let your profits run on." In other words, do not back bad luck at all, and let good luck have a large swing. When you are in bad luck you are on the high road to poverty, although you may be at a great distance from it, but still you are on a road which you cannot afford to travel; therefore *don't travel it any faster than you are obliged to*, and remember, when you are in bad luck, you are apt to lose on *strong hands*.

If more arguments need to be adduced in support of a small limit game, let me remind the reader that life is short, and that a few good reasons are as good as a great many. The only other reason that I shall here mention is that in a small game cash payments can be rigidly enforced, and without cash payments the game of Draw-Poker becomes a fertile source of trouble. Whoever invented the credit system at cards was an enemy of human happiness. Endorsing for your friends is a bad habit, but it is nothing to playing Poker on credit, that is if you are an honorable man. For in the excitement of a large game you are under a spell in the direction of borrowing which renders you unfit to undertake such speculations. Yet this is the very time when you undertake them most fiercely. How different is the position of the man who plays a small limited game and sits down for a few hours amusement with a hundred dollars in his pocket, *sure* that he cannot lose all of it, and *sure* therefore that he can rise from the table out of debt. In such a game the banker can demand cash for all chips furnished, hence at the end of the game all chips are redeemed in cash. Debit and credit ought never to interfere with the fine intellectual calculations of this game.

Nearly all Poker-players that eventually abandon the game do so because they have suffered by large play, of which some "sharp" has reaped the benefit. No one ever abandons Poker that plays it on small limited stakes. Sharps will not play such a game, and as it never leads to ill results it prospers forever by its own merits, like the simple, healthy and unforced growth of a plant that is nourished by Nature.

PUG PEARSON

FROM *Fast Company*

BY

JON BRADSHAW

Jon Bradshaw (1937–1986) was a gifted journalist with the proverbial keen eye for detail. A high-living raconteur, he loved the world of gambling, and he loved writing about it, as evidenced by his now-classic *Fast Company* (1975)—an enthralling half-dozen profiles of raffish, high-rolling winners. These six were, in Bradshaw's introductory words, "blessed with a certain magic"; they shared in common a "joyful acceptance of risk," a "superb and enviable insouciance."

Such traits define the inimitable Pug Pearson, for many decades a legendary fixture on the Vegas poker scene. In Bradshaw's vivid portraiture, here's Pearson shortly before he won the World Series of Poker in 1973.

The Aladdin is no gaudier than any other hotel on the Las Vegas Strip. Given the ambiance, the names of the hotel's main rooms make as much sense as its mock-Byzantine façade—the Sabre Room, the Sinbad Lounge, the Gold Room, and the Baghdad Theatre. The card room is in the Sinbad Lounge, the large main room on the ground floor, where nightly some of the biggest poker games in the world are played. It is here that Pug Pearson holds court in a way Neil Diamond must have had in mind when he sang of "a high-rolling man in a high-rolling neighborhood." At first, it seems more than a little preposterous to find Pug, "a poor country boy from down yonder," in such an opulent environment, until one understands that here the American ideal has been carried to its most practical conclusion: a place where regardless of differences in background, taste, or intelligence, money makes everyone equal, or momentarily creates that illusion. On the wall above the card tables is a sign that reads: POKER—24 HOURS EVERY DAY. Above the sign is a spread royal heart flush. The card room is not a room at all, since it occupies a side of the Sinbad Lounge and is open to traffic between the slot machines in the lobby and the stage, from which pours the amplified noise of resident talent. Round about the card tables is the crowd of tourists and hopeful high rollers, as ridiculously dressed as jesters, the shills and stickmen, the security men and bad-credit boys acting as a kind of palace guard, and here and there an itinerant hooker. The people come and go like refugees, the places of the departed so quickly taken by new arrivals that there is little impression of real movement—just a kind of tense restlessness, and the garbled sounds of the machines and the music and the mob lifted in endless crescendo. It is here that Pug, who had never been as innocent as any of them, makes his daily bread.

Pug has lived in Vegas for ten years. Once before that he had come here but the local players broke him and sent him home. Now, however, he and his wife, Andrea, his son and daughter occupied a rambling house on the suburban edge of the city. His wife was also from Nashville and Pug claimed they still missed the hills and streams of Tennessee. But Vegas was where the action was and his wife accepted his way of life, because, as Pug explained, "There ain't no changin' it." Now, action does not mean easy money, though there is that, too. But some of the best poker players in the country live in Vegas. Almost to a man they are Southerners—from Texas, Oklahoma, and Kentucky, and, like Pug, poor boys become well-to-do because of a talent at cards. It is a curious fact that, like the American military (eighty percent of whom above the rank of major are Southerners), the majority of professional cardplayers (and cardsharps) are from the South. Thus, in one sense, by playing cards with his peers, Pug maintains a loose hold on his roots. Eliminate the slot machines and the vulgar Western crowds, listen to the players in the Aladdin Hotel and one might easily be in Abilene or Tulsa or Bowling Green.

The night I walked into the Aladdin Hotel, I was told I could find Pug at the poker table, where he had been for the past twenty-four hours. He was dressed as he always was—the striped trousers, the short-sleeved shirt, the colored shoes, and the wide straw hat. He looked no more outlandish than anyone else in the room; he looked perfectly at home. There was an air of permanence about him, the slightly bored authority of a teacher who has taught the same course for twenty years. He was in the middle of a hand and looked, as Nick the Greek had once been described, "like a guy sitting with an icicle up his ass." Looking around the crowded, noisy room, I remembered that this was the place that Pug had called his office, a place of business to which he came each night; his opponents, seated now round the green felt table in various attitudes of peevish dejection, he had referred to as his clientele. They were all there—Johnny Moss, Alabama Blackie, Treetop Jack Straus, Nate Raymond, Texas Dolly, and a group of lesser players, all of whom looked like they had ridden in that night from the ranch.

In Las Vegas Pug was deferred to, as parents defer to favorite sons. Everyone seemed to know him. Waitresses assured themselves his glass was always filled with water or tea or Seven-Up; passers-by stopped to chat or to whisper urgent messages in his ear; and players, en route to other games, paused to discuss old times or future plans. All of which Pug accepted as his due. "Of course, they know me," he said. "If you were the principal of the school, wouldn't all the kids know you? Folks know me real well out here. I could sit down in the middle of the freeway and get a game going, because people like to play with me. They like my action. They know I'm gonna give 'em a square gamble. That's what it's all about. I can beat 'em and beat 'em and they'll always come back. But fuck 'em out of a quarter and they'll leave forever. It gives 'em an excuse for losing."

Pug thought of himself as a winner; it was something he knew

about. As a winner he also figured he knew more about loss than losers did. "Losing," he told me, "is like smoking. It's habit-forming,
believe me. Some of the players at this here table couldn't beat Tom
Thumb at nothin'. But loss is inevitable. The question is how much
you control it. A winner is first and foremost a controller. That's why
in life, I'm just a little better than even—and an odds-on favorite to
stay that way.

"You've got to remember that in poker there are more winners
than losers. At least at the higher levels. I'd say there was a ratio of
twenty-to-one. But losers are great suppliers. One loser supplies a lot
of winners. And the better the player, the bigger the cut. That's what
they call the great pyramid of gamblin'. Sharks at the top, then the
rounders, the minnows, and at the bottom the fish—the suckers, the
suppliers. Scavengers and suppliers, just like in life.

"It's a funny thing—gamblin'. It's like running a grocery store. You
buy and you sell. You pay the going rate for cards and you try and sell
'em for more than you paid. A gambler's ace is his ability to think
clearly under stress. That's very important, because, you see, fear is the
basis of all mankind. In cards, you psych 'em out, you shark 'em, you
put the fear of God in 'em. That's life. Everything's mental in life. The
butt was made to lug the mind around. The most important thing in
gamblin' is knowing the sixty-forty end of the proposition and knowing the human element. Some folks may know one of 'em, but ain't
many know 'em both. I believe in logics. Cut and dried. Two and two
ain't nothin' in this world but four. But them suckers always think it's
somethin' different. Makes you think, don't it? I play percentages in
everything. Now knowing the percentages perfectly, the kind of numbers you read in them books, is all right, but the hidden percentages
are more important. The real thing to know is that folks will stand to
lose more than they will to win. That's the most important percentage
there is. I mean, if they lose, they're willin' to lose everything. If they
win, they're usually satisfied to win enough to pay for dinner and a
show. The best gamblers know that."

Pug continued to play poker until ten in the morning. I sat next to
him or just behind like a stowaway, and between hands or when he

folded early, we talked. There were usually five or six players sitting round the table with piles of one-hundred-dollar bills and various stacks of colored chips in front of them. Occasionally a player went broke, or another would leave and someone would take his place. There were no introductions. They all knew one another and Pug referred to them as "environment." They played limit poker—usually five- or seven-card stud—which Pug believed was the best kind of poker, because there was less jeopardy and the best player always won. Once, in the middle of a hand, Pug suddenly turned as though he had forgotten something and said, "Always remember, the first thing a gambler has to do is make friends with himself. A lot of people go through this world thinking they're someone else. There are a lot of players sitting at this table with mistaken identities. You wouldn't believe it."

The hands continued throughout the night. At midnight Pug's wife phoned to say good night. She had accustomed herself to his hours long ago. "Sometimes I'll phone him up," she said, "and say, 'Hon, you're tired, it's time to come home,' and he'll say, 'I'll be home in a few minutes.' And I might not see him for days." As she talked Pug continued to play, the telephone cupped on his shoulder. At one point he was almost ten thousand dollars ahead, but by four in the morning he had lost most of it. He was tired. He had been up too long. "When you get to slidin' in gamblin'," he said, "you better have enough strength to quit. When you get beat on and beat on, you bet when you should check and you check when you should bet. Folks get so they can read your mail." Pug, however, began winning again and his game was soon interspersed with running comment and criticism. Toward the end of one hand he turned up his cards and said: "This will beat your two queens, pally."

"Christ, Pug, how'd you know I had queens?" said his opponent. "You see through my cards?"

"Hell, no," laughed Pug. "I'm a gambler, not a mind reader."

Another player, a Texan, decided to leave, taking nearly eight thousand dollars with him. As he left, Pug said, "He'll be back. He's a great poker player, but like most gamblers he's got a lot of bad habits—craps, roulette, and the football." Beating another player for a small pot, Pug said to him, "Son, if I'd had your hand, I'd of won." He laughed. "That's the thing of poker," he said. "Ideally, you want the winning hands to pay and the losing hands to win. And the only way to do that is to control the game. You know how an actor is on the stage? He acts in such a way as to keep every eye in that audience on *him*. Right? Now, a poker player's the same way. I want all them players' eyes on *me*. I want them to sweat out what I'm doing. I want them all involved with me. And I'll do anything to get their attention. Otherwise I wouldn't be there. If you don't act the way you should, you ain't there. Most players will sit at a table right through the night and they might as well have been home in bed. They just don't act right. And they don't learn nothin'. Everyone's got habits and you've got to recognize them. You know how cows always take the same path to the watering hole, one behind the other? Well, we're the same way. People, I mean. Hell, even the beasts of the jungle, them elephants, take the exact same path when they go away to die. Poker players are just the same."

At ten in the morning Pug was about twenty-five hundred dollars ahead. He decided to play a final hand. The calls and raises went back and forth until there was some four thousand dollars in the pot. Only Pug and one other player had stayed in. Pug was very quiet. The seventh card was dealt. It was his call. He hesitated for a moment, then looked up and, pushing a pile of one-hundred-dollar bills into the pot, said: "I'm gonna raise you, son, 'cause you ain't got nothin' in your hand but dreams." Pug didn't wait for an answer. Turning over his hand he pulled in the pot. The other player put down his cards and, shaking his head in disbelief, said, "Puggie, you're the goddamnedest lucky player. You really are."

Pug grinned, lighting up a fresh cigar. He put his money in his pocket and we left. "They all think I'm the luckiest son of a bitch that ever lived," he said. "I like that. It brings 'em back. Hell, ain't no one can fill an inside straight quicker'n me. I'll tell you 'bout luck. I believe in it, sure, even though I know there ain't no such thing. But other folks believe in it and sometimes it's downright polite to go along with their beliefs. One thing's certain, though. Luck ain't never paid the bills."

That morning, Pug told me the story of the biggest hand he had ever won. "I was playin' Johnny Moss," he said, "at deuce-to-the-seven lowball. Kansas City lowball, they call it. Straights and flushes count against you. The perfect hand is two–three–four–five–seven. Now, I'm dealt a two–three–four–seven–jack. There were six or seven players in the game, a two-hundred-dollar ante. After the first round, there ain't but three of us left in the pot—Johnny, me, and another guy, who was sitting on my right. This guy opens with a thousand. I raise twenty-eight hundred, Johnny calls and raises five thousand and then this guy only calls. Well, I know this guy, see, and he's a tight player, and when he calls, I figure either he's got a perfect hand, what they call a bicycle, or he's gonna draw, and it's a hundred-to-one he's gonna draw. So I push all my checks into the pot—about twenty-five thousand—hoping to pick it up right there. Well, there's about forty-seven thousand in that pot now. Johnny sits there and stalls and stalls and does a lot of whispering with his confederate. I know he's got a real tough hand, possibly a two–three–four–seven and a ten or a jack. And I'm worried. Well, I know what Johnny's thinkin' and he's a good enough player to know that I know what he's thinkin', just like he knows what I'm thinkin'. Hell, we're environment, we know each other like hills and streams. Finally, Johnny calls for what he's got left, which is fifteen thousand. By calling, you understand, he thought he was getting two-to-one on his money. Which is what I thought. But, what happens, the guy on my right throws in his cards. He folds. Now Johnny knows he ain't but getting about six-to-five on his money and that just ain't the same investment. That's the main secret in cards—getting the right price on your money. Now, had the other guy drawn, I'm gonna get rid of that jack, but he drops, so I stand pat, figuring to make Johnny come off his hand. Hoping he'll dog it. Johnny is in last position. And he's uncertain. He knows I play kinda wild. Now, he stalls and stalls. I can see the BB's goin' round and round in his head, just like he sees mine, though not so clearly—Johnny's gettin' on. No more bets can be made, so he knows I'm not stealin'. He also knows I'm not bluffin'. I'm not. I'm playin' a fine line, son. I was reading my people real good and I knew it. I was like one of those guys with a baton in front of an orchestra. I was playin' it like Liberace. And Johnny, Johnny knows I got a hand. But what kind of hand do I have? He probably figures I've got a slick nine or an eight, so what does he do? He pooches it and draws. Now, once he hits that deck, I'm an eight-and-a-half-to-five or maybe an eight-to-five favorite to win. As he draws I flop over my hand and say, 'Johnny, you made a mistake, now beat that jack.' 'Oh, my God,' he says, 'I dumped the winning hand.' And I raked in the pot of sixty-two thousand. Now that's what I mean about knowin' your human element."

It was nearly noon. Pug took me round his garden, which he had reclaimed from the desert at the back of his house. "It's a long way from Jackson County, ain't it?" he said with a grin. Even here, in Las Vegas, Appalachia wasn't far away, it seemed, and it reminded me that for all his practicalities Pug would have to play and keep on playing in order to push it farther from his mind. But it was always there. It was why he talked so intimately of loss and why, suddenly, as if in answer to a question I had asked some time ago, he began to talk of it again.

"Losers," he said, " have an overwhelming ambition to win. They con themselves that they can win and that's why they keep on coming back. They make regular appearances. They *have* to, you understand, 'cause they'd hold a bad opinion of themselves otherwise. But, without 'em, there would be no winners. No me." He paused, then added: "And that would be contrary to the laws of nature. Wouldn't be right."

Pug believed in what he liked to think were the laws of nature, one of them being that he would always be a winner. Although he had been broke before, he believed the odds had set things right and that they had also promised something more. And perhaps they had— though it continued to evade him. Like his father before him, chasing rumors of work from one hollow town to another, Pug still pursued that dream of high elusive action. And in his darker moments he must have wondered why it had not materialized before. No matter. He was a patient suitor. Tomorrow it would come. Tomorrow . . . or the day after. It was in the cards.

Four Men and a Poker Game, or Too Much Luck Is Bad Luck

BY

Bertolt Brecht

This gem of a parable from the great playwright first appeared in a Stuttgart literary magazine in 1926. For Brecht, it was a time of traditional storytelling that predated the innovative themes of his major dramatic works. But as with the later work, the style here is direct, lean, and markedly absent of sentiment. In his dramas, Brecht sought an "alienation effect" by which actors were to steer clear of overinvolvement in their roles. There's a similar sense of sardonic remove in his short-story writing, as in the author's early setup: "It is sheer poetry from A to Z. It begins with cigar smoke and laughter and ends with a corpse."

They sat on cane chairs in Havana and let the world go by. When it got too hot they drank iced water; in the evenings they danced the Boston at the Atlantic Hotel. All four of them had money.

The newspapers called them great men. They read it three times and chucked the paper into the sea. Or they held the paper between their hands and pierced it with their toecaps. Three of them had broken swimming records in front of ten thousand people, and the fourth had brought all ten thousand to their feet. When they had beaten the field and read the papers they boarded ship. They were headed back to New York with good money in their pockets.

To tell this story properly really calls for jazz accompaniment. It is sheer poetry from A to Z. It begins with cigar smoke and laughter and ends with a corpse.

For one of them, it was generally agreed, could coax salmon out of a sardine tin. He was what they call fortune's child. His name was Johnny Baker. Lucky Johnny. He was one of the best short-distance swimmers in either hemisphere. But the ridiculous luck he enjoyed threw a shadow over all his triumphs. For when a man can't unfold a paper napkin without finding a dollar bill, people begin to wonder whether he is good at his business, even if his name is Rockefeller. And wonder they did.

He had won in Havana just like the two others. He had won the 200 yard crawl by a length. But once again it was an open secret that his strongest opponent couldn't stand the climate and hadn't been fit. Johnny of course said they would try to pin something like that on him and go on about his "luck" whatever happened, no matter how well he had been swimming. When he said it the other three just smiled.

This was the state of play when the story began, and it began with a little game of poker. The ship was a bore.

The sky was blue and so was the sea. The drinks were good, but they always were. The cigars smoked as well as any other cigars. In short, sky, sea, drinks and cigars were no good at all.

They thought a little game of poker might be better. It wasn't far short of the Bermudas when they began to play. They settled themselves comfortably for the game; each of them used two chairs. They agreed like gentlemen about the seating arrangements. One man's feet lay by another's ear. Thus, not far short of the Bermudas, they began to work their own downfall.

Since Johnny was feeling insulted by certain insinuations, they were only three to start with. One won, one lost, one held his own. They were playing with tin chips, each standing for five cents. Then the game got too boring for one of them and he took his feet out of the game. Johnny took his place. After that, the game wasn't boring any more. That is, Johnny began to win. If there was one thing Johnny couldn't do, it was play poker: but winning at poker was something he could do.

When Johnny bluffed, the bluff was so ridiculous that no poker player in the world would have dared go along with it. And when anybody who knew Johnny would have suspected a bluff, Johnny would innocently lay a flush on the table.

Johnny himself played stone cold for a couple of hours. The two others were het up. When the fourth man came back after watching potatoes being peeled in the galley for two hours, he observed that the tin chips were standing at a dollar.

This little increase had been the only way Johnny's partners could hope to get back some of their money. It was quite simple: they were to recoup in greenbacks what he had won in cents. Responsible family men could not have played with more caution in this situation. But it was Johnny who raked in the spondulicks.

They played six hours at a stretch. At any time during those six hours they could have left the game and lost no more to Johnny than the prize-money they had won in Havana. After those six hours of worry and effort they no longer could.

It was time for dinner. They polished off the meal in double-quick time. Instead of forks they felt straights between their fingers. They ate their steaks thinking of royal flushes. The fourth man ate much more slowly. He said he was really beginning to feel like taking a hand, since a little life seemed to have crept into their dreary diddling.

After dinner they were a foursome again. They played for eight hours. When Johnny counted their money about three in the morning they had left the Bermudas behind.

They slept rather badly for five hours and started again. By then three of them were men who, whatever happened, would be in hock for years. They had one more day ahead of them; at midnight they would arrive in New York. In the course of that day they had to make sure they were not going to be ruined for life. For among them was a lousy poker player who was sucking the marrow from their bones.

In the morning, when the appearance of several ships showed that the coast was near, they began to stake their houses. On top of everything else Johnny won a piano. Then they took two hours off at noon before squaring up to play for the shirts on their backs. At five in the afternoon they saw no choice but to go on. The man who had waited till after the Bermudas to take a hand and who was still eating calmly when the others had forgotten what their forks were for, offered to play Johnny for his girl. That is to say, if Johnny won, he would have the right to take a certain Jenny Smith to the male voice choir's Widows' Ball in Hoboken, but if he lost he would have to give back everything he had already won from the others. And Johnny took him up.

First of all he got his facts straight.

"And you won't be coming along?"

"Wouldn't dream of it."

"And you won't hold it against me?"

"I won't hold it against you."

"Or against her?"

"What do you mean against her?"

"Well, the girl, you won't hold it against her?"

"Godammit no, I won't hold it against her either."

And then Johnny won.

When you place a bet, win, pocket your winnings, raise your hat and leave, it means you have been in danger and emerged unscathed. But if you have too big a heart and give your partners another chance, then, unless you end in the poorhouse, your partners will be on your back for the rest of your life. They will eat your liver like vultures. When playing poker you have to be as hard-hearted as in any other form of expropriation.

From the moment when Johnny joined the game because another player left the table, he had let the others call the shots. They had forced him to look at several thousand cards, they had robbed him of his sleep, they had made him wolf down his meals in record time. They would really have preferred him to carry on playing and every six hours snatch the odd mouthful from a steak dangling on a string above the card-table. Johnny found it all distasteful.

When he got up from the table after playing for the girl—which so far as he was concerned had topped everything—he had in his naïve way thought they had had enough. They had taken him on knowing how lucky he was, because they thought he knew as little about poker as a traindriver knows about geography. But trains have rails which know their geography: a guy goes from New York to Chicago and nowhere else. That was exactly the system with which he had won, and the only thing left was for him to return his winnings without mortally offending them. Johnny's weakness was his heart. He had too much tact.

He said straight out not to worry, it had all been in fun. They didn't answer. They sat there as they had since the previous day and watched the seagulls, which were now more plentiful.

Johnny concluded from this that, so far as they were concerned, more than 24 hours of poker was no joke.

Johnny stood by the railing and thought. Then it came to him. He suggested that they should first of all have a meal with him that evening to restore their spirits. At his expense naturally. What he had in mind was a grand function, a blow-out, a really slap-up meal. He himself would mix drinks that would loosen their tongues. In view of the circumstances no expense need be spared. He even had caviar in mind. Johnny expected big things of this meal.

They didn't say no.

They took this without exactly showing enthusiasm, but at any rate they agreed to go along with him. It was time to eat anyhow.

Johnny went off and did the ordering. He went into the kitchen and ingratiated himself with the chef. He wanted a meal dished up for himself and his friends, a banquet which would outdo anything of its kind ever produced by any first class ship's galley between Havana and New York. Johnny felt a lot better after the conversation with the chef.

During this half-hour not a single word was spoken on deck.

Johnny set the table himself downstairs. Beside his own place he put a little serving table on which he arranged the drinks. No need for him to stand up to mix. He had the chef bring his guests down. They came with a look of indifference and sat down as if it were an ordinary meal. It was all a bit flat.

Johnny had thought that they would open up during the meal. People usually unbutton when they are eating, and this meal was excellent. They tucked in but they did not seem to be enjoying it. They ate the fresh vegetables as if they were porridge, and the roast chicken as if it were cafeteria ham. They seemed to have ideas of their own about Johnny's meal. At one point one of them reached for a beautifully glazed little porcelain pot and asked "Is this caviar?" And Johnny answered truthfully. "Yes, the best that a leaky old tub like this has to offer." The man nodded and emptied the pot with a spoon. Right after that another pointed out to his neighbor a little, specially packed speciality in mayonnaise. And then they smiled. Neither this nor several other aspects of their behavior escaped their host.

But it was only over the coffee that it dawned on Johnny what a piece of impertinence it had been for him to invite them to a meal. They didn't seem to appreciate his desire to apply some of the money he had won to the common good. It seemed as if they only realized the extent of their losses once they were forced to watch their money being spent on such senseless tidbits. It is more or less the same with a woman who wants to leave you. When you read her nice little parting letter, you may understand, but it is only when you see her getting into a taxi with another man that it really hits you. Johnny was quite taken aback.

It was eight in the evening. Outside you could hear the tugs hooting. It was four hours to New York.

Johnny had a vague feeling that it would be intolerable to sit in this cabin with these ruined men for four hours. But it didn't look as if he would be able simply to get up and go. Given the situation, Johnny realized that he only had one chance. He suggested playing again for the whole pot.

They put down their coffee cups, pushed the half-empty cans to one corner of the table and dealt the cards.

They played for money with the same tin chips as they had done at the beginning. It struck Johnny that the other three were unwilling to go beyond a certain stake. So they were taking the game seriously again.

At the very first hand Johnny was dealt yet another straight. Nonetheless he dropped out in the second round and threw in his hand. He had definitely learned a thing or two.

In the second hand and in the third when the stakes were raised he bluffed and strung them along as far as he could. But then one of them calmly looked him straight in the eye and said, "Play the game." Whereupon he played a few hands as he had done previously, and won as before. Then he had a curious desire to play it by ear and follow his luck where he saw it. Then he saw their faces again and noticed that they scarcely looked at their cards before throwing them in, and at that he lost his nerve. He wanted to start deliberately losing, but each time he had a chance to pull a fast one he felt them watching him so closely that he drew back. And when he played badly out of sheer ignorance they played even worse, because the only thing they believed in was his luck. They took his total uncertainty for sheer malice. More and more they came to think that he was just playing cat and mouse with them.

When once again he had collected all the chips in front of him the other three all got up, and he was left sitting alone without a thought in his head, amid the cards and the cans. It was eleven o'clock, one hour out of New York.

Four men and a poker deck in a cabin between Havana and New York.

They still had a little time. Since the air in the cabin was hot and stuffy they decided to go up on deck. They thought the fresh air would help. The idea of fresh air seemed to improve their spirits. They even asked Johnny whether he wanted to go on deck with them.

Johnny didn't want to go on deck.

When the other three saw that Johnny didn't want to go on deck they began insisting.

It was then that Johnny lost his head for the first time and made the mistake of not standing up immediately. This probably gave them a prolonged glimpse of fear on his face. And this in turn made up their minds.

Five minutes later, without uttering a word, Johnny went on deck with them. The steps were wide enough for two. It just happened that one of them went up ahead of Johnny, one behind him and one at his side.

When they reached the top the night was cool and foggy. The deck was damp and slippery. Johnny was glad to be in the middle.

They passed a man at the wheel who paid no attention to them. When they had gone four paces beyond him Johnny had a distinct feeling that he had missed a chance. But by then they were heading for the stern railings.

When they reached the railings Johnny wanted to put his plan into effect and give a loud shout. But he abandoned this idea, oddly enough because of the fog; for when people have trouble seeing, they think no one can hear them.

From the railings they heaved him into the sea.

Then they sat in the cabin for a while eating what was left in the half-empty cans. They consolidated what was left of the drinks, three men and a poker deck on the way from Havana to New York, and asked one another whether Johnny Baker who was no doubt swimming behind the ship as its red navigation light disappeared into the night, was as good at swimming as he was at wining poker games.

But *nobody* can possibly swim well enough to save himself from his fellow men if he has too much luck in this world.

THE TOUGHEST POKER PLAYER
IN THE WORLD

BY

CHRIS CALHOUN

Chris Calhoun, literary agent supreme, wrote the following piece for the *Village Voice* while visiting the 1988 Super Bowl of Poker with his friend Peter Alson. Anyone who's ever sat across a card table from Chris will attest to his talents as a master coffeehouser—which makes him a very tough read, a hard nut to crack. As his celebrated subject Johnny Moss once noted, "wit, spit, and bullshit" can take you a long way. And that may just be how Calhoun got the toughest poker player in the world to show his hand.

The most famous hand in poker, is, of course, aces over eights—the hand Wild Bill Hickok held when he was shot in the back of the head (if you count that bullet he had a full house). What's the second? If it's not Edward G. Robinson's straight flush in *The Cincinnati Kid*, it's gotta be the one held by Nick the Greek Dandolos when he was playing five-card stud head up against Johnny Moss in the first public no-limit game in Vegas in 1949. Johnny, holding a split pair of nines, laid in the weeds until he had $60,000 of Nick's money in the pot.

Nick, with unknown hole card and a garbage two-four-eight showing, incredibly kept shelling out until the last card when he drew a jack and then bet out. Johnny raised $130,000. Nick called, going all in, making the pot $500,000. Then he delivered the immortal line, "Mr. Moss, I think I got a jack in the hole." As the crowd gaped, Nick turned over the jack of diamonds.

But that's not a Nick the Greek story (Nick is most famous for tales of *losing* millions)—it's a Johnny Moss story because Johnny caught some sleep after the hand, rallied, and over the next five months beat Nick out of three million.

Johnny Moss, the world's toughest poker player and the only man to win the World Series of Poker three times (1970, '71, and '74), will turn 81 next month which is almost as hard for me to believe as anything I'm going to hear for the next hour. He looks a fit 65, tops. We're surrounded by players wearing Members Only jackets, Fila warmup suits, and western shirts and cowboy hats. But Moss is dressed like a dapper golfer in a snappy sports cap, maroon continental pants, patent leather loafers and black knit shirt. His voice is like his face, quiet and rugged; he speaks with a real molasses-and-gravel drawl but no twang.

I ask Johnny when he first got to Vegas and he rolls right into it: Benny Binion's invitation to come up and play no-limit against the Greek, the 1400-mile drive to the game on no sleep, how he played for four days straight, then went to bed for 20 hours, while Nick stayed up and shot craps. About the famous hand, Moss says simply, "I set a trap and the Greek outdrew me. Biggest pot of my life. Damnedest thing you ever saw."

Being outdrawn in a big pot is no good time—it's a stinking, sinking feeling. You moan about luck, about how only suckers try to "keep you honest," about how you can't fold out a bad poker player. Then you go on tilt and start playing for the last card too. And now you're just another weak dog consoling yourself that at least you got some action ("The next best thing to playing and winning is playing and losing," Nick the Greek once said). But if you're tough as a three-dollar steak you smile like Johnny did after losing that half a million dollar pot. Smile because you know that the guy who sticks around paying to see the last card is going to lose in the end just like Nick lost his three million.

"Most players today only got one game, ace to five, hold 'em, stud, sumpin'," says Johnny. "Used to be you had to play *all* the games to be a pro. Ya got me?" Johnny learned gambling as a boy selling newspapers in East Dallas domino halls. At 15 he was making a living shooting dice in alleys and spotting cheats and thieves for local gambling houses. He later spent time loading crackers at a Nabisco plant and also roped some cattle but the only real steady job he's had has been as a gambler. "Gambling and work don't mix," he explains.

Johnny introduces me to his wife, Virgie, who is also wonderfully fit with short, curly hair and a sweet face with lots of lines. She married Moss when she was 19. They patched through the Depression with Johnny playing cards all over Texas, a .410 shotgun in the back seat of his car. In 1939, during the Texas oil boom, Johnny won $250,000 in a very hot game. He told Virgie to pick out the nicest home in Dallas. A couple of weeks later, she came back to describe her choice. "You looked too long," Moss said. He'd hit a bad run and was broke again.

Virgie's been controlling the household money ever since (she runs the Mosses' big pad in Odessa, Texas). "Virgie's a millionaire," grins Moss, "though I could run broke on any day."

It's been said that Moss was a better golf hustler than a poker player but he quit golf after a car accident in the '50s. He asks if I play. Yeah, I say, with a big slice. "Here's what ya do," he says. "Put ya some Vaseline on your woods and irons and you'll hit that ball right down the middle. Word got out I was doing that in the '40s. I musta sold a million bottles of that stuff for 'em. They shoulda paid me." Johnny's rolling now. "Listen here, 12 years ago, I was goin' to have a bypass surgery on my heart. I got from the doctor I had a 25 percent chance of not gettin' off that table. Well, I didn't like them odds. I got up, took the pictures of my heart with me. Doc said, 'Where you goin'?' I said I'm goin' to buy me another opinion. I ain't never looked back."

I wanted to hear about the time Johnny shot an 81 playing with only a four iron and won $200,000, or about the time he got a hole in one to win by a stroke and ran Virgie's last $800 up to 40 grand. But Johnny wanted to riff on his health. "Listen here, a couple years ago I bent down to tie my shoe and my glasses dropped off. I'd been wearing bifocals for 25 years and now I can see my shoes better without 'em. Well, I go to the eye doctor and I just read that whole damn chart. I got 20-20 vision again. Lookee here, see what I'm sayin'?" He opens his wallet and points to "no restrictions" on his driver's license. Moss looks older in the photo than he does today.

I'm reminded of a group shot of the players in the first World Series in 1970. Most of the guys haven't aged a bit—not Doyle, not Slim, not Johnny, not Jack Binion either. Some gained a little weight and a few lines, but man, they all look terrific. It's dawning on me now that 40 years sitting on your ass playing cards in smoky rooms must be pretty healthy. I've been wearing glasses since I was seven; maybe if I up my poker to five days a week my eyes will go to 20-20 too. "Lookee here, here's a little exercise I do to keep the blood agoin'," Johnny says. He tilts back and forth on his chair, sort of like a push-up but without the weight. Seeing I'm interested he says matter-of-factly, "It's in the repetitions."

Johnny adds that "in the really long sessions I used to catnap. I watched the action with my eyes almost all closed. A player would nudge me to tell me it was my bet thinking I was asleepin'. I'd come out raisin', pushin' *all* my checks in. Well, they just didn't know what to do then."

Now this is all I need to hear. He's been breaking suckers in his sleep. You don't even have to be awake to play! This is the life. I start looking for an empty seat at a $10 and $20 stud table. It's time for some exercise.

COUNSEL TO THE PRESIDENT

CLARK CLIFFORD

President Harry Truman was an inveterate card player whose frequent White House poker games would run long into the night. The following brief passage, from Clark Clifford's 1991 memoirs as a presidential aide, relates the story of a poker game that took place on the cross-country train trip preceding Winston Churchill's famous Fulton, Missouri, "Iron Curtain" speech of 1946.

After working on his speech, Churchill rejoined us for drinks and dinner. President Truman showed him the redesigned Presidential seal, which was on the wall of the car, and said, "This may interest you. We have just turned the eagle's head from the talons of war to the olive branch of peace." Churchill looked at the seal for a moment and said dryly, "I have a suggestion to make. The head should be on a swivel so that it can turn from the talons of war to the olive branch of peace as the occasion warrants." Churchill added, teasingly, that the berries on the olive branch looked more like atom bombs to him.

During dinner, Churchill, who loved to play cards, turned to President Truman and said the magic words: "Harry, I understand from the press that you like to play poker."

"That's correct, Winston. I have played a great deal of poker in my life."

"I am delighted to hear it. You know, I played my first poker game during the Boer War. I like poker—a fine game. Do you think there is any possibility that we might play during this trip?"

"Winston, the fellows around you are all poker players, serious poker players, and we would be delighted to provide you with a game."

A few minutes later, with dinner completed, Churchill excused himself for a moment. The moment he had left, the President turned to us, and in total seriousness, said, "Men, we have an important task ahead of us. This man has been playing poker for more than forty years. He is cagey, he loves cards, and is probably an excellent player. The reputation of American poker is at stake, and I expect every man to do his duty."

Churchill returned to the dining room, dressed in his famous World War II zippered blue siren suit, which I thought looked a bit like a bunny suit. The stewards had put a green baize cover over the dining room table and six of us—the President, Churchill, Charlie Ross, Harry Vaughan, Wallace Graham, and I—sat down for the most memorable poker game in which I ever played.

The truth emerged quickly: however enthusiastic and proud of his poker skills, Churchill was not very good at the game. I learned later that, when playing his own card games in England, such as gin rummy and bezique, he was excellent. But in poker, with its bluffs and the value of deception and a certain code with which we were all familiar, he was, so to speak, a lamb among wolves. In addition, his terminology for the cards was foreign to us, and this required constant clarification, which only increased our advantage. He called a straight a "sequence," and the jack a "knave," a bit of routine British terminology so vastly amusing to Harry Vaughan that he could hardly keep from laughing aloud.

After about an hour, Churchill excused himself briefly. The moment the door closed President Truman turned to us, with a grave expression. "Now look here, men—you are not treating our guest very well." He looked at Churchill's dwindling stack of chips. "I fear that he may already have lost close to three hundred dollars."

Vaughan looked at his friend of thirty years and laughed. "But,

Boss, *this guy's a pigeon!* If you want us to play our best poker for the nation's honor, we'll have this guy's pants before the evening is over. Now, you just tell us what you want. You want us to play customer poker, okay, we can carry him along all evening. If you want us to give it our best, we'll have his underwear."

President Truman smiled. "I don't want him to think we are pushovers, but at the same time, let's not treat him badly."

Those were our ground rules for the rest of the trip. Churchill "won" some splendid pots, lost some others. At one point, I dropped out of a hand of stud poker, and noticed that Charlie Ross, who was sitting next to me, had an ace showing and an ace in the hole. I watched Ross raise Churchill and raise him again. Churchill, with only a jack showing, stayed right with him. Then, at the end, Churchill bet a substantial amount of money, perhaps a hundred dollars, right into this ace. Charlie studied what he knew to be a winning hand, with its two aces, looked over at the President, gave what I thought sounded like a sigh, and folded.

Finally, however, as the evening was drawing to a close, we moved in a little on our guest. When the dust had settled and we tallied up, Churchill had lost about $250. He had enjoyed himself thoroughly, but he had dropped just enough money so that he could not go back to London and, as Vaughan put it, "brag to his Limey friends that he had beaten the Americans at poker."

SILVER DOLLARS

BY
BILLY COLLINS

This whimsical treatment of Wild Bill's demise is from *Pokerface* (Kenmore, 1977), the first collection of poems by the former U.S. poet laureate Billy Collins.

However historically suspect, the poem bears no relation to Collins's poker talents, which are quite real—provided the stakes are kept small.

> *My great grandfather*
> *was the man who held*
>
> *queens*
> *over fours*
>
> *in the hand*
> *that Wild Bill Hickok*
> *had aces and eights.*
>
> *It turned out to be*
> *the second best hand*
> *(nobody else had shit)*

so he took the pot,
Wild Bill having been shot
in the back
by a runt.

Everybody thought
he should have kicked it in
for the great man's funeral expenses

but he didn't
and that is why my family
today
is so enormously wealthy.

A POKER GAME

BY

STEPHEN CRANE

Stephen Crane's short-shortish poker story was written three months before his death in 1900. It would eventually appear in *New York City Sketches*, a posthumous collection published by his widow. An editor's footnote in that volume suggests that Crane himself was a poor poker player, yet a good sport—not unlike his happy-go-lucky Bob Cinch, who manages to win even when he loses.

Usually, a poker game is a picture of peace. There is no drama so low-voiced and serene and monotonous. If an amateur loser does not softly curse, there is no orchestral support. Here is one of the most exciting and absorbing occupations known to intelligent American manhood; here a year's reflection is compressed into a moment of thought; here the nerves may stand on end and scream to themselves, but a tranquility as from heaven is interrupted only by the click of chips. The higher the stakes the more quiet the scene; this is a law that applies everywhere, save on the stage.

And yet sometimes in a poker game things happen. Everybody remembers the celebrated corner on Bay Rum that was triumphantly consummated by Robert F. Cinch, of Chicago, assisted by the United States courts, and whatever federal power he needed. Robert F. Cinch enjoyed his victory four months. Then he died, and young Bobbie

Cinch came to New York in order to more clearly demonstrate that there was a good deal of fun in twenty-two million dollars.

Old Henry Spuytendyvil owns all the real estate in New York, save that previously appropriated by the hospitals and Central Park. He had been a friend of Bob's father. When Bob appeared in New York, Spuytendyvil entertained him correctly. It came to pass that they just naturally played poker.

One night, they were having a small game in an uptown hotel. There were five of them, including two lawyers and a politician. The stakes depended on the ability of the individual fortune.

Bobbie Cinch had won rather heavily. He was as generous as sunshine, and when luck chases a generous man, it chases him hard, even though he cannot bet with all the skill of his opponents.

Old Spuytendyvil had lost a considerable amount. One of the lawyers from time to time smiled quietly, because he knew Spuytendyvil well, and he knew that anything with the name of loss attached to it sliced the old man's heart into sections.

At midnight Archie Bracketts, the actor, came into the room. "How are you holding 'em, Bob?" said he.

"Pretty well," said Bob.

"Having any luck, Mr. Spuytendyvil?"

"Blooming bad," grunted the old man.

Bracketts laughed and put his foot on the rung of Spuytendyvil's chair. "There," said he, "I'll queer your luck for you." Spuytendyvil sat at the end of the table. "Bobbie," said the actor presently, as Cinch won another pot, "I guess I better knock your luck." So he took his foot from the old man's chair, and placed it on Bob's chair. The lad grinned good-naturedly and said he didn't care.

Bracketts was in a position to scan both of the hands. It was Bob's ante, and old Spuytendyvil threw in a red chip. Everybody passed out up to Bobbie. He filled in the pot and drew a card.

Spuytendyvil also drew a card. Bracketts, looking over his shoulder, saw him holding the ten, nine, eight, seven, and six of diamonds. Theatrically speaking, straight flushes are as frequent as berries on a juniper tree, but as a matter of truth the reason that straight flushes are so admired is that they are not as common as berries on a juniper tree. Bracketts stared, drew a cigar slowly from his pocket, and placing it between his teeth forgot its existence.

Bobbie was the only other stayer. Bracketts flashed an eye for the lad's hand, and saw the nine, eight, seven, six, and five of hearts. Now, there are but six hundred and forty-five emotions possible to the human mind, and Bracketts immediately had them all. Under the impression that he had finished his cigar, he took it from his mouth and tossed it toward the grate without turning his eyes to follow its flight.

There happened to be a complete silence around the green-clothed table. Spuytendyvil was studying his hand with a kind of contemptuous smile, but in his eyes there was perhaps to be seen a cold, stern light expressing something sinister and relentless.

Young Bob sat as he had sat. As the pause grew longer, he looked up once inquiringly at Spuytendyvil.

The old man reached for a white chip. "Well, mine are worth about that much," said he, tossing it into the pot. Thereupon he leaned back comfortably in his chair, and renewed his stare at the five straight diamonds. Young Bob extended his hand leisurely toward his stack. It occurred to Bracketts that he was smoking, but he found no cigar in his mouth.

The lad fingered his chips and looked pensively at his hand. The silence of those moments oppressed Bracketts like the smoke from a conflagration.

Bobbie Cinch continued for some moments to coolly observe his cards. At last he breathed a little sigh and said, "Well, Mr. Spuytendyvil, I can't play a sure thing against you." He threw in a white chip. "I'll just call you. I've got a straight flush." He faced down his cards.

Old Spuytendyvil's fear, horror, and rage could only be equaled in volume to a small explosion of gasoline. He dashed his cards upon the table. "There!" he shouted, glaring frightfully at Bobbie. "I've got a straight flush, too! And mine is Jack high!"

Bobbie was at first paralyzed with amazement, but in a moment he recovered, and apparently observing something amusing in the situation, he grinned.

Archie Bracketts, having burst his bonds of silence, yelled for joy and relief. He smote Bobbie on the shoulder. "Bob, my boy," he cried exuberantly, "you're no gambler, but you're a mighty good fellow, and if you hadn't been you would be losing a good many dollars this minute."

Old Spuytendyvil glowered at Bracketts. "Stop making such an infernal din, will you, Archie?" he said, morosely. His throat seemed filled with pounded glass. "Pass the whiskey."

HOW NOT TO PLAY POKER

BY

RUSSELL CROUSE

Broadway playwright Russell Crouse wrote this wry assessment of his poker experience for *Life* magazine in 1941. For twelve years prior to that, Crouse had bumped heads with fellow actors, directors, and producers in a weekly game held in a New York City hotel room. After the fashion of many a "friendly" Friday-night game, the Runyonesque tone is as self-deprecating as it is grouchy—friendly, yes, but with an edge.

So many compilations of misinformation have been foisted upon the public under the general title of "How to Play Poker" that I have come to the conclusion that most of the authors are disgruntled and unsuccessful gamblers seeking to regain, in the form of royalties, their losses at the green baize table.

If I were to write a book on the subject—or even an article for *Life*—it would be entitled "How NOT to Play Poker." I would choose that title not only because I consider it the most important phase of the game, but also because it is the phase in which I can qualify as an expert. If anyone believes that statement is braggadocio I can refer him to the Morris Plan Bank, which has perhaps the largest collection of my autographs extant. I have often said that poker is the greatest game in the world for my money—and I use "for my money" not just as a figure of speech.

Now the simplest way not to play poker is just not to play poker. However, as is the case with so many simple things in life, that is not so simple as it sounds. To tell a poker player he should not play poker is like telling an opium addict to lay off smoking. So if you are a poker addict I will not tell you not to play poker. I will merely tell you how not to play poker when you play poker.

Let us assume, then, that you are going to play poker. What you want to know is what to do with certain hands that are dealt to you in the course of an evening and probably part of the next morning.

Where most of the poker experts who write books on the subject make their mistake is in telling you only what to do with the good hands. I maintain that if you have a good hand—let us say three aces and a pair of queens, known technically as a full house and by the less pedantic as a stuffed cottage—you do not need Ely Culbertson or Oswald Jacoby or even Edmund Hoyle, if anybody happens to pick him up on a Ouija Board, to tell you what to do. Anyone who is not blind, or paralyzed in the right, or betting hand, knows what to do.

What to Do with Bad Hands

But what about the bad hands? Statistics show that there are 1,302,540 possible poker hands of less value than one pair. That's just what the statistics show. I do not have to depend on statistics. I have held all of those 1,302,540 hands and a few thousand more that statistics never heard of.

Poker experts have no chapter in their books telling you what to do with those hands. But I will tell you. Throw them away. Do not throw them out the window because that makes the deck thinner and someone will notice it sooner or later. To prove this statement I need only say that in 1,302,540 hands there are 6,512,700 cards and you can see how these would be missed out of a 52-card deck. Just throw them back to the dealer and let him use them in the next deal.

Now this advice is not easy to follow but I assure you it is worth its weight in gold. It requires patience above everything else. Let us take the case of Franklin P. Adams, for instance. If you have listened to Mr.

Adams on *Information Please* you know that he is a very bright man. It has been my good fortune to play with him for years and by glancing over his shoulder, in an honest way, of course, I have been able to study his game.

I have seen Mr. Adams start an evening of poker a patient and resolute man. I have seen him glimpse and reject bad hands. And then I have seen his patience ebb as the tide. His hands have begun to twitch, his eyes to harden until finally from sheer ennui I have seen him draw three cards to a flush, two cards to a straight and, on one occasion, four cards to a slice of rye bread. But we won't go into that.

Now let us take the opposite side of the picture. Mr. Frank Hall, a portly but patient soul, once caught a straight flush using live bait. I will tell you how he made that straight flush and how you can make one, too. Statistics show that a straight flush appears, according to the law of averages, every 64,974 deals. He just waited patiently 64,974 deals.

You, too, can have a straight flush if you follow my system. I am going to have one. I am waiting patiently for the law of averages to operate. Only with the luck I have had lately I am laying 18 to 5 that on the 64,973rd deal the Supreme Court will declare the law of averages invalid by a vote of 7 to 2, Frankfurter and Black dissenting.

So you see how simple poker is after all. And you see how much more important it is to know how not to play poker. You will save more money not betting on bad hands than you will win betting on good hands.

That, of course, brings up the question of betting. There are several schools of thought with regard to betting. The school which has probably turned out more successful graduates than any other is the "don't bet unless you've got 'em" school.

In line with my policy of telling you how not to play poker, however, I believe it is my duty to warn you against some of the other schools. Let us take one in particular, that of Mr. Ely Culbertson, who advocates studying your opponent's face before betting.

WHY NOT TO STUDY YOUR OPPONENTS' FACES

I do not know the class of faces with which you play poker but in my set it is not advisable to study your opponent's face unless you are prepared to go slightly nuts. You should see the faces I see at the weekly sessions of the Hoyle Club.

Let us take the face of Mr. Theron Bamberger for instance. Do *you* want to study it? I would rather study the Einstein theory or take a short course, let us say, in tropical diseases. It has been said of Mr. Bernard Hart that he has a kind face. What probably was meant was that he has a kind of face.

Take Mr. Howard Lindsay's face. I have written several plays with Mr. Lindsay and they have been completed only because I have worn blinders to keep me from studying his face. Have a look at Mr. Michael Wallach. The Chinese make a great deal of to-do about "saving face" but I don't think they would save Mr. Wallach's. I might add that I am no Rembrandt myself.

Mr. Edward G. Robinson, the cinema star, often has played in our game. Now if I want to study Mr. Robinson's face I will not do so at a poker game. I will go to a movie theater and put my money on the line on the chance that Miss Myrna Loy's face or Miss Hedy Lamarr's face will be thrown in.

No essay would be complete without a bit of advice on general demeanor. In order to maintain your charm of manner in a poker game I suggest that you win. But if you lose, be a cheerful loser. After all, what have you lost? Just money. And what is money? Nothing more than a common medium of exchange in trade.

There are many types of cheerless losers. There is the "persecuted loser." As an example, I will cite Mr. Marc Connelly, the brilliant and charming playwright. When Mr. Connelly loses it is not because he has played badly. It is because a malevolent fate has suspended all the laws of science for the sole purpose of plaguing Mr. Connelly. If you think Mr. Connelly takes this lying down you should sit next to him.

There is also the "aggrieved loser." In this category you will find Mr. Alfred de Liagre Jr., the theatrical impresario and snappy dresser.

When Mr. de Liagre loses he turns his big brown eyes upon you with an expression which can only say: "How could you do that to *me?*"

The commonest type, however, is the "crying loser." In this classification we find Mr. Theron Bamberger, who carries with him his own portable wailing wall. He is a remarkable example because he has been known to cry himself even and then go right on crying after becoming a winner.

It is well always to remember the words of the philosopher: "It isn't whether you win or lose, but how you play the game." I would like to meet that philosopher. I would like to invite him to our game. I would like to hold, say, three queens against his three jacks. And I would like to make him a little bet that he would quit being a philosopher.

FROM

FORTY YEARS A GAMBLER ON THE MISSISSIPPI

BY

GEORGE DEVOL

In 1839 at the age of ten, George Devol left home to become a riverboat cabin boy; within a few years, he'd learned to palm cards and stack decks with the precocious flair of his eventual calling as a card sharp. After a lifetime spent cleaning out the poor saps who traveled mid-American waterways, he wrote his candid, unremorseful memoirs in 1887.

While Devol was said to have won over two million dollars in his day, he died penniless in 1903. The style of these vignettes is brusque, dry, and even a bit formal, yet the odd mix of braggadocio and humility offers a sepia-toned glimpse of a true American legend: the gentleman hustler.

HE KNEW MY HAND

We were on board a Red River packet called the *J. K. Bell*, and we had not made any preparations to gamble. After a while a gentleman came up and asked me if I ever played poker. My partners, Tom Brown and Holly Chappell, and some of the officers of the boat, were sitting there and heard the conversation. They had to put their handkerchiefs in their mouths to keep from laughing, when they heard my answer, "No, I did not." "Well," said he, "I will teach you if you will sit down." He got a deck of cards at the bar, and commenced to show me which were the best hands. I at last agreed to play ten-cent ante. We played along, and I was amused to see him stocking the cards (or at least trying to do so). He gave me three queens, and I lost $10 on them, for he beat them with three aces. Presently he beat a full hand and won $25. That made him think his man was a good sucker. I always laughed at my losing, and kept telling him that after a while I would commence to bet higher. I pulled out a big roll of bills and laid it on the table. Finally I held out four fives, and then I went a big blind on his deal, so that if he did not come in I would throw down my hand, and perhaps there would be no pair in it. About this time he commenced to work with the cards, but I paid very little attention to his work. After playing a while I got three jacks, and then we commenced to bet high. He raised me, and I raised him back, and at last he thought we had enough up. Then I got away with the hand he gave me, and pulled up the four fives. Then the betting became lively. I made him call me; and when he saw my hand, and I had got the money, he grabbed at me and said, "That is not the hand you had." How the d——l do you know what I had?" "Well," says he, "where are the other five cards?" "I don't know what you are talking about." He counted the cards and found the jacks, for I had palmed them on top of the deck. Then he pulled out his knife and said, "You are a gambler, and I want my money back." "Oh, is that all? I did not understand. I will give it back, as I don't want to keep your money if you think I did not win it fairly." I let on as though I was taking out the money, when I pulled out old Betsy Jane. He saw her looking him in the face, and he wilted like a calf. I made him apologize, and you never saw a man get such a turning over as they all gave him. They told him he must not pick out such apt scholars, for they learn too quickly. What hurt my feelings more than anything else was, that he would not speak to me all the way up to where I got off. As I was leaving the boat I said to him, "Good-bye, sir. We are never too old to learn."

MY CARDS

The first trip the steamer *Eclipse* made I was on board. There were five games of poker running at one time in the cabin. I was invited into one, and I represented myself as a horseman. I played on the square, as I wanted to gain their confidence; so when the game closed for the night, they all thought me a square man. After all my new friends had retired to their little beds, I got out six decks of my marked cards and went to the bar. I told the barkeeper what I wanted, but he objected, as he did not own the bar, and was afraid it would be found out, and then he would be discharged. I told him that no one but old gamblers could detect the marks, and not one in fifty of them, as it was my own private mark. I had been a good customer at the new bar, so the new barkeeper finally consented to take my cards and send them to the table where I would be playing. The next morning after breakfast the games were started, and my new friends wanted me to sit in. I accepted the invitation, and when the barkeeper put the checks and cards on the table, I saw my old friends (I mean the cards). The game was five-handed, and it was pretty hard to keep the run of all the hands; but I quit the game a few hundred dollars winner. After the game one of the gentlemen came to me and said: "I don't like a five-handed game; suppose we split up and make two games." That was just what I wanted, provided I could get in the game that had the most suckers, so I said to him: "I do not care to play, if you gentlemen can make up your game without me; but as we are all going through to New Orleans, I will play a little to pass the time. You can arrange the games to suit yourselves, and can count me in if you are short a man." The gentleman arranged two nice games, with me in one of them. I had no partner, so I had to depend entirely on myself and my old friends, the marks on the back. We played until the engines were stopped at the landing in New Orleans, and I was $4,300 ahead. I might have won a great deal more with the assistance of a good partner, but then, you know, I would have had to divide with him; so I was very well pleased with my last day on the new steamer. I did not forget the new barkeeper, but gave him $50 for using my cards at one of the tables in place of his own.

LOST HIS WIFE'S DIAMONDS

I was playing poker with a gentleman on board the steamer *John Simonds*, bound for Louisville, late one night, and had won a few hundred dollars from him, when he got up without saying a word, and went to the ladies' cabin. In a short time he came back with a small velvet-covered box in his hand, and said to me, "Come, let us finish our game." He opened the box, and I saw it was full of ladies' diamond jewelry. I said: "What are you going to do with those?" Said he, "I will put them up as money." "Oh, no; I have no use for ladies' jewelry." "Well," says he, "if I lose I will redeem them when we get to Louisville." I told him I was not going above Vicksburg. "Well," says he, "if you win, leave them with the clerk and I will pay him." I then loaned him $1,500 on the jewelry, and we sat down to play. It was about 3 A.M. when we commenced, and before they wanted the tables for breakfast I had won the $1,500 back. We drank a champagne cocktail, and he went to his room. The barber was at work on me, so that I was a little late for breakfast, and the steward had to take me into the ladies' cabin to get me a seat. There was a gentleman, a very beautiful lady, and a sweet little child at the same table; the lady's eyes were red, as if she had been crying. I looked at the gentleman, and saw it was the same person who had lost the diamonds. Somehow, my breakfast did not suit me; and the more I looked at that young wife and mother, the less I felt like eating. So at last I got up and left the table. I went to my room, got the little velvet box, wrapped it up, and carried it back. They were just leaving the table when I returned. I called the chambermaid, and told her the lady had left a package, and for her to take it to her room. After it was gone I felt better, and I eat a square meal. The gentleman came and thanked me, and wanted my address; but as I never had any one to send me money lost at gambling, I told him not to mind the address; for I knew if I did not give it, I would not expect anything, and therefore would not be disappointed.

The 1876 assassination of Wild Bill Hickok in Deadwood, South Dakota, is one of the most enduring stories of the American West. When he was shot at point-blank range at a card game in the #10 Saloon by Jack (Crooked-Nose) McCall, Wild Bill was said to be holding aces and eights. These two pair have long since entered poker vernacular as the "dead-man's hand."

Pete Dexter, author of *God's Pocket* and the award-winning *Paris Trout*, wrote *Deadwood* (1986) as a novel based on real-life characters living in the lawless limbo of their time. Historical accuracy aside, Dexter's evocative prose vibrates with the beauty of Western myth, as it re-creates the abrupt endgame of the legendary gunslinger.

It was dusk before Bill got back into town, walking sightless up the street, slow and straight with his eyes dangerous. The dog stayed a few feet in front of him, panting, and Bill followed the noise all the way to the bar. He thought the dog understood that there were times he went blind.

The place had filled up in the hours Bill had been gone, he could tell that from the noise. He found the bar and Harry Sam Young brought him a gin and bitters. He tasted it, and his eyes began to see shapes again. The pilot shouted to him across the room, "We got you a chair saved, Bill."

Bill pushed the gin and bitters away. "Let me test something different," he said. "This is lost its bouquet."

The bartender moved the glass in front of a pilgrim a few feet down the bar—half of the badlands was drinking pink gin by then—and poured Bill a shot of whiskey.

The whiskey tasted healthy and familiar, and Bill wished Charley would come in the door so they could drink one together. No matter what had gone wrong between them, they couldn't be so far apart that a bottle of American whiskey wouldn't bridge it. He waited while the bartender poured him another, and then picked the bottle up and took it with him to the table where Pink Buford, Carl Mann, Charles Rich, and the river pilot, Massie, were playing poker.

Massie was still in Bill's customary seat. The seat they'd left for Bill offered his back to the door. "I don't sit with my back exposed," he said.

"I got your lucky seat," the pilot said.

Bill looked at him unkindly. He had his rules, and his reasons. With all the local talk of Indians and bandits and poisonings, the citizens and visitors of the badlands visioned themselves as charmed men in dangerous times, but the truth was there wasn't a man at the table anybody had ever tried to kill.

Bill had been shot at frequently. Once he had believed he was charmed too, but that feeling had ebbed from the moment he shot the policeman Mike Williams in Abilene. He never mentioned the change to a soul, not even Charley, but killing Mike Williams by accident told him he could be killed by accident too. And he was accordingly careful in places accidents happened. He never filled his right hand in a bar, he never sat with his back to the door.

It was a strain, always watching for accidents, and he was tired.

Nobody at the table moved, and Bill saw they weren't going to. It was like a test. He set the bottle of whiskey in front of the empty chair and sat down. The river pilot winked at him and patted the dollars he had already won.

The bulldog lay at Bill's feet and sighed. Bill took the winnings from the night before out of his pocket and laid them next to his bottle. The room seemed wrong, he couldn't say why.

Pink Buford dealt cards. They played dollar ante, table-stakes draw poker. Bill couldn't catch a hand; the river pilot's cards continued their winning run. He drew one card into Bill's three tens, and caught his straight. He drew into Pink Buford's aces, and made three fours.

The more the river pilot won, the more reckless he got. And the cards still defied all the laws of probability and common sense, and stayed with him. "I can't lose, boys," he said. Bill had seen runs before, and waited him out.

In two hours, Bill lost close to a hundred and fifty dollars, and finished the bottle of whiskey. He was feeling the need to relieve himself, but he hated to leave the table and miss it when the laws of common sense caught up with the pilot. It wasn't anybody's time forever.

Number 10 had filled, as it did most nights, with tourists and miners of all kinds and quality. Captain Jack Crawford had come in and was standing behind him, just out of sight. There was a professor at the piano, and the upstairs girls took turns singing ballads of the West. The tourists paid them to sing, the miners paid them to stop.

It was a hot night and even with the front and back doors open, all the smoke and noise hung inside. Bill decided to leave the table. He began to stand up, but the dealer, Carl Mann, gave him the first card of a new hand, and he stayed to finish it.

Jack McCall came in through the back door and went to the bar. He picked up a glass of gin and bitters sitting in front of a tourist and drank it before Harry Sam Young could stop him. The bartender fixed the cat man a hard look. "A whiskey thief is unwelcome everywhere," he said. "Even thieves won't have a whiskey thief around . . ."

But there was something loose in Jack McCall's eyes that Harry Sam Young had seen before, and he stopped himself in mid-sentence. Jack McCall walked away from him, down the bar, pushing through whores and miners alike. He was holding a gun in his hand now, and the ones who saw it moved out of his way.

At the end of the bar was the poker table. Bill had picked up his cards and was holding them against his chest. Across the table, Pink Buford noticed the change in the way Bill protected his cards, and prepared to abandon his hand.

Captain Jack Crawford saw the cat man and the gun, and backed out of the way.

Jack McCall fired into the left side of Bill's head from a distance of less than a foot. The ball exited through his right cheek, then broke all the bones in the river pilot's left wrist. Telling it later, the pilot would say he saw smoke before he heard the shot.

A moment later, Jack McCall shouted, "Damn you, take that," and Bill's head, which had been turned to the left by the force of the ball exiting his cheek, lowered slowly to the table. He could have been taking a nap. William Massie fell out of his chair, covering his wrist with his body; Charles Rich sat frozen. Only Carl Mann moved, and McCall pointed the pistol at his face and pulled the trigger. There was a snapping noise, but no shot. Mann would sell his half of the business the next week and move to New Orleans.

It was a few seconds before most of the bar patrons had realized what had happened—it was nothing out of the ordinary for somebody to fire into the ceiling—and in those moments Jack McCall ran out the front door, snapping his gun at Harry Sam Young and half a dozen others. He turned in the street and yelled at the bar, "Come on, you sons of bitches," and then ran south and tried to take the first horse he saw.

The bar emptied out after him, with no one in a hurry to be at the front. The horse belonged to Mayor E. B. Farnum, who was a considerate man and always eased the animal's cinch when he left him saddled. The saddle turned over, dropping McCall into the mud. He got up and ran into Farnum's store, and hid in back behind freshly butchered meat. The crowd followed him in and took McCall prisoner. Not as much as a piece of penny candy was stolen.

In the crowd now was Boone May, who assumed authority, being the closest thing to a law officer there. He took McCall to the Gem Theater, holding him by the back of the collar. He allowed anybody so inclined to cuff McCall in the face, and by the time they arrived at the Gem, the prisoner was bleeding from the nose.

A miner's jury was already waiting at the bar. Al Swearingen closed all downstairs activities and forbade howling upstairs while the trial was in progress. Howling had become as fashionable as pink gin. Two hundred men crowded into the establishment to watch, and that many again stood outside, unable to get in. Word of what happened was spreading everywhere in town.

Jack McCall testified that Bill had killed his brother in Abilene, and then threatened to kill him too, if their paths ever crossed again. "As soon as I saw Wild Bill, I knewed it was him or me," he said.

The jury took an hour to decide. Al Swearingen opened the bar while they made up their minds, and then closed down again for the announcement. The foreman was a soft-brain who had once been a Confederate soldier. He was called Swill Barrel Jimmy, and owned what was conceded to be the oldest coat and shoes in Deadwood, but always wore a clean white collar. "We find the defendant not guilty on account of his mortal grudge against Wild Bill, and self-defense," he said.

And Jack McCall was released. He took a horse that belonged to Al Swearingen and rode for Fort Laramie.

Elliot "Doc" Pierce was called from his house to administer to the corpse. He lived in the quarters behind his barber shop. He brought along his nephews, Mutt and Buster, to carry the body. They went into Nuttall and Mann's and found Bill lying on the poker table. The cards he had been holding were in his lap. Pink Buford's bulldog was asleep at his feet. There wasn't much blood.

Carl Mann, who had looked into the barrel of Jack McCall's gun, was still sitting on the other side of the table, drinking. Everyone else had gone to the trial. Doc Pierce felt for a pulse at the neck and the wrist, and noted to Buster that it was strange to find the most famous man in the West dead with so little company. There was about seventy dollars under him on the table.

He had the nephews carry the body back to the barber shop, and laid it on a table. Doc Pierce sent Buster to Charley Utter's camp for Bill's Sunday clothes, and any other personal effects that would be appropriate for the funeral, such as his derringer.

He shaved Bill and then closed the wound in his cheek and covered it with pancake makeup. It was a perfect cross. He cleaned Bill's nails and cut ten locks of his hair from the back, where it wouldn't show as Bill lay in his box. The nephew came back and they dressed Bill in a clean shirt and the Prince Albert frock coat that was his favorite.

They laid him in the box with his guns on and the derringer in a coat pocket. The white handles of Bill's pistols looked beautiful against the green lining of the box. They combed his hair. They put Charley's carbine in the box too, trying it on both sides to see which way it looked best.

A. W. Merrick of the *Black Hills Pioneer* arrived sometime after midnight, out of breath, shaking. He asked Doc questions and wrote down the answers. "What was the hand he was holding?" the newspaperman asked.

"I didn't notice," the barber said.

"Some said it was aces," the newspaper man said, "and some said it was eights . . . Exactly how did you find him?"

Doc Pierce didn't have much use for the printed word. "Lookit," he said, "I got things to do here. How the hell do you think I found him?"

"How did he look?"

Doc Pierce sighed. "This is for the people who loved the deceased," Merrick said. "This is the last they'll hear of him, so it ought to be good . . ."

"Well," the barber said, "Bill was the prettiest corpse I ever encountered. His fingers looked like marble."

"The place where the assassin's bullet come out, it was a perfect cross." Doc Pierce brushed past the newspaperman then, pretending there was more left to do than there was. "You want to make yourself useful," he said, "you could print up some funeral notices."

By morning the notices were posted all over town

NOTICE

Died, in Deadwood, Black Hills, August 2, 1876, from the effects of a pistol shot, J. B. Hickok (Wild Bill), formerly of Cheyenne, Wyoming.

Funeral services will be held at Charley Utter's camp, on Thursday afternoon, 8/3/76, at three o'clock, p.m.

All are respectfully invited to attend.

The Woman with Five Hearts

by
Stephen Dunn

Stephen Dunn is a Pulitzer Prize–winning poet who also gambles. "We're betting we're smart and talented," he writes in an essay ("Gambling: Remembrances and Assertions"), "and/or lucky enough to lean but not fall. Sometimes we are." And at other times we aren't, as in the case of the "man without enough clubs" who makes the costly mistake of underestimating a woman's strength.

The woman with five hearts knew what she had,
knew what we lacked. She bet high and then
higher; it was what any of us would have done.
    A woman with five hearts,
we concluded, was a dangerous thing.
She did not think it romantic, what she had.
  She knew it was better
than two pair, better than anything straight.
She was sure I, for example, had weakness,
three of something at best.
    The man to my right
clearly resented the woman with five hearts.
He touched her arm, as if this were a different game.
He tried to be ironic, but instead was mean.

The woman with five hearts saw him
as a man with clubs, one fewer than he needed.
A man without enough clubs can be a pathetic thing.
Each of her bets demanded he come clean.
            It was simple prudence
to yield to such a woman, a woman with all that.
The rest of us did, understanding so many hearts
could not be beaten, not with what we had.
But the man to my right decided to bluff.
    He raised her with what seemed
his entire body, everything he had been and was.
The woman with five hearts raised back,
amused now, as if aware of an old act—
            a man with nothing puffing himself up.
He stayed because by now it had all gone
too far, a woman with five hearts and a man
            without enough clubs.
And when she showed him all five, beautifully red,
he had to admit that was exactly what she had.

FROM

THE GENTLEMEN'S HANDBOOK ON POKER

BY

WILLIAM J. FLORENCE

Shakespearean actor William J. Florence won a substantial wager by completing his *Handbook* within a month's time in 1890. A potpourri of anecdotes, rules, advice, and history, the treatise is a forerunner (of sorts) to similar books that would appear over the next century. The following segment, "Advice to Players," is offered more for its author's quaint sincerity than for any suggestions as to his expertise. "Always keep cool," for example, is harmless enough boilerplate guidance; but the suggestion to keep "trying to fill (straights and flushes)" in order to "equalize" one's chances is outright quackery.

There are no rules for playing poker so as to win. Advice may be given so as to limit losses. All absolute laws as to how you must play end in disaster. A good player varies his game. He may play a poor game for a while on purpose. To deceive is the acme of poker playing. The strong point in poker is never to lose your temper, either with those you are playing with or, more particularly, with the cards. There is no sympathy at poker. Always keep cool. If you lose your head you will lose all your chips. Poker being as much a criterion of character as anything else, keep in the shade your personalities. As Mr. Cable has it, "a man who can play delightfully on a guitar and keep a knife in his boot" would be a perfect poker player. Always believe in the equalization of chances. If your king flush is beaten twice hand running by an ace flush today, tomorrow you will hold the ace flushes and your adversaries the king flushes. If you begin to draw for flushes and straights and cannot fill them, you must continue trying to fill them, otherwise you throw away your chance of equalizing your draw. Patience is one of the strong points of poker, just as much as cheek. He who waits longest finds his opportunity. A player who never bluffs at poker is not in sympathy with the game. His battery is never masked. The enemy gives him a wide berth; when his guns are shotted no foes ever approach. He fires a volley and kills a lame duck. Too much curiosity is ruinous. All the money saved at poker comes from not seeing. To be over-timid is an equal fault. It is perfectly legitimate to tell stories at poker. All is fair in love, war, and poker.

To adhere to anything but the strictly truthful brings with poker no moral obliquity. As it is impossible for some players not to lie when they play, this want of veracity brings its own cure. It is not, however, a good rule to tell stories about your hand. You may, if you have the talent for such things, assume an innocent guise with your face alone. This is the most effective of lures. It is best never to show your hand at all, if not called, and to remain silent in regard to its merits. A solemn mystery in regard to your cards is the most effective. Though a hand which is miscalled when shown rests solely on its face value, avoid doing this. It should, in fact, never be permitted. It induces fraud. An adversary might throw down his cards, the winning ones, when another player announced something which he did not have. As the holder of the best cards has thrown them away, they cannot be found again, and he loses, whereas he should have won. It is, at the least, an ungentlemanly trick. It irritates the best-tempered players. When a player leaves the room no hand should be dealt him. No two persons ever ought to have an interest in the same hand. The reasons for this are legion. The strongest is, that it prevents rascality. Then, again, when another player takes the hand of a person who is not present, and enters or makes a bet, it gives an additional strength to the hand, which is unfair. Never play poker without a limit. It is then the most dangerous of all games.

A Disreputable Family Holiday in Las Vegas

BY

Hal Goodman

Some of us children of non-gambling parentage might regard this piece (from a 1988 *New York Times* Travel section) with no small envy. What better bonding than a poker trip to Vegas with Dad (albeit as adults)? After a teenaged apprenticeship mixing drinks for the guys, Goodman, a former editor at *Business Month* and *Men's Health*, cut his poker teeth on his father's weekly game. The father, Walter Goodman, was a longtime editor/critic at the *Times* and an avid player who, as mentioned in this article, shied from betting into his kids. But that's all right, as Hal Goodman recalls: "If I could weasel a pot out of sympathy, I'd take it."

It is not true, as a foul rumor circulating among family friends has it, that while other fathers were out tossing baseballs or visiting zoos with their kids, my dad was sitting at the kitchen table with my brother and me, teaching us not to draw to inside straights. Nonetheless, when it was decided that 1988 was the year for a wholesome family vacation, this wholesome family headed for Las Vegas to catch the nineteenth annual World Series of Poker.

For a week in mid-May, the three of us reveled in the company of some very grubby characters indeed—and what's more, did our best to pattern our behavior after theirs. Other families hike in Yellowstone or tour Disney World; we played poker across the airplane aisle, lit cigars and dealt the cards in the hotel room at 8 A.M., hurried past pool and tennis court to get seats in a casino poker game. Say what you will about a father introducing his young sons to the wonders of nature, there is something just as touching in the sight of a papa and his devoted children, overnight bags clutched in one hand, cash in the other, stumbling out the door of the Las Vegas airport wearing demented grins, ready to box the town, wrap it up and bring it home for mom.

The buy-in for the poker championship, which is held each year at Binion's Horseshoe Club in downtown Vegas, was a bit above our means at $10,000 a person. But we spent many contented and educational hours (every good vacation should be educational) wedged in among the four-deep spectators at the rail, watching the 167 entrants who had come up with the tariff.

The game that determines the championship is a brutal from of poker called Texas Hold 'em, in which each player gets two cards face down, and uses those two plus five community cards in the middle of the table to make his best hand. The championship was no-limit; players could bet all they had at any time. In the late stages of the tournament, this was often several hundred thousand dollars before any cards were exposed. The drama of seeing someone slide half a million bucks into a pot rivals the tension in the bottom of the ninth in the seventh game of the World Series (the other World Series). Even the side games among players who'd been knocked out of the tournament were incredible. Watching a tableful of men playing $400–$800 draw lowball with six-inch-high stacks of hundred-dollar bills was like being out in the wild at night, staring awestruck at the aurora borealis or some other glorious natural phenomenon.

In the evenings, the poker cloth was our campfire, and we would sit around it, listening to the calls of the wildlife at the craps table ("Yeeeee-HAH! Whoop! Whoop!"), and when marshmallows sat down looking for some action, we would toast them. That was the plan, anyway. As it happened, I got toasted a couple of times myself—charred, in fact. The $3–$6 hi-lo game at the Fremont was no problem, but when I ventured into a small-stakes Hold 'em game, in emulation of the big boys at Binion's, I proved easy meat for the local players, who spend their days waiting patiently for people like me to come along. The locals at the hi-lo game were a more profitable crowd, and far more entertaining. I sat there bantering with Pineapple and Colostomy Joe, making side bets on other players' hands. I declined, however, to join a pool on when the decrepit codger at the next table would kick off, though I was told that "July and August are still open." I'd have bet, but even July looked like a poor risk.

In our effort to immerse ourselves in thoroughly disreputable pursuits, we received plenty of encouragement from the city itself. It doesn't take long for Las Vegas to warp one's values, and this goes well beyond the simple disregard for money that the town does its best to induce in all visitors. Win or lose, one soon starts to feel that any time not spent pushing chips across green felt is time wasted, that an hour away from the tedious routine and numbing conversation of the tables is an hour blown. The guilt I felt upon settling down in my room for a quiet 30 minutes of reading after four hours at poker is exactly what I would feel in normal life if I left work early to play cards. Even a quiet morning stroll through downtown, watching the light bulb truck make its round of the casinos, was poisoned by the thought of the straights and flushes I could have been drawing at the poker table. I hurried back, only to find, sure enough, that all the straights and flushes had been drawn when I was gone.

Most of the players in the World Series of Poker looked as if they'd spent all their lives behaving the way we did for a week. T-shirts and dirty sneakers were the rule; I saw only three suits, and one of them was on the owner of the casino. We did our earnest best to fit in with the prevailing customs, refusing to shave, wearing baseball caps promoting obscure places and events ("I'm Appreciated at Tulsa Truck Plaza," mine read), speaking casually of the top players, whom we'd never met, as T. J., Doyle and Johhny. I tried to cultivate a Texas accent, though I don't think I fooled anyone. It pains me to report that despite these sincere efforts, a most unjust double standard prevailed. Prowling around the poker tables at Binion's after the day's play had concluded, my brother and I were approached by a thoroughly scruffy young man. "Damn," he said, looking us over. "Don't you guys ever shave?"

The tournament organizers may not actually encourage grubbiness, but they're certainly aware that the expressionless, rough-hewn, three-days-with-no-sleep appearance of many top-notch players is part of the allure of high-stakes poker. These dudes look dangerous, and that never kept anyone out of a casino. Similarly, the organizers know that the legend of the big-time gambler is tied in with the legend of the big-time crook, and they play off it with sly humor. On the fourth and final day of play, Eric Drache, the tournament director, was giving me his prediction of how long the tournament would last when an assistant ran up with a message. Drache raised his eyebrows, then turned to me. "Excuse me," he said. "I've got a collect call from a guy doing life in prison."

It's lucky for me that Drache got that call. His prediction that the tournament would end within a half-hour seemed ridiculous; the final two players had been going head-to-head for almost three hours, and neither had a huge advantage in chips. I was considering betting a hundred or so that it would go longer, and I would have lost. Ten minutes later, 30-year-old Johnny Chan, the defending champion, wiped out Eric Seidel, a 28-year-old former options trader from New York. The crowd screamed, the cameras moved in, and $980,000 in cash was dumped on the table—$700,000 to Chan, $280,000 to the runner-up. I'd been rooting for my fellow New Yorker, but I applauded heartily when the end came, relieved that I'd be able to get in a few hours at the hi-low game before dinner.

Where our wholesome family vacation failed was in promoting togetherness. It's tough when the most respectful and affectionate thing one can do for a relative is take a seat at a different table. We played together a few times, and though I made a few quick shekels off my father's strange reluctance to bet into his children, it would have been more satisfying to take the greenery from strangers. So we got into the pattern of breakfasting together (Binion's $2 breakfast special, we found, amply fortifies a family of degenerates for a long day of hard labor), then heading off to steep ourselves in our respective decadences, checking in occasionally throughout the day. ("How'd ya do?" "Up 50. You?" "Down a couple. Heading back?" "Yep. You?" "Yep." "See ya." "Bye.")

Finally we cashed in, packed up and checked out, leaving an extra-large tip for the chambermaid—hazard pay for enduring the nicotinic atmosphere. Talked over the morning's poker hands in the cab to the airport ("How in hell could the guy fold trip twos on board?"), and, as soon as we were airborne, pulled out the cards and chips. We can now claim that we played in the highest poker game in the world. "My God," said the stewardess. "Didn't you guys get enough of that in Vegas?" "No," we answered as one.

The flight was smooth, and the Grand Canyon was spectacular in the early afternoon light, but I had three queens at the time and could spare it no more than a glance.

POKER FACES: THE LIFE AND WORK OF PROFESSIONAL CARD PLAYERS

BY

DAVID HAYANO

Culled from ten years' "field work" by the author, *Poker Faces* (1982) is a shrewd and intelligent sociological study of the poker subculture of Gardena, California—longtime home of legal card play. In his introduction, anthropologist/poker player David Hayano writes that as an ethnographer, his interest lies in "documenting the social mechanics of face-to-face confrontation." In this passage, he accomplishes that in spades with an insightful read on the inevitable trash-talking that occurs when regular players repeatedly square off against one another.

THE POWER OF WORDS AND ACTION: INTIMIDATING AND MANIPULATING OPPONENTS

Much of the playful and serious character of game interaction derives from manipulating talk and game-related symbols. Some players are even known as specialists at "talking" a good game—deceiving, intimidating, and cajoling novices into making bad judgments and costly playing errors. Indeed, lies and insults (up to a certain level) are a standard form of poker table interaction. Verbal duels and one-liners, while sometimes delivered in jest, also serve as potential warnings and not-so-subtle criticisms of another player's action:

God, are you rocky! They even named a movie after you. If I played your discards, I'd probably make a million bucks.

You're so rocky you probably shit bricks.

I've played with tight players, but you're tighter than a nun's cunt.

Players openly call one another rocks, pigeons, donkeys, and other pejorative terms and publicly insult opponents' actions and playing competence. Anthropologists have found that in many societies verbal abuse or "ritual insults" accompany situations of play, perhaps to ease tension and express aggression in relatively harmless form. Insults in poker games may fulfill these same functions, and they may also have the intended or unintended effect of changing, destroying, or weakening opponents, thereby making them more likely to commit errors or begin "steaming." Raking in the chips the winner tells the loser to "get a job" or threatens to send him and other "poker bums" back on the freeway forever. These gabby methods of intimidation are highly effective in many instances, especially against players who are easily flustered.

Another reason for obnoxious or aggressive actions is to loosen up tight players or drive them out of the game. Rocks and ultraconservative players who give little action are the most obvious targets of abuse. Sometimes the battles of intimidation and name-calling reach comical proportions, as in this incident, pitting an impatient loser against two rocks:

M.T., who was losing heavily and steadily, was called, pot after pot, by two players who played a tight, conservative game. Repeatedly, M.T. would bet his hand, get called, and lose the pot. After several identical outcomes, in frustration he took out a pen and wrote "No Action" on the green felt tablecloth with arrows pointing in the direction of the two players. Following that, he kept shouting, "N.A., N.A." (for No Action) every time either of them was in a pot. He tried to convince the rest of the table that they did not deserve any play because they were too rocky. The other players were laughing too hard to pay any attention.

Almost no player escapes verbal abuse. Winners with good playing reputations are sometimes singled out as targets for the barbs thrown by needlers, or "needle artists," particularly when the former have blown back a lot of chips or are losing to the worst players in the game:

I see the elephant's been in town. [Meaning: You used to have a lot of chips but they look like they've been stomped on by a large animal, and now you don't have any.]

Look here! The carrots are eating the rabbits. Marge [a chip-girl], bring this here boy a *turkey* sandwich and a glass of water. This fish needs plenty to drink.

Winners also needle losers whom they do not like by giving them "instructions" on how they should have played a losing hand, no matter how they played it, or asking them irrelevant questions such as what cards they caught on the draw.

Players in aggressive games express much of their table talk in the idioms of power and dominance. They threaten to "punish" or "take care of" others. To punish another player means to beat him out of future pots or to "burn up" his money by excessive raising. Among some of the more vibrant players, splashing chips and money around, presenting an aggressive front, and talking a game indeed act as effective symbols of power. These players can "buy" pots by frightening and intimidating opponents who are too confused to defend themselves.

Intimidation, threats, and needles can arise out of unpremeditated spite or can be carefully constructed ploys to change the playing style of another—to make a good player bad, a bad player worse. These aggressive attacks, however, are not applied indiscriminately. There is an unwritten rule among regulars that obvious live ones, wealthy losers, and cardroom strangers should never be criticized publicly or made to feel bad about their poor play and the extent of their losses. Losers or "feeders" should by all means be kept in the game. Warning several regulars about their irritating conduct at the table, a pro said: "You guys better tone down on all your yelling and fooling around during the game. You're going to lose all the feeders, and then who're you going to be left with? Just yourselves jerkin' off as usual. Who's going to support you then?"

Another unwritten rule stipulates that losers should never be "educated," that is, given poker lessons over the table on how and what kinds of hands should be played. When a bad player does win a pot, regardless of how poorly he played the hand, he is aided by regulars who push him the chips and congratulate him on his hand. Meanwhile, to each other, the regulars exchange collusive glances whose meaning signifies that they have a live one in their midst. When a loser leaves the table, a lesson in cardroom group alignment can be learned. Regulars resume their insider talk free of censorship and hidden meanings. Once the loser has left the cardroom, he is the butt of many jokes. When a medical doctor, after dropping several thousand dollars, finally gave up and left the game at five in the morning, a winner asked rhetorically, "How would you like to be operated on by him today?" When a gas station owner left broke, another player commented, "It's all right. He'll be back. Tomorrow he'll just raise the price of gas to $10 a gallon and won't accept credit cards."

Not all professional poker players are slanderous and scurrilous. Many pros and winners are calm, silent players who survive in the cardroom without needles, insults, or fights. The intensity and type of verbalization seems completely a matter of personal style. And I repeat that most spiteful table talk is usually packaged with humor. All experienced poker players know that unfortunate circumstances and going busted are not the exclusive province of unskilled losers. To wit, they know that the cards and words may turn against *them* at any time.

FROM

DRAGOON CAMPAIGNS TO
THE ROCKY MOUNTAINS

BY

JAMES HILDRETH

**This selection is from a published soldier's diary (1837)
chronicling early nineteenth-century military life in the
Wild West. For our purposes, the text becomes historically
relevant for having the first documented mention of poker
in literature. However brief, the gambling sequence res-
onates loud and clear with what would eventually risk
becoming a hackneyed close to a number of poker tales—
four aces over four kings.**

My Dear Sir,

I thought, at the date of my last, that I should not again write you
before our return from the prairies, but an occurrence which took
place last evening furnishes me with a little amusing material.

It was about half an hour after tattoo, when I was about returning
to my bunk, somewhat fatigued with the toils and heat of the day,
when two of my companions, Corporal Ned Stephens and Harry Benson, came into the barrack-room and gave me the wink to follow
them.

Accordingly, throwing my guard-cloak around me, I left the quarters, and in a few moments our party was joined by our friend Long Ned, who had been waiting without the sentry-walk for our arrival.

"Boys," said he, "this is perhaps the last evening that we shall spend here. Now, as you know we have a long journey in prospect, and have had some months of temperance in arrears, I've no notion of letting the last chance slip by of partaking of a little *rational enjoyment.* What do you agree to?"

"Let's go to Rodger's," said Corporal Stephens, "and talk about old times, over a venison steak and a drop of whiskey."

"Not so," said Benson. "The M— lost some cool hundreds last night at poker,* in camp, and is to meet some brother officers at Rodger's tonight. So that won't do."

"Well," said Long Ned, "the moon shines bright, and as the weather bids fair, let's take an outdoor sitting for want of better quarters. So toss up who goes for the whiskey, and then hurra for the hollow beyond the *bayou.*"

This was agreed to, and it fell to my lot to act the part of caterer. So off they started for the *bayou,* while I trudged across the prairie to our mutual friend old Rodger's cabin.

It was strictly forbidden that any man should leave the barrack-ground after dark without a written pass, upon any pretense whatever; and moreover, whiskey was a contraband article among the soldiers, probably because the officers deemed the supply not more than sufficient for *home consumption*; therefore the business that I had in hand was one of double risk and severe penalty in case of detection.

However, I walked boldly up to the house and commenced reconnoitering. First I creeped under the window and saw that the room was lighted, but could not distinguish anyone distinctly; presently I heard the major and the captain talking loudly, and soon discovered what was going on.

"I'll stake you ten," cried the M—.

"Done," said the Captain.

"Twenty more," said the M—.

---

*A favorite game of cards at the south and west.

"Done," said the Captain.

"Fifty more," said the M——.

"Done," said the Captain.

The M—— hesitated; the coolness of the Captain threw him off his guard; at last he struck his fist upon the table and roared at the top of his voice,

"I'll stake you another hundred."

"Done," said the Captain.

The M—— dared not risk more, and throwing down his cards exclaimed,

"There's four kings! What have you got?"

"Only four aces," said the captain coolly, as he began to scrape the money together.

"D—m—n!" roared the M——, at the same time splitting the pine table with a blow of his fist.

That's enough, thought I, the M—— has lost again, and we shall probably have an hour's extra drill in the morning to make up for it.

Some one now came into the hall, and I skulked down into the grass until I should see who it might be; the fellow, however, came into the moonlight, and I discovered him to be one of old Rodger's slaves.

"Ben—Ben—Ben," I whispered as loud as I dared. "Ben—Ben, I say." He heard the last call and came to where I was sitting in the grass.

"Ben," said I, "here's a dollar—hurra for a quart of whiskey in a twinkling."

The fellow was used to such calls, and obeyed *instanter*; and in a few minutes more I was "making tracks" toward the trysting place . . .

With best-selling biographies of Laurence Olivier, Tchai-kowsky, and Prince Charles to his credit (and some twenty-odd books published), Anthony Holden counts *Big Deal* (1990) as his personal favorite—"the only one it was as much fun to write as to research." No small claim, since research amounted to a rollicking, yearlong stab at pro-fessional poker. Besides finishing in the black (sort of—net profit: $12,300), Holden's odyssey resulted in a cult classic among poker readers—a warm, amusing, and provocative account of swimming with the sharks. His sketch of Amarillo Slim adroitly captures the homespun craftiness of one of the game's wiliest and most celebrated characters.

Many of today's younger poker pros, physical as well as mental ath-letes, belie the game's unhealthy image by arriving at the table in track suit and trainers, fresh from the squash court or the jogging track. The rest get fat. And then there's Amarillo Slim.

Forget yon Cassius' lean and hungry look. Slim is so tall and thin that even his friends say he looks like the advance man for a famine. "Slim?" says the man himself. "Hell, when I was a kid, I had to get out of the bathtub before they pulled the plug."

Thomas Austin Preston, surely the only Arkansan christened for one Texas town and nicknamed after another, weighs 170 pounds and stands six-feet-four—six-nine or more if you count the huge Stetson which never leaves his head. You can see Slim coming two blocks away—and hear him, too, for "Amarillo" is one of poker's greatest talkers. This is not just his natural *joie de vivre*. Table-talk, to Slim, is a wily tactic, designed to throw his opponents off their game. Variations on such themes as, "Hey, neighbor, you better not call that big bet o' mine, I got six titties [three queens] down here," or, "This man's slower than a mule with three broken legs," or (if there are no ladies present), "This sucker's tighter than a nun's doodah" have won Slim a handsome fortune for years, and helped to make him the most celebrated poker player of his time.

When challenged to take on the world's top woman player, à la Bobby Riggs vs. Billie-Jean King, Slim accepted with glee, forecasting that "a woman would have a better chance of putting a wildcat in a tobacco sack than she would of beating me." Betty Carey, then the reigning women's world champion, allowed herself to be table-talked to defeat. She had arrived demurely dressed, but Slim claimed after the game that, "ah could see that left little titty of hers throbbin' every time she tried a bluff." A rematch was arranged, for which Betty arrived displaying a little cleavage. "All the easier to see that tell o' yours," cried Slim repeatedly, throughout the game, and won again. For the third and final contest Betty arrived with a dramatic *décolletage*—and, more to the point, a Sony Walkman to shut out Slim's ceaseless chatter. This time she won.

Slim's own victory in the 1972 World Series of Poker surprised even him: "Neighbor, at one point I had a better chance of getting a date with the Statue of Liberty than I did of winning that tournament." But he put it to extremely good effect. A wise-cracking appearance on the Johnny Carson show, swiftly followed by a bestselling poker manual, made him poker's only household name since "Wild Bill" Hickok. These days he may no longer be the best player alive, but he is certainly the best known. Home-town card-sharps making their first, wide-eyed visit to Vegas nudge each other, point and whisper excitedly as Slim lopes by. Even those who have tired of his antics at the table concede that he has been a great ambassador for poker over the years. Anywhere he is invited he will go—"My passport looks like a chicken scratched on it"—so long as the terms are right. When, to this day, amateur enthusiasts hail Slim as "Mr. Poker," few of his fellow professionals can find it in themselves to protest.

Born in Johnson, Arkansas, some seventy years ago—he is one of the few poker pros to be bashful about his age—Slim was less than a year old when his folks "saw the error of their ways" and moved to Texas. There was no gambling at all in the Preston family background. "My parents were average, church-going, hard-working people. Daddy had some cafés and ran a used-car business in Amarillo for many years." Today, likewise, the private Slim is very much the family man on his huge spread outside Amarillo. He travels in the winter, and stays home in summer to be with his family. "So far as I know, my wife, Helen Elizabeth, has never played a game of chance in her life. She thinks a king is the ruler of a country and a queen is his bedmate."

In that chicken-scratched passport, to this day, Amarillo Slim lists his occupation as "professional pool player," which is indeed how his career began. In high school, young Preston used to cut sixth-period study, head for the pool hall and "bust everybody in sight." He graduated from pool to cards at about sixteen, though his pool skills continued to come in handy. In the Navy he hustled his way up and down the West Coast, using an official car when off-duty as a captain's yeoman and chauffeur. On one famous occasion, so the story goes, he won five Cadillacs in San Francisco after cleaning his opponents out of cash. "I came out of the Navy with over $100,000 in my pocket. I was still a kid, just twenty, and I thought it was all the money in the world. I lost it all within a year."

When war came Slim traveled Europe giving pool exhibitions as a civilian member of the U.S. Special Services. Though he could never beat England's legendary world snooker champion, Joe Davis, he bested America's equally legendary Minnesota Fats in two out of three public challenges. Or so he says. Fats has always disputed Slim's memories of these occasions; but they have long since passed, like many another story too good to check, into the Preston folklore.

These days, the U.S. Statute of Declarations also enables Slim to reminisce gleefully about the lucrative black-market trade he ran among Allied troops in Europe. "Them GIs were just *amazed* what they could find in the back of my wagon." By war's end pool-hustling was no longer a gravy train rich enough to sustain his taste for the high life, so Slim shifted his center of gravity to poker. In the fifties he went on the road in a playing partnership with Doyle Brunson and Brian "Sailor" Roberts, sharing their wins and losses as they chased action all over the western United States. "When we moved on, the town looked like a vacuum had been through it."

Another of Slim's ploys was to hang around in the early mornings in the bars outside state prisons. Newly released prisoners, their savings ripe for the plucking, would head here first in search of a drink and a woman; and here they would find Slim and a partner playing a deceptively amateur game of dominoes, the only gambling game allowed in American jails. Challenges would inevitably be issued. Slim would let the jailbirds win a couple of small games, innocently offer to up the stakes, and ruthlessly clean them out.

Doubters of this particular legend—including, to his cost, Steve Wynn, owner of the Golden Nugget—were silenced only recently, when Slim accepted and won a dominoes challenge from a celebrated ex-con then appearing in the Nugget's showroom, the country-and-western singer Willie Nelson. Celebrities seem to love taking a crack at Slim. A few years ago it cost Larry Flint, the proprietor of *Hustler* magazine, nearly two million dollars to find out that Slim really *can* talk his way to victory in a two-handed poker game—especially with the kind of pots he loves best, "higher than a dawg could jump over."

Poker players tend not to penetrate each other's homes, but it doesn't take much persuading for Slim to tell you about the Waterford crystal chandeliers which adorn his lavish Texas ranch, or the head of cattle wandering about outside, within sight of the Olympic-size swimming pool. He used to own a string of thoroughbred racehorses, but "you should never have a hobby that eats." Most yarns emanating from Slim's home on the range carry glancing references to the stockmen who tend his herds, the grooms who care for his horses, the hands who ride for days without leaving the Preston patch. It was one of these who loyally killed and skinned the rattlesnake which bit Slim ten years back, and now winds for eternity around his Stetson, its emerald-green eyes matching the large, uncut rocks with which he buttons his monogrammed shirts.

You don't believe him? He'll show you the rattler's bitemark on his hand. You've never seen him win? He'll offer you a (modest) discount at one of the chain of fast food stores for which he owns the franchise in three western states. Then he'll tell you how much he paid for the dead-weight of jewelry which sets off his tailor-made western suits. The Imelda Marcos of poker footwear, Slim wears five-figure boots of calf, alligator, lizard, even ostrich, kangaroo and anteater skin. "I know I live high on the hog, but it's something you've got to do when you're hunting high-stakes poker . . .

"It never hurts for potential opponents to think you're more than a little stupid, and can hardly count all the money in your hip pocket, much less hold on to it. That's one reason I wear a big cowboy hat, cowboy boots and western duds—especially when I'm globe-trotting and looking for high action. People everywhere assume that anyone from Texas in a ten-gallon hat is not only a billionaire, but an easy mark. That's just fine with me, because that's the impression I'm trying to give. The approach puts those dudes in the category of guessers, and guessers are losers. That's my meat, to make the other guy guess."

"Live high on the hog"—that was Slim's first piece of advice when I sought a few tricks of his trade. The finery, moreover, is functional: "Why do you think I like to wear this big-brimmed Stetson o' mine? A man's eyes show 90 percent of what he's thinking. When I'm wearing my hat, you can only see my eyes when I want you to."

Having tried on the hat, which weighed a couple of tons, I decided to go for dark glasses. Headgear, to Slim, is even a source of poker metaphors. "Just as important for home-town players as for the World Series pros are things like psychology, position, the percentages and trappin'. Ah love to trap—and it ain't all trappers wear fur caps."

Slim offered me a lexicon of poker advice too eloquent to hug to my chest. For starters, he confirmed one of my pet theses: that although poker is an institutionalized form of dishonesty, the relationships between its regular players are among the most honest to be found in this murky world. "Tony," he said with feeling, "I've got two or three cigar boxes full of bad checks I've been given by businessmen, but I ain't got one from a professional gambler."

There followed Slim on the need to be observant: "You want to be able to see a gnat's keester at a hundred yards or hear a mouse wet on cotton." Slim on knowing whom you can trust: "In this game, if a true friend tells you that a goose will pull a plow, then hook him up, because he'll damn sure move it out . . ."

On feeling pity for friends who are losing: "I like you, Tony, but I'll put a rattlesnake in your pocket, and ask you for a match." On going for the kill: "You can shear a sheep many times, but you can only skin him once." Slim on optimism: "I'm kinda like that guy who got a big box of horse shit from some joker for his birthday, and when this optimist opens it up, he's happy as hell and starts digging in all that horse dung—looking for the horse."

Slim knows how to make the most of a strong hand: "You don't come in like a wildcat gusher. Wait till you think you've got this cat, then introduce him to Mr. More." He chooses his opponents carefully: "Ah'd rather have early frost on my peaches than play stud with that guy." He knows when to quit: "You can damn sure stick a fork in me because ah'm done. Ah'm slicker than a wet gut." And he knows how to take defeat philosophically: "Sometimes the lambs slaughter the butcher."

One of Slim's best lines, however, distills the art of the dignified exit: "If they ask you where you're goin', just tell 'em: 'No one knows where the hobo goes when it snows.'"

FROM HERE TO ETERNITY

JAMES JONES

James Jones joined the Army a few months after graduating high school in 1939. He served until 1944, then spent several years writing this epic novel of soldiers in the Pacific, which won the 1952 National Book Award. Jones's biting portrayal of a weak-willed private's struggle at the card table delves subtly into the psychological frailties of a chronic loser. After building up a $20 stake in a nickel-dime barracks game, Prew seeks out higher-staked action with one goal in mind: win two hands, only two, and enough money to buy the favors of the prostitute he's in love with.

Prew slid onto the empty seat and pushed his little ten and two fives over to the dealer as unobtrusively as possible. The money boys kept the takeout low on Payday, so you could get in, but they stared at your twenty bucks contemptuously, when you did. He got back a stack of 15 cartwheels, 6 halves, and 8 of the plastic chips and fingering them did not any longer mind the contempt because the old familiar alchemy, the best drug of them all against this life, spread over him as he flipped a red chip in there with the others. His heart was beating faster with louder, more emphatic thumps, echoing in his ears. The gambler's flush was spreading across his face, making it feverish. The bottom of his belly dropped away from under him leaving him standing on the edge of which the world stopped moving.

Here, he thought, just here, and only here, held in these pieces of pasteboard being tossed facedown around the table, governed by whatever Laws or fickle Goddess moved them, here lay infinity and the secret of all life and death, what the scientists were seeking, here under your hand if you could only grasp it, penetrate the unreadability. You may shortly win $1000. You may more shortly be completely broke. And any man who could just only learn to understand the reason why would be shaking hands with God. They were playing table stakes and in front of the winners lay thick piles of greenbacks weighted down with silver. The sight of all this crisp green paper that was so important in this life swept him with a greediness to take these crinkly good smelling pieces of paper to himself, not for what they would buy but for their lovely selves. All this was contained in the slow, measured, inexorable dropping of the cards, like time beating slowly but irresistibly in the ears of an old man.

Around the table twice, twice ten cards, once down, once up. Somebody's watch beat loudly. And the known familiar faces took on new characteristics and became strange. The bright light cast strange shadows down from the impassive brows and noses, making of each man an eyeless harelip. He did not know these men. That was not Warden there or O'Hayer there, only a pair of bodyless hands moving the top card under the holecard for a secret look, only an armless hand clicking a stack of halves down one on top the other, then lifting all and clicking them down again, and again, perpetually, with measured thoughtfulness. An unreasoning thrill passed down his spine, and all the unpleasantness his life had become in the last two months fell away from him, dead, forgotten.

The first hand was a big one. He had hoped for a small one, his $20 would not go far in this game. But the cards were high, and the betting heavy. He had jacks backed up and by the third round he was all in, for the side pot his twenty shared, unable because this was table stakes to go into his pocket for more money if he had it which he did not. The pot he could win was shoved to one side and the betting went on in the center, and all he could do was sit and sweat it out. On the fourth card O'Hayer caught the ace to match his holecard that all of them knew he had because Jim O'Hayer never stayed for fun. He raised fifteen. Prew's belly sagged and he looked at his jacks ruefully and was very glad he was all in for the pot. But on the last card he caught another jack, making a pair showing. He felt his heart skip a beat and cursed silently because he was all in for the pot.

There was nearly a hundred and fifty in his pot. O'Hayer won the other, the smaller pot. Warden looked at O'Hayer and then at him and snorted his disgust. Prew grinned, dragging in his pot, and reminded himself that if he won the next one he would quit and check out and Warden could really snort then.

He didnt need to win the next one. What he had from the first was plenty. But he had promised himself two hands, not one, so he stayed in. But he did not win the second hand, Warden won it, and he had dropped $40 which left him only about a hundred and now he felt he needed the second win before he dropped out so he stayed in. But he did not win the third hand either, or the fourth, nor did he win the fifth. He dropped clear down to less than $50, before he finally won another one.

Raking in the money he sighed off the tenseness that had grown in him in ratio to the shrinking of his capital; he had begun to believe he would never win another one. But now though he had a real backlog to work from. The second win put him up to over two hundred. Two hundred was plenty capital. And he began to play careful, weighing each bet. He played shirtfront poker, enjoying it immensely, completely lost in loving it, in matching his brain against the disembodied brains against him. It was true poker, hard monotonous unthrilling, and he truly loved it, and played steadily, losing only a little, dropping out often, winning a small one now and then, playing now against the time when he would win that really big one and check out.

He knew of course all the time that it could not go on indefinitely this way, $200 was no reserve to put up against the capital in this game, but then all he wanted was just one more big win like the first

two, one that would be bigger because now he had more money, one
he could quit on and check out for good. If he had won the first two
like he promised he would have quit then but he hadnt won them he
had only won one and now he wanted this last one to quit on, before
he finally got caught.

But before the big win he was just waiting for to quit on came they
caught him, they caught him good.

He had tens backed up, a good hand. On the fourth card he drew
another. On the same card Warden paired kings showing. Warden
checked to the tens. Prew was cautious, they were not *trying* to play
dirty poker in this game but with this much on the table anything
went. Warden might have trips and he was not being sucked in, he was
not that green. When the bet had checked clear around to him he
raised lightly, very lightly, just a touch, a feeler, a protection bet he
could afford to abandon and lose. Three men dropped out right away.
Only O'Hayer and Warden called, finally. O'Hayer obviously had an
ace paired to his holecard and was willing to pay for the chance to
catch the third. O'Hayer was a percentage man, twenty percentage
man, O'Hayer. And Warden who thought quite a while before he
called looked at his holecard twice and then he almost didn't call, so
he had no trips.

On the last card O'Hayer missed his ace and dropped out, indifferently. O'Hayer could always afford to drop out indifferently. Warden
with his kings still high checked it to Prew, and Prew felt a salve of
relief grease over him for sure now Warden had no trips. Warden had
two pair and hoped the kings would nose him out since O'Hayer had
two bullets. Well, if he wanted to see them he could by god pay for seeing them, like everybody else, and Prew bet twenty-five, figuring to
milk the last drop out of him, figuring he had this one cinched, figuring The Warden for his lousy pair to brace his kings. It was a legitimate bet; Warden had checked his kings twice when they were high.
Warden raised him sixty dollars.

Looking at Warden's malignant grin he knew then he was caught,
really hooked, right through the bag. By three big kings. Outsmarted.
Sucked in like a green kid. The first time somebody checked a cinch

into him. His belly flopped over sickeningly with disbelief and he made as if to drop out, but he knew he had to call. There was too much of his money in this pot, which was a big one, to chance a bluff. And The Warden knew just how high to raise without raising too high to get a call.

The hand cost him two hundred even, he had about forty dollars left. He pushed the stool back, and got up then.

"Seat open."

Warden's eyebrows quivered, then hooked up pixishly.

"I hated to do that to you, kid. I really did. If I dint need the money so goddam bad I'd by god give it back."

The table laughed all around.

"Ah, you keep it," Prew said. "You won it, Top, it's yours. Check me out," he said to the dealer, thinking why dint you drop out you son of a bitch after that second win like you promised, thinking this is not an original lament.

"Whats wrong, kid?" Warden said. "You look positively unwell."

"Just hungry. Missed noon chow."

Warden winked at Stark who had only just come back. "Too late to catch chow now. You better stick around? Win some of this back? Forty, fifty bucks aint much take home pay."

"Enough," Prew said. "For what I need." Why didnt he let it go? why did he have to rub it in? The son of a bitch bastard whoring bastard.

"Yeah, but you want a bottle too, dont you? Hell, we all friends here, just a friendly game for pastime. Aint that right, Jim?"

Prew could see his eyes clenching into rays of wrinkles as he looked at the gambler.

"Sure," O'Hayer said indifferently. "Long as you got the money to be friendly. Deal the cards."

Warden laughed softly, as if to himself. "You see?" he said to Prew. "No cutthroat. No hardtack. The take out's only twenty."

"Beats me," Prew said. He started to add, *"I've got a widowed mother,"* but nobody would have heard it. The cards were already riffling off the deck.

As he moved back Stark goosed him warmly in the ribs and winked, and slipped into the seat.

"Heres fifty," Stark said to the dealer.

Outside the air free of smoke and the moisture of exhaled breath smote Prew like cold water and he inhaled deeply, suddenly awake again, then let it out, trying to let out with it the weary tired unrest that was urging him to go back. He could not escape the belief that he had just lost $200 of his own hard-earned money to that bastard Warden. Come on, cut it out, he told himself, you didnt lose a cent, you're twenty to the good, you got enough for tonight, lets me and you walk from this place.

The air had wakened him and he saw clearly that this was no personal feud, this was a poker game, and you cant break them all, eventually they'll break you. He walked around the sheds and down to the sidewalk. Then he walked across the street. He even got so far his hand was on the doorknob of the day-room door and the door half open. Before he finally decided to quit kidding himself and slammed the door angrily and turned around and went irritably back to O'Hayer's.

"Well look who's here," Warden grinned. "I thought we'd be seeing you. Is there a seat open? Somebody get up and give this old gambler a seat."

"Aw can it," Prew said savagely and slipped into the seat of another loser who was checking out and grinning unhappily at The Warden with the look of a man who wants to do the right thing and be a sport but finds it hard.

"Come on, come on," Prew said. "Whats holding things up? Lets get this show on the road."

"Man!" The Warden said. "You sound like you're itchin for a great big lick."

"I am. Look out for yourself. I'm hot. First jack bets."

But he was not hot and knew it, he was only savagely irritated, and there is a difference and it took him just fifteen minutes and three hands to lose the forty dollars, as he had known he would. Where before he had played happily, lost in loving it, savoring every second, now he played with dogged irritation, not giving a damn, angered by even the time it took to deal. You dont win at poker playing that way, and he stood up feeling a welcome sense of release that came with being broke and able to quit now.

"Now I can go home and go to bed. And sleep."

"What!" The Warden said. "At three o'clock in the afternoon?"

"Sure," Prew said. Was it only three o'clock? He had thought they'd played Tattoo already. "Why not?" he said.

The Warden snorted his disgust. "Punks wont never listen to me. I told you you should of quit while you was ahead. But would you listen? A lot you listen."

"Forgot," Prew said. "Forgot all about it. Hows for loanin me a hundred, and I'll remember." It got a laugh around the table.

"Sorry kid. You know I'm behind myself."

"Hell. And I thought you was winnin." It got another laugh, and he felt better, but he remembered it did not put money back in his pocket. He elbowed his way out.

"What you want to awys be pickin on the kid for, First?" he heard Stark say behind him.

"Pick on him?" Warden said indignantly. "Whatever give you that idea?"

"He dont need you to pick on him," the K Co topkick, a bald fat man with drinker's hollowed eyes, said. "From what I hear."

"Thats right," Stark said. "He doin all right by himself."

Warden snorted then. "He can take it. He's a punchy. He's use to bein hit. Some of them even like it."

"If I was him," the K Co topkick said, "I'd transfer the hell out of there."

"Thats all you know," Warden said. "He cant. Dynamite wont let him."

"Come on," Jim O'Hayer's voice said nasally, "Is this a sewing circle or a card game? King is high, king bets."

"Bet five," Warden said. "You know, thats what I like about you,

Jim. Your overwhelming sense of human compassion," he said quizzi-
cally. In his mind Prew could see the eyes clenching themselves into
those somehow ominous rays of wrinkles.

He let the shaky door swing shut behind him, cutting off the talk,
wishing he could find it in him to hate that bitchery Warden but he
couldnt, and remembering suddenly he had not even in his passion
thought to get a sandwich and coffee from O'Hayer's free lunch for
the players. But he would not go back in there now.

He could also remember, suddenly, a lot of other things he had
meant to do with part of that money before he risked it. He needed
shaving cream and a new bore brush and a new Blizt rag and he had
wanted to stock up some tailormades. It was lucky he had a carton of
Duke's still stashed away.

Because you are through, Prewitt, he told himself, your wad is
shot, your roll is gone, you're through till next month now, and there
will be no Lorene for you this month. By next month she may have
retired and gone back to the States already.

He jammed his hands in his pockets savagely and found some
change, a small pile of dimes and nickels, and brought it out and
looked at it, wondering what it was good for. It was enough to get
into a small change game in the latrine, but the hopelessness of ever
running that little bit back up to two hundred and sixty bucks hit
him and he threw it down into the railroad bed viciously and with satisfaction watched it spread like shot but glinting silver, then heard
with satisfaction the clink of it hitting the rails.

FROM

TELLING LIES AND GETTING PAID

BY

MICHAEL KONIK

As the original gambling columnist for *Cigar Aficionado*, Michael Konik knows whereof he writes. He's had off-and-on success on the periphery of big-time poker and even qualified (via the arduous, long-shot satellite tournament route) for the World Series of Poker in 1998. But in the recognized spirit that gamblers will more readily call up (and more passionately relate to) past losses than past wins, the offering here is of the author's tragicomic tourney exit of 1992. Welcome to bad-beat country.

J es drinkin' and gamblin', boys," he says, laying down his cards. "Drinkin' and gamblin'! Evuh day's a party and evuh night's a Saturday night!"

He's got the "nuts," the unbeatable lock hand, a hand he wasn't supposed to have—and he's letting the other nine players at our poker table know it. "Gimme that money, honey!" he implores the dealer. "I'm jes a po' boy from Texas and I need as much money as I can git." Raymond—that's what we'll call him—is one of the most successful bookies in Houston. He doesn't need the $600 pile of poker chips the dealer, inevitably, shoves his way. (His organization clears more than $100,000 a week; winning or losing $600 concerns him about as much as it would you or me if a quarter fell through a hole in our pocket.) Indeed, the $600 in chips is not even worth $600. It's tournament money, a bunch of tokens. Still, Raymond intends to crow long and loud enough that his opponents get sufficiently fed up with him to do something stupid.

It's 1992. I'm playing with Ray and a school of other sharks in a satellite tournament at the World Series of Poker at Binion's Horseshoe in downtown Las Vegas.

The main event, the World Championship, is a grueling four-day affair that costs $10,000 to enter. Some competitors, such as two-time World Champions Johnny Chan and Doyle Brunson, are too busy playing in side games laden with $1,000 chips—real $1,000 chips—to waste time dabbling in satellite tournaments. But for working stiffs like me, satellites are mandatory. The PGA Tour has them, and so does the tennis circuit. For those without full-time playing privileges, these golf and tennis mini-tournaments are a weekly odyssey. The winner of the satellite earns a coveted spot in the big show. It's the same at the World Series of Poker. The Horseshoe conducts daily $220-buy-in tournaments that award winners a $10,000 seat in the World Championship. The losers watch on television. Or get press credentials.

I've played in dozens of satellites leading up to my 1992 campaign, winning a few minor events and finishing in the money (the final table) at some major ones. But I've never won a satellite for the Big One, the World Series of Poker main event. For years I've *written* about the championship, enjoying intimate access to the greatest tournament poker players on Earth, observing the insights and judgments and character that place these wizards on a slightly elevated plane, a place where studying and reading (and writing) about the game are woeful substitutes for talent and experience. Years of chronicling the exploits of the best players in the game have afforded me the kind of training a young lad earned in the Middle Ages when he served as an unpaid and much-abused apprentice to, say, a pedophilic blacksmith.

Thanks to my assignments as an ink-stained wretch, I've effectively been mentored in the game of poker, though my mentors are blissfully unaware that they've taught me anything—except perhaps how to give a thoroughly uninteresting interview filled with a litany of clichés. (Most great poker players—as with most great artists—have difficulty articulating how they do what they do; they just do.) Armed with what I take to be an unimpeachably authoritative compendium of poker knowledge, I figure I'm ready to cross the threshold from voyeur to participant. If I can win my way into the main event, I'll know I deserve to play with the big boys. Thus far I haven't deserved it. Tonight, though, I'm seated with a bunch of fools like Raymond, and I've got a terrific chance.

We're down to 27 players. The top three will all win $10,000 seats in the main event; fourth, fifth, and sixth will earn several thousand dollars, and the remaining three at the final table will pocket several hundred. I'm feeling good.

Mine is one of those dream tables you sometimes encounter in Las Vegas, a collection of players who, lacking skill, compensate with outlandish theatrics. Dueling Raymond for the title of Loudest Voice is Jimmy, who raises fighting cocks outside of Lafayette, Louisiana. All week, Jimmy, who looks to be in his fifties, has garnered the admiration of his opponents by having two fetching teenage girls—one blonde, one brunette—accompany his every move, like a couple of Cajun geishas. When he makes an ill-advised bluff and gets raised, Jimmy turns to his girls and proclaims in a Creole growl, "I make a bet, *everyone* call me. Shit, guy at the next table call me! Guy across the street pick up the phone and call me!" His girls titter respectfully and return to preening.

Billy's at my table, too. He runs a gun shop in Alabama. Someone asks him how's business. "Bettuh'n evuh," drawls Billy. "Evuh-budy got *someone* they wanna kill." I tell myself that even if I fail to place in this satellite tournament, my cash investment has bought me an evening worthy of *Guys and Dolls*. What a cast! The Jew Boy writer and a chorus of redneck Bubbas. Earlier in the tourney, our table disposed of a 450-pound guy named Oklahoma Bob, owner of a port-a-potty concern. His baseball cap, tilted rakishly on his balding crown, proclaimed him to be "Number One in the Number Two Business!"

Across from the empty space that Bob's gargantuan girth previously occupied sits a taciturn enigma named John, whose dyed-black perm, smoky sunglasses, and necklaces entwined in chest hair recall a disco-era wild and crazy guy. Despite a gold-chunk bracelet around one wrist and diamond-encrusted watch around the other, John takes a distant second in the over-accessorized department. That honor easily goes to the gentleman on my left, Ed, who sports sparkling diamond rings on every finger of both hands.

Ray continues to yell about drinking and gambling. Jimmy is sending one of his under-aged ladies-in-waiting for an antacid. Ed is clipping his manicured nails. John has a few chips left. Billy is surveying the room, seeing if he can outlast 18 more players. And I look down and see my poker dreams have come true.

Aces in the hole.

It's become a mythic phrase applied to any situation where hidden power lurks, where a secret weapon waits to be unleashed. In almost any poker game—seven-stud, five-card draw—aces in the hole are strong. In no-limit Texas hold 'em, the game we're playing now, aces in the hole is the most powerful hand you can possibly start with. (Hold 'em is played with two hole cards and five "community" cards. Players make the best five-card hand from the quintet of "up" cards and the duo of "down" cards. "No limit" means just that—you can bet all of your chips at any time.) Like Stanley Cups in New York and pennants in Chicago, pocket aces show up with depressing infrequency, only .45% of the time, one in every 221 hands, or about once in every six hours of continuous betting, raising, and folding.

Not only do I have wired aces, I'm on the "button," the last player to act. With nine people before me, chances are good that someone will raise the pot, either because he's bluffing or because he has a legitimately strong hand. I'm hoping someone will make a large bet, which I can then re-raise. *Please!* I'm screaming in my head, *someone raise this pot!*

During the eternal 10 seconds it takes for betting to commence, I glance around the room: three tables left in the satellite; my birthday numbers up on the keno board; Doyle Brunson, playing with Chan, one table over in the corner, scooping up a pot larger than most people's yearly income. Doyle's book, *Super/System*, is the poker player's bible, a 605-page repository of secrets that every fledgling card sharp commits to memory. One of Brunson's maxims, buried in the chapter on no-limit Texas hold 'em, goes like this: "Most of the time, a pair of aces in the hole will either win you a small pot or lose you a big one." I'm displeased to remember that lesson at this particular moment.

In early position, Billy raises the ante $400. *(Yes!)* Everyone folds until it comes around to Raymond, who's grown unusually circum-spect. He scratches his beard, looks at Billy, and re-raises $1,200. *(Yes!!)* John folds. Jimmy folds. It's up to me. I don't want to put on too much of a show, but I don't want to act too quickly either. I want to suggest uncertainty, even though I'm completely certain of what I must do. I peek at my hole cards, look at the pot, scan my stack of chips, and deadpan, "Raise." I match Raymond's $1,600 and shove $2,200 more—all my money—toward the center. "All in," announces the dealer.

Billy sighs and folds without hesitation. Raymond stares at me glumly. "You got somethin' there, writer boy?" he asks, riffling chips between his long fingers. I stare beyond him, at Doyle Brunson. "I'm gonna have to call you," Raymond snarls. *(Yes!!!)* He puts in nearly all his chips. The spot has swelled to more than $8,000. Winning it will virtually guarantee me a spot at the final table and an odds-on chance at grabbing my first seat at the $10,000 World Championship.

"You got a pair?" Raymond asks me weakly. I nod confidently. "Shit," he groans, turning over two little deuces. "I was hoping you had ace-king or something." I show him my two aces, and he nods. "Shit." He knows the probabilities, and they're the poker equivalent of having Shaquille O'Neal posted up on Mugsy Bogues: The only card that can help him now is a deuce, and only two remain in the deck. I'm close to a 5–1 favorite. The dealer flops the first three community cards: six-nine-king of various suits. He turns the next card, "fourth street." Another six. Only one card, "the river," remains. One card between me and poker nirvana.

It's a deuce.

"How *'bout* that!" Raymond yelps, gathering in the spoils of his improbable full house. I try unsuccessfully to force a smile and wish everyone luck, but my face feels frozen, as though the fateful deuce has splashed a large puddle of novocaine onto my cheeks. I'm speechless. I'm catatonic. I'm done.

As I depart, hoping I'll make it back to my room before I start whimpering, Doyle Brunson glances my way. The dealer at his table is pushing Johnny Chan a pot that appears to have nearly $100,000 of Doyle's money in it. Brunson, the old master, sits placidly, unmoved. His expression is blank, unreadable. I briefly consider telling him about my $8,000 bad beat, about his aces-in-the-hole maxim getting proven one more ugly time. But I sense this might not be the best moment.

Doyle Brunson reaches into a black shoulder bag and pulls out $75,000 more to play with. I walk past the Horseshoe's Gallery of Champions, a pantheon of the World Series of Poker's past winners, and trudge off toward the nickel slots.

POKER'S PROMISE

BY

LEONARD KRIEGEL

Renowned essayist Leonard Kriegel is the author of *Flying Solo*, an artful blend of memoir and social history about growing up in the 1940s and '50s. At the age of eleven, Kriegel contracted polio, effectively shattering a Bronx kid's dreams of becoming a pro baseball player. Here (from a 1992 *New York Times Magazine* column) he writes lovingly about just how purely American our *other* national pastime can be.

Like me, the friends who introduced me to poker in the early 1950s were the children of immigrants. And that, I suspect, explains our infatuation with a game that seemed quintessentially American. No game commanded greater loyalty and no game promised more. Along with the intricacies of baseball, poker was a cultural bridge that helped you cross over into a wider world.

As a game, poker is pedestrian. As gambling, it is prosaic. A short drive from our Bronx neighborhood was Yonkers Raceway. An evening with the trotters there offered a more exciting prospect than the run of cards on somebody's kitchen table. But as a rite of passage, poker eased us into American aspirations, suggesting how each of us might bankroll his sense of belonging.

Among my vivid adolescent memories is listening to a group of

middle-aged men—furriers, countermen, garment workers, taxi drivers—vehemently discussing in Yiddish the trials and tribulations of
their weekly poker game. I can still hear the echo of those voices dripping with derision as a player's efforts were dismissed with the contemptuous, *"Er speelt vee ah greener."* ("He plays like an immigrant.")
No condemnation could have been more formidable, no dismissal
more damning. For to play like an immigrant was to deny those very
entitlements America offered like some generous uncle dispensing
unheard-of largesse. Even in the golden land, one listened carefully
for opportunity's knock.

I remember a Holocaust survivor who had arrived in our midst in
1949. Defined by the horror of his past and limited by the paucity of
his English, he searched our fears as closely as we searched his. One
night, someone brought him to our poker game. Almost immediately,
he established a reputation as a daring, skillful player. It was as if the
nightmare of Europe could be expunged by the mundane triumph of
drawing an inside straight. I can still see him as he dealt, slamming
the cards down, blue numbers tattooed on his arm seeming to quiver
beneath the living flesh. I remember him holding his own cards like a
sweeping fan of affirmation as he said in his thickly accented yet suddenly triumphant English, *"I* open!"

The pedestrian run of cards might have been a mundane gift, but
what else could have so quickly transformed a refugee dependent
upon our psychological charity into a man secure in his reputation as
a player? In poker, one made one's own choices, avoiding catastrophe
by paying attention to what was on the table. Even a losing hand provided security in American games.

No game better embodied the enormous sense of possibility we
felt was ours by right of having been born in this America. A man
could shed the past in poker. What could possibly be more American
than that? Poker was never meant for heroics, nor is it, despite those
movie close-ups of faces sprinkled by sweat as the cards are dealt, a
game in which bluffing usually works. Its scale is too human, its
rewards too commonplace.

I don't mean that playing poker allowed our Holocaust survivor to create a successful business, marry, raise a family—to become what we admiringly called "a proper citizen." Yet, in a small way, it helped. His syntax might have remained redolent of Europe, but the knowledge that he, too, now possessed choices reinforced his right to think of himself as an American.

My own father, who came to this country at the age of 30, never learned to play poker. Tied to an immigrant psychology until the day of his death 44 years after his arrival in America, he was contemptuous of card players. When he spoke about gambling, his natural gentleness was overwhelmed by anger at a profligacy he could not afford to imagine. But my father sensed that, like his never having learned to drive or his inability to understand baseball, not knowing how to play poker was another way he had shut himself off from a country he loved but could never decipher. My father never realized that playing poker had more to do with the ease of a man's stance in this country than with gambling. The cards dealt not a way to wealth but a way to an America in the mind, where each and all might claim a proper citizenship.

My father distrusted what lay beyond his grasp. Yet when I myself began to play, he didn't discourage me. Unable to overcome the stigma of psychologically remaining a refugee himself, he didn't want his sons to share his spiritual exile. Unable to comprehend what motivated Americans, his challenges grew half-hearted. If he himself could not participate in wooing America, he might yet capture it vicariously. When I would return from a game, he would question me closely. One night, I came home $40 richer (not an insubstantial sum in a nickel-and-dime game in 1952). My father laughed delightedly as I spread the coins out before him. It wasn't the money, although that was almost a week's salary for a workingman like my father. It was simply that I had won. And winning was an affirmation of the worth of American sons.

I never became an accomplished player. As happy as I feel at the prospect of a game, I am bored once the cards are dealt. Poker demands not skill but concentration and allegiance to the run of the cards. I lack concentration—I do not follow the cards as serious players must—and the traditional demands of poker irritate me.

Not that my ambition was to be a good loser. Winning in poker may not be a metaphor for winning in life, but neither is losing. Poker does not test character—it defines it. Even a quarter-ante game demands a mask of patience. One may believe that winning doesn't matter, but one still plays for that brief but decisive glimpse into another's mind. A singular American lesson—and one I unfortunately must master over and over.

When I was a graduate student in the late 1950s, I would occasionally break the grind of libraries and classes by seeking out a game. Studying for exams or working on my dissertation, I would devour books as if I were a contestant in a Fourth of July hot dog eating contest. That was my signal to seek a game out. Merely envisioning the flow of cards restored balance and proportion to the world. When Emerson on compensation or Frederick Jackson Turner on the significance of the frontier proved too much, I could turn to the game that embodied *my* American aspirations.

One evening, unable to follow Thoreau for the hundredth time to Walden Pond, I went instead to the apartment of a friend where I knew a game was in progress. Ted's New York acquaintances and fellow émigrés from Indianapolis also needed the assurance of cards. For the next four hours, faces drifted in and out of the game. My cards were good, I was winning, my eyes drifted from face to face. I was happy to be here, even happy to be playing. Neither a game of daring, nor of skill, nor particularly esthetic, poker was just one more American game—and mine.

A Girlhood Among Gamblers

FROM *Poker Face*

BY

KATY LEDERER

Katy Lederer's unusual family background includes an alcoholic mother/actress who becomes a bookie's assistant and quiz show finalist; a father/prep school teacher who writes a best-seller; and an older brother and sister/sibling rivals who respectively jump from homelessness and motherhood to the highest ranks of professional poker. In searching for her own identity (and a semblance of family unity), Lederer follows her brother and sister to the Vegas card rooms before heading for the University of Iowa poetry program. Not a bad choice. Her poker talents may have failed her in the end, but her sensitive reflections from *Poker Face* (2003) are stone-cold winners.

Though I remember many days that I spent in Las Vegas, the nights I recall only vaguely. Session after session playing cards at my low-limit table, lost to memory. I played with great fervor—I remember that—and waking to the rustling of leaves, the skin around my eyes as dark as coffee rings. At dusk I would go to play poker again, mechanically shifting the gears of the car, darting from corner to corner till I reached the Mirage. It was a gleaming, incredibly beautiful building, bright and sublime as a new bar of gold, and I loved walking slowly through its glass double doors, toward the room where my sister and brother played cards. Was I there to play poker or to feel like a part of the family? I guess both.

Those early hands lost, though I wrote them all down on a small pad of paper that I'd filched from the card room. The other players would look on in amusement at the terribly serious girl who wrote down their plays: "Man in first position: raise. *His right hand is shaking.* Woman to his right: call. Ninth seat: reraise. First seat: call. Call. Flop comes 8-3-6, different suits. Check, then bet. Raise. *Woman's jugular pulsing.* Call. Call. Ace of spades. Bet. *Man's hand still shaking.* Call. Ninth seat folds. (Man must have an ace?) Final card comes: Jack. Bet. Woman hesitates. *Covers her mouth with her hand.* Call." After checking my opinions with Howard at dinner, I would stuff the notes in a clear plastic binder. All those notes, all those hands. Even if I'd kept them, I wouldn't now remember the way those hands played out, the way, for example, the woman's head listed when she brandished her ace-king of hearts. Or the way that the first seat had tilted his hat while his right hand, *still shaking,* had thrown in his cards.

"And what do you think happened there?" Howard asked after hearing me narrate this hand.

"I think the first seat also had an ace, but his second card was smaller."

"I think you're exactly right," Howard said. "Nice job. Now when are you going to stop with the notes and just remember?"

"I don't know," I said, picking at the lukewarm baked potato on my plate. "I don't know if I'll ever be able to remember. All the hands just bleed into one another, you know? And all the people."

"No, I don't know," said Howard. "You can't just spend your whole life taking notes while you play. I know they must *feel* real, but they're not real."

All my life it had struck me that my sister and brother had better memories than I. When I was much younger, I would notice how easily and quickly they'd study for their tests, how well they could learn any fact or statistic. I'd always assumed that this uncanny ability had come from my mother, who, my father would regularly remind us, used to borrow his notes back in graduate school, memorize them in a single sitting, then proceed to do better on the test than he. My father just loved to extol my mother's knack for rote memorization (a knack that had helped her through the years with all her plays), yet even then, when I was young, I doubted the value of this particular variety of photographic memory. It seemed like a cheat.

Not that I wasn't impressed. I can remember listening to Annie and Howard as they'd talk about cards. They could narrate almost any hand exactly as it had happened, even those hands that had happened several years before, and in such a thick and impenetrable jargon that I'd have trouble just following along. I knew I didn't have that kind of talent, but I also knew that a player could be very good without it, so I didn't despair. Besides, I had my own equally inane type of photographic memory: for colors, for scenes, for the way that people said things. This more visceral way of remembering the past meant that I was able to "read" people well, but it proved problematic. I would sit at my table, look around at my opponents, and try my best to assess them by their postures and expressions, but it would be strangely painful. Or, not painful. It would make me feel *dirty*. A poker table is one of the only places in the world where people are encouraged to downright stare at one another. A player's entire body becomes part of the game, an extension of the cards—in fact a stand-in for the cards— and so I'd stare. I'd stare and they'd stare, and then I'd become uncomfortable at staring, at watching the other players staring. Their faces would grow tired, ashen, their expressions severe. We would sit there, growing filthy together, handling our cards and the dirty plastic chips, trying not to bite our nails for fear of what had lodged itself beneath them.

The cardinal sin in poker, worse than playing dud cards, worse even than figuring your odds incorrectly, is becoming emotionally involved. While the game requires that you fully engage with other players at the table, that you pay attention to their quirks and personalities, you're not supposed to identify with them in any way. You are, in other words, expected to empathize with your opponents while remaining devoid of all compassion. It is very hard to do.

While my sister and brother would remember their hands with a mechanical precision, their opponents merely actors, nothing more, I'd remember mine in such a sensory fashion that I'd often lose the logic of the hand as it had happened, and when I stopped taking notes, I felt suddenly unmoored. It was exposing to sit there, no pencil to keep my hands busy. I was just this little girl, I'd think, a *child*, though by then I was twenty-two. The other players at my table would regularly pity me, advising me to fold when they knew they had me beat, refraining from raising in spite of the fact that they'd read my poor odds in my face. In this way, I gained an advantage by being a woman in Vegas, an advantage that, in and of itself, may have accounted for my tiny $2-an-hour edge. I knew it couldn't last, however, and one day I met up with a man with no pitying bone in his body.

Mealy Joe was an elderly man, maybe sixty years old. His skin resembled oatmeal, a yellow sort of brown, pocked on his cheeks and his neck by old acne scars, and this is why I called him Mealy Joe. I could never figure out why Joe played low. His skills at the table were, if not flawless, then at least profitable, and he should have moved up long before. From the bits of conversation I'd overheard him engaging in that night, I gleaned that he'd been in the navy at some point, stuck on some long band of blue, waiting for orders that took a few months to arrive. "Nothin' to do but play cards," he grumbled. "All the day and all the night. The best time of my life I had on that boat."

By the time I was seated, Joe had already drained a good deal of the money from the table. His stack was as wide and as tall as a bread box, and his face, which was normally sallow, was flushed. The other players at the table had not simply been unlucky; to a one they were terrible. In poker parlance, they would be deemed "calling stations," which means they were willing to play almost any hand, no matter how much of an underdog to win, and call it all the way to the end just to see how things turned out. They never raised, but they hardly ever folded, and this made it difficult to know what they were holding. My way of dealing with this problem was to sit on my hands until I held premium cards, cards that I felt would beat anything. A more experienced player like Mealy Joe, however, had another way of playing such a table. He would check-raise and bluster his way to big pots, playing hands that he knew were unbeatable weakly, and soaking up the action like a sponge. When he didn't have much, he would wait till the end, observing the other players' postures. If it looked as if they hadn't hit (something he could ascertain in an instant, he was that good), he'd raise—and they'd fold.

After watching Mealy Joe dominate the table in this way for some hours, and after playing just a couple of hands myself, I was dealt a king-queen of different suits in the sixth position, which means that I was right in the middle of the order of play. Everyone after the second seat had folded, and so, in large part to bully the remaining players out of the pot, I raised.

The player in the eight-seat called, but all the other players folded. I thought I was home free, but when it came to Mealy Joe, who was waiting rather slyly in the first seat for the action, he raised.

"You're not getting away with anything tonight, little miss," he said, crossing and uncrossing his slim sailor's legs. "I call your three dollars and I raise you three more."

I reraised.

The eight-seat folded.

"I'll call you," said Joe, his face cracking open in a rictus. "I guess it's you and me, young miss. Alone."

I remember my cheeks welling up with blood—and the tremor in my hands and wrists. Mealy Joe was smart enough to know that this could mean anything. Maybe I was sitting on a strong pair of cards. Or maybe I had nothing. Whatever I was holding, I was terrified—terrified of Mealy Joe. Terrified of losing.

But then the flop came: two queens and an ace, three different suits. I now had three queens and a king, a strong hand, a hand almost nothing could beat, but Joe bet into me. He didn't even hesitate. I raised. But then he raised me back. We capped it. (Did he have the other queen? I wasn't any good at reading Joe.)

The dealer dealt a jack of hearts, then neatened up the cards: queen of hearts, queen of spades, ace of diamonds, jack of hearts. The action was with Mealy Joe. He bet. "Sure are a lot of face cards on the table," he said.

"No shit," I said. "Raise."

He reraised. I called. The dealer called, "King." (Did Joe have a king? An ace-king? I was thinking too much, and my hands were still shaking.)

"What do you have?" I asked.

"That's for me to know and you to find out," he replied. There was no single trace of trepidation in his voice, but I had a full house, so I raised.

We capped the bets.

"Show your cards," said the dealer. I turned my hand over.

"I have queens full of kings," I said, choking back something. (Not tears, it was drier than that.)

"Well, what d'ya know?" said Mealy Joe. "I got myself a full house too. I got myself *trip-aces and two queens.*"

I played with Mealy Joe only one other time. My father was in town. He was staying with me, and I'd drive him around, showing him sights that neither of us cared for much but that both of us believed it was our duty to take in: the great, grinning sphinx crouched in front of the Luxor; the volcano that erupted on the hour at the Mirage; all the tourists who walked down the street, their feet shuffling exhaustedly along.

One night, after driving back and forth in this fashion, I'd insisted that my father watch me play a little poker, a demand to which he acquiesced, if not enthusiastically then at least cordially. Looking back now, I can see that I was jealous, jealous of my sister and my brother for their giant stakes, jealous of the fact that they'd redeemed the family's unremarkable impoverishment.

When we got to the poker room, I was dismayed to see that the only available seat was next to Mealy Joe. I sat down and put my chips on the table, the two of us warily eyeing each other.

Though I cannot remember the hands that were played, I can vividly remember stealing glances at my father, who was sitting right behind me. I explained every move I made to him with excessive pride. I played a lot of hands that night I had no business playing, just to keep him entertained. There is an old saying that watching a person play poker is just about as interesting as watching paint dry, and I was worried he was bored. He kept leaning over, putting his hands in the shape of a steeple, putting the point of the steeple to his chin, resting his face on the steeple.

"Are you bored?" I asked.

"No," he said. "I'm having . . . I'm having a *wonderful* time."

"Because if you're bored we can go. Or maybe Annie and Howard will get here and play. We can watch them play?"

"No, no."

But he was clearly bored.

And then Mealy Joe, who kept looking and looking. I managed to win a small pot from him then, but otherwise we didn't play (ever again, for that matter).

In my mind, I suppose, I will always associate my father with old Mealy Joe, their boredom, their amusement at watching me play.

No Game for a Woman

BY

Mignon McLaughlin

This poker piece, from a 1963 *Atlantic Monthly*, ends with a decidedly nonfeminist perspective (hence the title). It's too bad, for McLaughlin—an editor at *Glamour* at the time—obviously knew her way around a card table. What she couldn't possibly know back then was that one day, many women would actually make a living beating men at poker. But even if the cautionary side rings a bit retro, hers is still a well-crafted take on the familiar gut-wrenching self-analysis endemic to all levels of play.

Baltimore was made habitable for us by all those lovely racetracks. Friends of ours would come down from New York nearly every weekend, and we'd go out to Pimlico or Laurel on Saturday afternoons and then, after dinner, settle down to a nice long night of poker. The games started modestly—fifty-cent limit—but we soon switched to table stakes. It seemed sensible to play it that way, knowingly. In a limit game there was all that nonsense at the end of the evening, "roodles," where the stakes would be doubled for the final rounds, and the losers never wanted to quit. In table stakes, you knew right from the beginning that the going would be rough and serious—that is, delicious.

I had learned poker the hard way, from a lively, tough Manhattan game where I fast dropped two weeks' salary. More than by the money loss, I had been scorched by a remark of one of the men. We had been playing stud, and I had stayed for a raise and bought a card which did not help my hand but would have helped his. He spoke bitterly of people who didn't know when to drop out, adding automatically that poker was "no game for a woman."

I thought his attitude jerky and unjust. I had paid for the card, hadn't I? Didn't I have the right to throw away my own money? Even later, when I was good at the game, I disagreed with his premise. My own poker credo held that when you had a good hand you made the others pay and pay, and if suckers insisted on staying, so much the better. Of course, I did see what he meant: that you might wish to preserve a smaller but surer pot by driving out the inferior hands with raises, and if they were too dumb to leave, it increased the chances that someone might draw out on you. But I still thought it was a niggling, play-safe way of gambling.

We had rented the Baltimore house furnished, for we expected to be there only a year or two. Outside, it was like any other shingled, two-story house; inside, like no other. One's first impression of the living room was of a jungle, with antimacassars. There were tropical fish and sinister plants everywhere, and cozies on anything that would take a cozy, including the keyboard of the piano. The dining room was dominated by the devil and his wife, a pair of seven-foot statues carved in wood by demented Italians and garishly painted. The statues inspired a lot of bad jokes, for it was at the circular dining-room table, in the cross fire of their malevolent gaze, that we gathered for our Saturday night poker games.

We never had trouble finding a quorum. Sometimes ten players would show up, requiring us to stick to stud, which I preferred to draw, anyway. Among the regulars were two men whose wives always came but did not play. It took me a long time to realize that the homelier wife, the one who wore glasses, was having a blazing love affair with the pretty wife's husband. There was a third couple, both of whom played, and both abominably. They had three children and could not afford their repeated losses but could not be kept away from the game. They loved each other dearly in those days (later, he fell or jumped, and she did not even go to the funeral). The only times I ever saw them harsh with each other was at the poker table, where each saw, and loudly criticized, the suicidal gambling habits of the other.

Hal was also a regular: he was flashy and erratic, and it was impossible to know when he really had the cards and when he didn't. He seldom folded before the third or fourth card and always bet heavily if he stayed. As a result, he was usually the evening's biggest winner or loser. George and Perry were basically more conservative, but nevertheless capable of reckless changes of pace, so you could never rule out the possibility of a bluff or a strong hand. If you saw one of them with a four, six, seven, and eight showing, it could be a straight—he just might have stayed at the beginning with a five and an eight. There was my husband, of course, but I would no more comment publicly on his poker playing than on his lovemaking.

And there was Fritz: steady, successful, the most conservative, and to me the most readable of all the regulars. The reason I understood his game so well was because I followed much the same psychology, the same percentages, that he did. But I felt I did it with some style, a certain amount of dash. I would even let myself be caught bluffing on a hand or two early in the evening, just so that no one could ever be sure of me.

I was, in fact, very proud of my conduct, skill, and acceptance at the poker table. In New York, I had been the only woman allowed in a first-rate weekly game that was something of an institution. Fritz never drank while playing. I despised such ungentlemanly prudence and always had at least four highballs during the game. I was a careful dealer, calling the cards clearly and accurately, never prematurely exposing one. I did not bet or fold out of turn. I never yielded to the temptation to "cry a hand in" or to hold endless postmortems when the hand was over. I was reasonably cheerful and gay but didn't overdo the conversation either. In short, Fritz was a pretty good poker player, but in my opinion, I was even better.

*   *   *

Then one night Fritz and I had our big showdown hand. I had a pair of tens back to back; it was pretty clear from the betting that Fritz had wired sixes. My husband and George folded early. Hal and Perry, each with jacks showing, stayed. On the next two cards, no hand openly paired, but Fritz drew a king and I an ace.

I bet heavily, and he called. Hal and Perry dropped out. The final card was dealt: to me another ace, to Fritz another six. With a pair of aces showing, I bet fifty dollars, hoping he would think I had three aces. With a pair of sixes showing, he hesitated, looked again at his hole card. Then he called my bet and raised me a hundred dollars.

I was a long time deciding. A lot of things flashed through my mind, not all of them relevant. I remembered having told a friend who could not understand the gambling fever, "There's no more exciting way in the world to spend a hundred dollars. You're not betting it on a horse, or a card—you're betting it on yourself. What really baffles me is the kind of person who'd spend it on a useless piece of china like a Chelsea lettuce leaf." I also remembered some outstanding household bills and the run of bad luck we had been having at the track. I thought of a red tweed dress I had liked but had not bought because it cost ninety dollars.

But mostly I thought about Fritz, and the absolute certainty that he had three sixes and the winning hand. Why not just fold, then? I simply couldn't. For the first time (and this hadn't happened even during my disastrous beginner's game) I felt fear that was close to panic. Whatever I did would be irrecoverably wrong. If I called, I'd be throwing away a hundred dollars. But I pictured myself refusing his raise and his smug expression as he neatly folded his cards into the rest of the pack and raked in the pot. He would succeed in convincing me, convincing everybody, that safe, careful Fritz had bluffed me out of the pot. If only it had been Hal or Perry or George—they would possibly have kings up, or even just a pair of sixes. To win from them was a pleasure, to lose to them no disgrace, for no one could ever be sure what cards they held. With Fritz though—The worst of it was to know so positively and to be the only one to know, to know from the inside. The others were too easygoing. They underestimated his caution. Not I. So what was I to do?

Well, what exactly was at stake? Money, of course. But more than that. Pride. Judgment. The public and private image of myself as a poker player.

I looked across at Fritz, and there was something in his eye, in his typically stodgy expression, in the faint tremble of his fingers on the table that convinced me that, this once, Fritz was trying to bluff his way to a pot.

"I call," I said, and pushed in the hundred dollars—not so certain of my intuition that I would raise him with the fifty dollars I had left.

He showed me his hole card—the third six. We both smiled as he leaned forward to gather in the chips. His smile was relieved, prissy, triumphant. Mine, I hoped, was gallant.

I finished out the session, and even played several more times in Baltimore and back in New York. But it was really all over for me. I was the pilot who is not cured by walking away from a crash and taking up another plane. With that night, that hand, I lost my poker nerve totally and forever and with it all joy in the game, or in any form of gambling.

But I never quite understood it till the other day, when I ran into Fritz on Fifth Avenue. We had a drink at the Louis XIV bar and caught up on what had become of everyone. The man with the pretty wife was now remarried, and so was she. The homely wife was still with her husband but, I gathered from Fritz's giggle, still playing around. We lamented the death of the bad poker player and clucked at his wife's lack of grief. George and Perry were partners in a firm making some tiny electrical gadget. We agreed that they might be overextending themselves. Hal had gone into politics and was now involved in an investigation of alleged election fraud.

Fritz offered these tidbits with undiscriminating enthusiasm. They interested me, but it made me uneasy to hear a man gossip so. We assured each other that we were looking marvelous. For my part, I lied. Fritz looked like an old woman.

That was it, of course! He was a womanish sort of man, and a womanish sort of poker player too. And so, for all my pride, had I been myself. Secretly thrifty, jealously conservative, avoiding risks, willing to bet heavily only on a sure thing—all that is a woman's way, not a man's. (I exclude professional gamblers, who seem nearer to machines than to men or women.) The honest-to-God good poker player is a man, with a man's reckless temperament, his sense of humor on the edge of a precipice, his unguessable courage, his mystical personal feelings about the wooing of luck. Those are the ingredients, and Fritz didn't have them, and neither did I.

We are what we are: it's the only way to be happy. Oh, once in a while I miss the chills and theater of those evenings with the devil and his wife standing guard above the poker table. But, being a woman, I'm pretty realistic about things. And there is something I keep on the mantel as a sort of reminder. It's a little Chelsea lettuce leaf.

LET'S GET RID
OF THE RIBBON CLERKS

BY

ROBERT MCLAUGHLIN

Robert McLaughlin—husband of Mignon McLaughlin, author of the article on the preceding pages—worked during the 1950s and '60s as an editor for *Time* magazine. He wrote this gritty short story of barracks poker while serving as a lieutenant in World War II (it appeared in *The New Yorker* in 1945). Wilson, McLaughlin's Dostoevskian antagonist, is a poor soul burdened with a hubris common to all desperado losers—the inability to know when to quit.

On Saturday the company went out to Alligator Point to make spacing tests with the new smoke generators. Now they were coming back into camp, a long column of jeeps and trailers, the men tired and dirty and looking forward to Saturday night in Tallahassee, to getting away from the post for a few hours.

But Lieutenant Fred Wilson's problem was to figure out a way of staying on the post tonight. He and his wife, Dottie, were supposed to go swimming at Wakulla Springs with the Robinsons. Dottie would blow her top if he told her he wanted to drop out of the party. He could almost hear the piercing accents of her complaining voice.

He wanted to stay because there was going to be a big game at the

Officers' Club tonight. Not the usual ten-and-twenty poker, where you nickel and dime yourself to death, but table stakes with a couple of brass hats from Washington sitting in. There would be pots of fifty, a hundred, maybe a couple of hundred dollars, even. A guy could really clean up in a game like that.

"I've got to make it," Wilson told himself, feeling the anticipatory thrill of gambling, the elation that accompanies the snap around of carefully dealt cards, the gathering up of the hand, close-held against the face, the looking at each card separately and with mounting excitement.

Wilson's was the leading jeep of the motor convoy, and the driver halted at the fire station, as usual, to let the rest of the column close up before resuming the motor march at the slower speed required in the camp area. Overhead, P-40s from Dale Mabry Field were circling, preparatory to making their practice bombing and strafing runs out at the tip of the Point. Tremendous clouds were piled along the limitless horizon, but the sky above was clear and the late-afternoon sun held a midday heat. As always there along the Gulf, the sky was vast and the land flat and meagre, the sea flat and unruffled.

What the hell could he tell Dottie, Wilson wondered. He could say he was O.D. tonight, but she could check up on that. Or that there was a night problem. Or an officers' call. The trouble was she could check up on any alibi he gave. It would be better not to go home at all. He could borrow a change of clothes from someone and send Dottie a message. Robinson would do it. He'd tell Robinson to take Dottie out to the Springs, that he'd be along later. O.K. Now, about money. He had ten dollars and could cash a check for another ten bucks at the Club, but of course he'd need much more than that. He thought, I don't want to get caught with a big hand and not have any dough in front of me. And it was bad psychology to write a check at the very beginning of a game. Especially since one of his had bounced recently.

His jeep driver said, "O.K., sir?"

"What?" Wilson demanded. Then he realized that they were still halted. He glanced back down the line, said "O.K.," and the driver gave the arm-and-hand signal for go ahead and edged the jeep forward.

*   *   *

Wilson stopped at battalion headquarters to see if there was any mail. There wasn't, but he found Lieutenant Robinson and gave him the message for Dottie.

Robinson was a little uneasy. "You'd better tell her yourself," he said. "She'll want to know why—"

"Just say I'm held up. I'll come out later with Myer."

"Is he going to Wakulla? I thought—"

"If he isn't, I'll get a ride with someone else. I'll see you out there," said Wilson with finality. He left Robinson and took Lieutenant Jones by the arm.

Jones was a new lieutenant recently assigned to the battalion, about Wilson's size but four or five years younger. He was only a kid and not too bright a one at that.

Wilson said, "Say, Jonesy, lend me a shirt and trousers for tonight, will you, chum?"

"Well, gee . . . " Jones said.

Wilson glanced at his watch. "I've got to get out of these fatigues and haven't time to go home. Hell, I'll send it to the laundry for you, if that's what's the matter."

"No, that's all right."

"Let's go, then," said Wilson.

Half an hour later, showered and wearing a chino shirt and trousers of Jones's, with fifteen additional dollars in his pocket that Jones had reluctantly given him in exchange for a check, Wilson walked along the broken duckboard walk to the Officers' Club. It was a tar-paper shack illuminated by blue fluorescent lights and containing a pool table, a short-order kitchen, a bar that dispensed bottled beer, and a number of chairs and tables. A large fan, whirring in a corner, stirred the humid air.

Wilson saw Captain Myer standing at the ice-water barrel with Major Kelly. They were two of the poker players, but Wilson didn't join them. He got a beer, cashed a check for ten dollars—the limit at the Officers' Club—and went over to a chair by the pool table, so that he could keep an eye on Kelly and Myer. His strategy was to pretend an elaborate disinterest in poker until the players sat down and then join them, ostensibly for a few hands. This deviousness was inspired by the fact that he owed Captain Myer twenty-five dollars. The chances were that Myer wouldn't say anything about it if Wilson just popped into the game that way. He decided to pay Myer out of his first good pot. He liked to pay his debts that way, largely because money at a poker table didn't seem like money to him.

The two officers from Washington came in shortly. They were Major Brinton and Lieutenant Colonel Le Clerc. Brinton was short and bland-faced and had the special rotundity of majors; Le Clerc was an elderly man with a sharp eye and frequently pursed lips.

Wilson watched them while they talked to Kelly and Myer. Presently Kelly called over to Lieutenant Lopez, another poker regular. They all moved to the poker table and sat down. Major Kelly opened a new pack of cards while the others laid money before them and ordered beer and hamburgers from the bar.

Wilson got up and walked over to the table. He slipped into a chair between Lopez and Myer and said, "Deal me in," to Major Kelly. Then, looking at his watch, he added quickly, "I can only sit in for a few rounds. Dottie wants me home early. God knows why—so we can stare at each other, I guess."

Myer said, "I thought you were going out to Wakulla Springs with Robby."

"Couldn't make it," said Wilson, smoothing out his little pile of bills and arranging his change in neat stacks.

Kelly gave Wilson a long stare and asked, "What have you been telling your little woman about me? She's been bending my frau's ear about how I lead you astray."

"She must have been kidding."

"From the reports I got, she wasn't kidding. Keep me out of your troubles, man."

"What's the game?" asked Wilson, his face petulant.

"Dealer's choice," said Kelly. "Draw or stud. Fifty-cent ante on draw."

Brinton said, "Aren't we going to use chips?"

"There's a war on, Major," said Captain Myer. "We have none of the amenities of civilization here."

"There's no limit to the buy-in, either?" asked Brinton.

Kelly said, "You bet with what you've got in front of you. After a hand you can put up more money if you want to. That O.K.?"

Brinton nodded. "If that's the way you want to play, it's all right by me." His eyes had the intentness of a cat that has just sighted some pigeons.

"This is draw," said Kelly. "Jacks or better to open."

Wilson got four spades and a diamond. He drew to the flush but didn't make it.

He took two pots in the next hour and that enabled him to stay even. He was playing very carefully, staying out of most pots, watching the others play, listening to the clichés of poker, weighing the ability of the officers from Washington. Brinton was pretty fair, but Wilson didn't think he pushed a strong hand the way he should have. Le Clerc was terrible but shot with luck. He knew about Myer, who was a steady player, and Kelly, who was erratic, and Lopez, who stayed in too many pots. "I should clean this gang," he said to himself.

The big fan throbbed at Wilson's elbow and the Florida night came swiftly outside the screened windows, with practically no twilight. At nine o'clock the players heard the metallic squawking of the open-air movie down the street, and then the bigger-than-life harmony of an orchestra's strings. It was a Deanna Durbin picture.

They played on steadily and the only conversation was the odds and ends of poker phrases—Kelly saying, "You can never go broke taking a profit," as he pulled in a small pot, or Myer, when asked if he had a pair showing, replying, "Yeah. Paregoric," or Lopez muttering, "What do you have to do to get a hand?"

Around eleven, Wilson's cards improved. He won four pots in a row and the mound of bills and change in front of him was so impressive that he amiably pushed over twenty-five dollars to Myer. "Thanks, pal," he said. But then his cards began to run second high, and at one o'clock, when the Club closed and they moved the game down to Captain Myer's hutment, Wilson was down about fifty dollars and had already written two checks. Lopez and Kelly were losing, too.

They carried a case of beer to the hutment with them. It was very dark and they moved carefully over the duckboards. The pine trees that grew in the sandy earth rose motionless against the distant, star-pierced sky. Frogs and cicadas were chorusing out in the swamps and there was a sense of timelessness to the hot, insect-ridden night.

Wilson's luck stayed bad and he looked resentfully at the money in front of Captain Myer, convinced that paying his twenty-five-dollar debt was what had started it all. He waited impatiently for his run of cards to change, still confident that with any break at all he was bound to win. He smoked and drank beer and wrote checks when necessity required. His thin face sharpened as he watched the fall of the cards.

Then he won a pot, and another, stayed out of the next few, and had a couple of more wins. He had sixty or seventy dollars in front of him when the big one came up. And he dealt it himself.

He dealt around two down cards and then turned the next card up.

"Hey, what *is* this?" demanded Major Brinton. "What's the game?"

"Seven-card stud," said Wilson.

Brinton said, "I thought we agreed to play only draw and stud, and no wild games."

"Nothing's wild," said Wilson.

"But this isn't poker," said Brinton irritably. "You might as well be playing all spades wild—"

"It's dealer's choice," replied Wilson. "You can fold your hand if you don't like the game." To Myer, he said, "Your ace is high."

Myer opened for a half-dollar. Wilson had a six of hearts up. He looked at his hole cards. A pair of tens. A tremor of excitement went through him. When the bet came to him, he raised Myer a dollar, saying, "You can't insult my deal." Lopez dropped.

Wilson's next card was the queen of hearts. Myer got a king to his ace but no one else seemed to have improved. Myer bet a dollar and Wilson said, "I'll just raise that five. Let's get rid of the ribbon clerks."

"What the hell are you so proud of?" demanded Kelly, studying

Wilson's hand. Then he folded. Myer, Le Clerc, and Brinton stayed.

Wilson dealt himself another six. He had two pair now, and he bet ten dollars. Brinton hesitated briefly, then called, and Wilson, whistling tunelessly, felt happy. He knew Brinton was annoyed with him and hoped his annoyance would keep him in the game. Le Clerc pursed his lips a long time and kept re-examining his hole cards. Then he said, "I'm through." Myer said, "Against my better judgment," and pushed out one of Wilson's checks for fifteen dollars and took five dollars change.

Wilson dealt around. He gave himself the seven of hearts. He still had his two pair, and now he had four hearts. He had a possible full house, a possible flush. He was sure that his luck was in.

"Pair of sixes are high," said Brinton.

Wilson counted his money very deliberately. "Twenty-five dollars," he said.

Brinton and Myer stayed, Myer saying, "I ought to have my head examined." He was shooting for a flush. It was hard to read Brinton's hand—he had a jack, ace, nine, and four showing. He might have two pair.

As Wilson started to deal the last card, Myer said, "This one is down!"

"I know it's down," Wilson answered. He dealt, laid down the pack, and put his card with his two other hole cards. Then he brought the three cards up to his face, separated them. He'd got the deuce of clubs. He hadn't improved. He put the cards back on the table. Brinton and Myer were looking at him.

"Your bet," said Brinton.

Wilson knew he should bet, that this was the time to bluff, but his nerve failed. He tapped his cards. "Check," he said.

Brinton leaned forward. "How much money have you got there, Lieutenant?"

Oh, God, he's got me, thought Wilson. He said, "Bet your hand, Major."

"I'm going to bet, all right," said Brinton. "I just wanted to save bookkeeping." He counted out money. "Thirty bucks," he said.

Myer turned down his up cards. "I didn't fill," he said sadly.

Wilson felt trapped. Brinton's bluffing, he thought. I've got to call him. But he didn't make a move. He looked at Brinton's hand and at his own.

"Anybody calling?" asked Brinton.

"Wait a minute, can't you?" demanded Wilson. Suddenly, he pushed out the thirty dollars. That left him with seventy-five cents.

"Jack-high straight," said Brinton, showing his hand. Wilson reached, unbelieving, for Brinton's cards, his lips moving as he counted the straight. Then he snapped over his own cards. "God damn, look at that!" he said.

"Consolation prize," said Lopez, putting a bottle of beer beside him.

Wilson complained in a strained voice, "I had two pair from the first four cards. I had four hearts to a queen-high flush, and then he makes a lucky last-card draw on me."

Brinton was pulling in the pot—nearly two hundred dollars.

"I had to see him," Wilson declared to uninterested listeners. "Somebody had to keep him honest. I couldn't let him steal the pot."

"You should know by this time that I never bluff," said Brinton.

"Whose deal is it?" asked Myer, and then he said to Wilson, "The crying room is the third door to the left."

"Give me your pen," said Wilson to Lopez.

Le Clerc began to shuffle with the maddening deliberation of a winner. Wilson wrote a check for twenty-five dollars and said defiantly, "This is my last check, damn it."

"You said that before," said Lopez.

"I mean it this time."

"I'll bet you do."

Wilson couldn't keep silent. He said, "I've always heard there wasn't any rank at the poker table, but the lieutenants are getting it in the neck, as usual."

"My heart bleeds," Major Kelly told him.

Colonel Le Clerc finally finished shuffling. Wilson cut and then Le Clerc felt in his pocket for cigarettes.

"Let's go, let's go," said Wilson.

It was draw poker this time and Wilson got a bust hand.

Brinton said, "It's nearly three. What time shall we quit?"

No one answered, but Le Clerc gave him an encouraging look.

Wilson said, "Hell, we can quit right now, if you want to. I know how sleepy winning a big pot makes a man."

"You're the loser," said Brinton. "When do you want to quit?"

"If it's up to me, I'm good for twenty-four hours."

Brinton laughed. "Well, I'm not."

Wilson said, "Any time you're tired, Major, just pull out."

Brinton looked at his watch and addressed the Colonel. "What do you say to four o'clock?"

"That's good by me," answered the Colonel.

Now that a time had been set for quitting, the minutes raced by. Wilson's face had a bruised look. He tried to bluff his way through a hand, but Kelly called him and won with a pair of treys. Wilson wrote another check.

When they stopped, he was down a hundred and sixty dollars.

"How about one more round?" he asked, wetting his lips.

Brinton gave him a brief glance. Le Clerc rubbed his eyes tiredly.

"We agreed to quit at four," said Myer.

"*They* said that," Wilson answered, indicating the Washington officers. "We don't have to quit because they're quitting." He turned to Lopez, desperate for allies. "How about you, Joe?"

"I've had enough," said Lopez. Kelly pocketed his money and pushed back from the table. Myer stretched prodigiously.

Wilson looked around at them, searching each face with a kind of desperation. Without another word he got up and left.

Outside, Wilson walked blindly along the duckboards, then stepped off them to the yielding sand and stood for a moment just beyond the screened window of the hutment.

He heard Lopez say, "How much did he drop? It must have been a couple of hundred, at least."

Kelly said sententiously, "Men who can't afford it shouldn't play poker."

Brinton, who had most of Wilson's checks, asked anxiously, "Are these going to bounce?"

Kelly laughed. "That's a good question."

They started toward the door and Wilson moved quickly around the corner of the hutment and stood there while they went up the walk toward the latrine. He felt alone in the sleeping camp. A dog was barking far off and the stars trembled above him. He heard the dull clamor of the frogs and the beer he had drunk was heavy in his stomach.

Dottie was back from Wakulla Springs, he knew. She'd be sleeping lightly against his coming, ready to make the night hideous with complaints. And Brinton would be sure to put the checks through on Monday. "I've got to get some money," thought Wilson. He could get fifty from his mother, maybe more. And Dottie'd have to touch her old man.

"I'm in a jam," he told himself, "a real jam this time."

Strangely, that made him feel a little better. It would shut Dottie up, anyway. When he got home she'd raise a stink and he wouldn't say anything. He wouldn't answer her at all. Then, sensing that something was really wrong, she'd say more quietly, "What's the matter?" and he'd tell her. Even Dottie would recognize that it was serious.

Maybe she can get her father to wire the money, he thought. They'd call him long distance tomorrow.

He shivered a little and set off for home.

FROM

BLACK MAGIC

BY

JAMES McMANUS

How good does it get in the insular world of poker writing? Consider James McManus, a poet-novelist (and the author of this book's introduction) who teaches a course in poker literature at the School of the Art Institute of Chicago. Assigned to cover the 2000 World Series of Poker for *Harper's*, he risked advance monies by entering a satellite tournament, which he won for a $10,000 seat at the main event. From there he played his way to a remarkable fifth-place finish worth $250,000. He would later parlay an excellent article about the experience into a critically acclaimed best-seller, *Positively Fifth Street*. An old poker saying suggests it's better to be "lucky than good." McManus is both.

The following is from an essay in a 2002 issue of *American Poetry Review*, parts of which also appear in *Fifth Street*.

God may play dice with the universe, despite Einstein's last hope, but serious gamblers, scorning metaphysical crapshoots and the casino's house edge, prefer no-limit Texas hold 'em. Each hold 'em session comprises a miniature global economy laid out on a baize oval table. Taking part satisfies not only our atavistic desire to play but our more modern urge to keep score. As Jack Binion, the Texas-born host of the

World Series of Poker, told the English poet A. Alvarez back in the hey-day of the Cold War: "In the free enterprise system, you have to assume that each guy is the best judge of what he does with his own money . . . So if a guy wants to bet twenty or thirty thousand dollars in a poker game, that is his privilege. Society might consider it bad judgment, but if that is what he wants to do, you can't fault him for it. That's America." A skeptical Alvarez commented: "That, too, is Las Vegas—the only place on earth where they justify gambling as a form of patriotism."

The fact, however, is that financial markets around the planet continue to authorize gambling for vastly higher stakes, and national economies flounder or flourish with the net results. And what better metaphor for democratic free-market risk-taking than poker? Like national security advisors or stem-cell research teams, poker players make educated guesses under radically uncertain conditions. That a few of them wind up with most of the chips is what makes the game terrifying, ugly and beautiful. It's what makes it *work*. As Walter Matthau dryly observed, "The game exemplifies the worst aspects of capitalism that have made our country so great." Because in no sense is poker a socialist or totalitarian enterprise. Instead, the game is a stimulating arena in which money-management, pluck and intelligence combine to determine who will get hacked limb from limb. Wealth gets created, egos deflated, blood spilled. Not for nothing are poker tables shaped like the floor of the Colosseum—the better to concentrate the butchery, the better to observe it up close. Lions and tigers and bears, oh my! Thumbs up or thumbs down on the river.

No limit hold 'em has also been called black art, requiring players to broadcast and decipher fake tells, master complex (mis)information and amoral psychology, all of it illuminated by bolts of hideous and beneficent fortune. Folding, the thoroughly passive gesture at the heart of strong play, can be understood in religious or spiritual terms—as humble acceptance, for example, of a metaphysical order beyond our comprehension, sometimes known as the shuffle. While to *not* fold then backdoor a flush on the final card after your all-in-opponent fills a bellybuster straight requires voodoo theology and titanium nerves to get your mind around, not logic or math prowess.

Thank Shango or Oloddumare as you rake in the pot, or perhaps your lucky stars. As my daughter Bridget has been known to explain rare phenomena: "Whatever what*ev*er, okay?"

Despite poker's nonrational dimension, philosopher John Lukacs was moved to call it "the game closest to the Western conception of life, where life and thought are recognized as infinitely combined, where free will prevails over philosophies of fate or of chance, where men are considered moral agents, and where—at least in the short run—the important thing is not what happens but what people think happens." With everyone's hole cards lying facedown on the table, the hand perceived to be the strongest in effect *is*.

Poker is also a game in which freely willed decisions prevail over class, race or fate, since the cards your opponents believe you are hold-ing makes everything else quite irrelevant. Above all, the game requires each player to account for deceit by the others. "Owing largely to the bluff," writes A. D. Livingston, "poker has influenced our thinking on life, love, business, and even war." Bullfighting, by con-trast, better expresses Spain's traditional gaming spirit, as *futbol* does for Brazil and Go for Japan, just as Dostoyevsky argued in *The Gambler* and elsewhere that "Roulette is a preeminently Russian game." Dos-toyevsky believed that go-for-broke betting, whatever the game, was more "poetic" than frostily measuring the odds "like a German."

More recently, the American poet Stephen Dunn observed: "Good high-stakes poker players are neither noble nor greedy. They've sized up their fellow players, know a good deal about probabilities and ten-dencies, and wish like poets that their most audacious moves be per-ceived as part of a series of credible gestures." Dunn also points out that, "The great gamblers, and there are not many, don't need any-thing. They simply wish to prevail. And we all know how dangerous people are who don't need anything." As Cool Hand Luke hand-somely drawled, "Sometimes nothin's a pretty cool hand."

To feel this dangerous ourselves, even for only a couple of minutes, can be severely intoxicating. It makes both erotic and emotional sense to say that we *love* it, and sometimes we love it too much. "When I'm rushing on my run / and I feel just like Jesus' son" is Lou Reed's (and later, Denis Johnson's) blasphemous apotheosis of going too far. Another menacing quality of the rush is to make us want more of it, and getting more makes us want *more*. At the poker table, this can be good. Feeling both endangered and dangerous, we tiptoe barefoot along the business end of a scalpel and never get sliced, and it quickly becomes possible to imagine that our state of grace *never* will pass. Players use expressions like "playing my rush" or "having a horseshoe up my ass" to describe surfing a wave of big hands and successful bluffs, and they often report the experience to be more stimulating than amphetamines, barbiturates, alcohol, music or sexual intercourse. Certainly synapses fire at the poker table, and serotonin drips faster—or slower. Electrons and corpuscles rush to the pleasure centers of the cerebral cortex, and others rush lower. We blush. Pink and orange chips and green money, foot-thick wads of it sometimes, flood our burgeoning coffers. To moderate our breathing becomes a pivotal challenge, but surely we're up to it. Right? We haven't renounced *all* control of ourselves. Far from it, in fact. Dunn defines intoxication as: "That sensation of 'fine excess' Keats wanted from poetry, the adjective gracing the noun, keeping it alert." Focus, grace, poetry, black magic, fucking, too-muchness—the feeling that *I am invincible*. Even if you kill me I'll come back from the dead, just like Jesus. And if Jesus made love, I'm His son.

There's downside to excess, of course. Antisocial urges like hitting and lying and thievery need outlets in games, but even in games we need limits. Or do we? No-limit hold 'em rarely is favored in home poker games, since it tends to make for less than convivial evenings. For one thing, it routinely forces your house guests to risk all their chips; when they lose them, buy more, then go broke, their feelings get hurt. They tend to prefer more approachable varietals, with wild cards, split pots, limited bet sizes and bans against check-raising, all of which tend to make luck the most dominant flavor. Anyone can win at these games, since whoever is dealt the best hand takes the pot. It's the shuffler who has all the power, in fact, though he doesn't have any control . . .

Serious players are at war with the shuffle. They tend to prefer no-limit or pot-limit hold'em because big-bet poker gives them the leverage to win pots *without* the best hand. The most talented among them don't even need a small pair to take down a pot; one large, well-timed raise, in response to some flicker of doubt in the bettor's retina or a twinge along the side of his neck, does the trick. Latter-day maestros like Jennifer Harman, Erik Seidel, Men "The Master" Nguyen, Kathy Liebert, and Chris "Jesus" Ferguson can deduce with mind-bending precision from your facial tics and body language, and from how you played earlier hands, what cards you hold now; they play *you* and the size of your stack as much as they play their own cards, ruthlessly taking advantage of whatever anxiety you betray about your hand. If you've raised them with anything short of the mortal nuts—those rare pocket cards that combine with the board to make an unbeatable hand—they can feel your level of confidence *drip . . . drip . . . drip* a quarter-notch below one hundred percent; and the meek won't inherit this pot. Extortionate reraises are called "coming over the top" of the initial raiser, often abbreviated to, simply, "coming." To come at most stages of a no-limit tournament requires shoving in all of your chips. For one of you, then, should your opponent have the nerve to call your huge bet, it's all over. Since the raiser has already expressed the strength of her hand with some confidence, to insist that your own hand is "nuttier" takes major-league chutzpah. By this hairy process as many as eight hundred players compete until one of them has all the chips.

Here's another way to think about it. After Michael Corleone gets back to Nevada from Washington, D.C., where he fraternally intimidated Frankie Five Angels into recanting his testimony before the Senate, he immediately begins plotting to kill both his big brother Fredo and their father's old friend Hyman Roth. Even the news of his wife's miscarriage (actually an abortion, of course, because Kay literally can't bear another male Corleone) fails to daunt Michael's single-minded bloodlust. Exasperated, Tom Hagen pleads, "C'mon, Michael. You won. Do you feel you have to wipe out everyone?" In what is regarded as the clinching evidence of Michael's absolute ruthlessness, he tells his adoptive brother, "No, Tom. Only my enemies."

A no-limit tournament player's answer to Tom would be, "Yes."

THE THINGS POKER TEACHES

BY

DAVID MAMET

**Pulitzer Prize–winning dramatist (*Glengarry Glen Ross*)
David Mamet is a long-time connoisseur of the art of
poker. He's also one very tough player (see Amis). The
beauty of this insightful essay (from a 1986 *New York Times
Magazine* column) lies in its contemplation of the ritual
behavioral modes that are routinely found among winners
and losers. Mamet's final dictum (that poker is about
character) might even be taken one step further: character
leads not only to improvement at the game, but to
acceptance of luck, good or bad. And that's a major key to
the *enjoyment* of poker.**

In twenty years of playing poker, I have seen very few poor losers.
Poker is a game of skill and chance. Playing poker is also a masculine ritual, and, most times, losers feel either sufficiently chagrined or
sufficiently reflective to retire, if not with grace, at least with alacrity.

I have seen many poor winners. They attribute their success to
divine intervention and celebrate either God's good sense in sending
them lucky cards or God's wisdom in making them technically superior to the others at the table. Most are eventually brought back to
reality when the cards begin to even out.

Any poker player knows that, despite what mathematicians say, there are phenomenal runs of luck that defy explanation. The poker player learns that sometimes both science and common sense are wrong. There is such a thing as absolute premonition of cards, a rock bottom *surety* of what will happen next. A good poker player knows that there is a time to push your luck and a time to retire gracefully, that all roads have a turning.

What do you do when you are pushing your luck beyond its limits? You must behave like a good philosopher and ask what axiom you must infer that you are acting under. Having determined that, you ask if this axiom, in the long run, will leave you a winner. For instance, you are drawing to a flush. You have a 1-in-4½ chance. The pot is offering you money odds of 5 to 1. It seems a close thing, but if you did it all day, you must receive a 10 percent return.

If the axiom you are acting under is not designed to make you money, you may discover that your real objective at the game is something else: you may be trying to prove yourself beloved of God. You *then* must ask yourself if—financially and emotionally—you can afford the potential rejection. For the first will certainly, and the second will most probably, ensue.

Poker is boring. If you sit down at the table to experience excitement, you will, consciously and subconsciously, do things to make the game exciting. You will take long-odds chances, you will create emergencies, and they will lose you money. The poker players I admire most are like that wise old owl who sat on the oak and kept his mouth shut and his eye on the action.

When you are proud of having made the correct decision (that is, the decision which, in the long run, *must* eventually make you a winner), you are inclined to look forward to the results of that decision with some degree of impassivity. When you are so resolved, you become less fearful and more calm. You are less interested in yourself and more naturally interested in the other players: now *they* begin to reveal themselves. Is their nervousness feigned? Is their hand made already? Are they bluffing? These elections are impossible to make when you are afraid, but they become easier the more content you are with your own actions.

Poker reveals to the frank observer something else of import—it will teach him about his own nature. Many bad players do not improve because they cannot bear self-knowledge. The bad player will not deign to determine what he thinks by watching what he does. To do so might, and frequently would, reveal a need to be abused (in calling what must be a superior hand); a need to be loved (in staying for "that one magic card"); a need to have Daddy relent (in trying to bluff out the obvious best hand), etc. It is painful to observe this sort of thing about oneself. Many times we'd rather suffer on than fix it.

The pain of losing is diverting. So is the thrill of winning. Winning, however, is lonelier, because those you've taken money from are not apt to commiserate with you. Winning takes some getting used to.

Many of us, and most of us from time to time, try to escape a blunt fact that may not tally with our self-image. When we are depressed, we re-create the world around us to rationalize our mood. We are then apt to overlook or misinterpret happy circumstances. At the poker table, this can be expensive, for opportunity may knock, but it seldom nags. Which brings us to a crass thought many genteel players cannot grasp: poker is about money.

The ability of a poker player is judged solely by the difference between his stack when he sits down and his stack when he gets up. The point is not to win the most hands, the point is not even to win the most games. The point is to win the most money. This probably means playing fewer hands than the guy who has just come for the action; it means not giving your fellow players a break because you value their feelings; it means not giving some back at the end of the night because you feel embarrassed by winning; it means taking those steps and creating those habits of thought and action that, in the long run, must prevail.

The long run for me—to date—has been those twenty years. One day in college I promoted myself from the dormitory game to the *big* poker game in town, up on the Hill. After graduation, I would occasionally come back for visits. I told myself my visits were to renew friendships, to use the library, to see the leaves. But I was really coming back to play in the Hill game.

Last September, one of the players pointed out that five of us at the table that night had been doing this for two decades. As a group, we have all improved. Some of us have improved drastically. Because the facts, the statistics, the tactics are known to us all, and because we are men of equal intelligence, that improvement can be due to only one thing: to character, which, as I finally begin to improve a bit myself, I see that the game of poker is all about.

FROM

DEALER'S CHOICE

BY

PATRICK MARBER

The characters in Patrick Marber's 1995 award-winning drama are an engagingly miserable lot—as dishonest with each other as they are with themselves. Against a poker backdrop of ever-shifting alliances, their sharp-edged interaction never quite eases up. Accordingly, the following scene builds to a bitter confrontation between Stephen, the restaurant owner, and Sweeney, the waiter/loser, a reluctant player to begin with. Nothing resolved, the game plays on.

ACT THREE, SCENE TWO

SWEENEY   *(singing to the tune of "I Could've Danced All Night")* I haven't seen a card all night, I haven't seen a card all night. I haven't seen a card all night. Right, everyone, if I lose this lot I'm going.

MUGSY   Bye, mate. The hospital for poker casualties is just along the road.

STEPHEN   Mugsy will show you the way.

SWEENEY   One last shot.

MUGSY   And the game is Mugsy's Nightmare.

STEPHEN   Deal me out.

MUGSY *(to* Ash)   Stephen doesn't like Mugsy's Nightmare.

STEPHEN   I like playing poker not bloody roulette.

FRANKIE   You don't like playing poker, Stephen. You like winning.

STEPHEN   Thank you, Sigmund. Come on, Mugsy, choose a grown-up game.

MUGSY   It's Dealer's Choice. I'm the dealer I'll play what I want.

SWEENEY   Just deal.

MUGSY *begins to deal two cards to each player.*

MUGSY   Out?

STEPHEN   Yes, OUT.

MUGSY   Ooo.

SWEENEY   Will someone remind me of the rules of this ridiculous fucking game . . .

MUGSY   Five-card stud, hi-lo, two down, three up, whores, fours and one-eyed jacks wild, cards speak, eight or better for the low, the wheel goes, suicide king up you lose automatically.

STEPHEN   It's not poker, it's bloody bingo for brain surgeons. The game is like its inventor—a freak mutation.

MUGSY   So don't play, Lemon.

STEPHEN   I'm not playing, Toilet.

MUGSY   Ash?

ASH   Pass.

STEPHEN   Very wise.

CARL   Call two.

MUGSY   Good boy.

SWEENEY   I call.

FRANKIE (*reluctant*)   Go on then.

MUGSY   No raise from the dealer.

He deals an up card to CARL, SWEENEY, FRANKIE *and himself.*

Three of clubs, jack of clubs, two-eyed, six of deemonds and ten of deemonds. Double deemonds. Jack to speak.

SWEENEY   Eight.

FRANKIE   Yeah.

MUGSY   One fat lezza going in.

SWEENEY   What?

MUGSY   Eight.

SWEENEY   Well, say it.

MUGSY   Ooo.

CARL   Call eight.

MUGSY *deals another up card to* CARL, SWEENEY, FRANKIE *and himself.*

MUGSY   Nine of hearts busted low, five of clubs possible flush, seven of spades straightening, queen of hearts wild. Tens are on the potty. What is it?

FRANKIE   Forty.

MUGSY   Mid-life crisis, forty.

CARL   Pass.

SWEENEY   Call.

FRANKIE   Yep. How old are you, Stephen?

STEPHEN   I can't remember.

FRANKIE   Enjoying your mid-life crisis?

STEPHEN   Yes, it began when you started working here.

SWEENEY   Can we play cards please?

MUGSY   We can, dunno about you.

He deals an up card to SWEENEY.

Eight of clubs, still possible . . .

And then FRANKIE.

King of hearts . . . bad luck, mate.

FRANKIE   What d'you mean?

MUGSY   Suicide king you lose automatically.

FRANKIE   You what?

MUGSY   Bye bye.

FRANKIE   You never said.

ALL   Yes he did.

Beat.

FRANKIE   What a stupid poxy little game.

STEPHEN   You were warned.

FRANKIE   WHAT A FEEBLE FUCKING FARCE.

SWEENEY   Could you please SHUT UP.

MUGSY   Shh, shh, everyone quiet for Sween, he's doing his bollocks, quiet.

SWEENEY   Deal, Mugs.

MUGSY   (*deals a final up card to himself*) Four of hearts. Check.

Pause.

SWEENEY (*to* FRANKIE)   You got that fifty?

Pause.

FRANK   . . . the fifty.

FRANKIE *gives* SWEENEY *fifty pounds in cash*.

SWEENEY   Let's see what you're made of, Mugsy. There's fifty plus forty . . . seven . . . that's ninety-seven all in.

MUGSY   Call.

SWEENEY   What you got, Mugs?

MUGSY   Five tens.

Pause.

SWEENEY   How the fuck can you have "five tens," there's only four in the pack and I've got one of them.

MUGSY   I've got queen four in the box, my son, four wilds.

MUGSY *turns over his cards*.

Beat.

SWEENEY   You win.

MUGSY   Yes! I wish you'd had more money, Sween, you'd have done your bollocks, roasted like a kipper, mate. It's my night, I told you, Mugsy's back, the Mug is back.

FRANKIE   You winning then?

MUGSY   No, but I'm on the way. What'd you have, Sween?

SWEENEY   Flush.

FRANKIE   You can't call with that.

SWEENEY   I just did.

FRANKIE   And you lost.

SWEENEY   Yeah, all right.

FRANKIE   Just trying to help.

SWEENEY   You winning?

FRANKIE   No but—

SWEENEY   Well, then, stop being such an expert Mr. Vegas.

STEPHEN   Lovers' tiff all over now, is it? Your deal, Frankie.

SWEENEY *gets up.*

SWEENEY   I'm out of here.

FRANKIE   Seven stud hi-lo.

SWEENEY   Can I grab a beer, Stephen?

STEPHEN   Yup.

SWEENEY *goes to the fridge but decides against taking a beer.*

FRANKIE *starts to deal.*

SWEENEY (*sings*)   I haven't seen a card all night, I haven't seen a card all night. I haven't seen a card all night, I—

STEPHEN   Sweeney.

SWEENEY   Good evening?

STEPHEN   There's a game on . . .

SWEENEY   Sorry, sorry.

FRANKIE (*to* MUGSY)   Your bet.

SWEENEY   I haven't seen a card all night, I haven't seen a card all night, I haven't seen a card all night—

STEPHEN   Sweeney.

SWEENEY   Your highness?

STEPHEN   You know the house rules, Sweeney, if you're not in the game you're not in the room.

SWEENEY   Sorry, I forgot.

FRANKIE   Mugs, you to bet.

SWEENEY   I HAVEN'T SEEN A CARD ALL NIGHT, I HAVEN'T SEEN A CARD ALL NIGHT, I HAVEN'T SEEN A CARD ALL FUCKING NIGHT—

STEPHEN   If you're not in the game you're not in the room. House Rules.

SWEENEY   What does it matter, Stephen, what the fuck does it matter?

STEPHEN   It matters, Sweeney, because rules are rules.

SWEENEY   They're *your* rules, Stephen, no one else gives a flying fuck. "No smoking"—have you ever heard anything so ridiculous for a poker school? No beers on the table unless they're on these poxy little beer mats. Oi . . . Ash, see this baize, this tatty bit of shit, he takes it home every Sunday night, religiously, and irons it, he fucking irons it, the c—

He is now close to tears.

He's got a computer, what does he keep on it? Accounts? Invoices? No, he keeps a record of all the games we've played, with lots of little colored graphs and charts. He lives for his poker. He can tell you who won the game and with what hand on Easter Sunday six fucking years ago.

STEPHEN   Yuh I can, you lost. You chose to play tonight, Sweeney, don't use your self-hatred as a weapon against us.

SWEENEY   Stephen, you are such a wanker, you are such an unbelievable fucking wanker.

STEPHEN   Good night.

SWEENEY   What is your fucking problem?

STEPHEN   I don't think I have a problem. I just want to play a quiet game of cards on a Sunday night without you in the background sloshing around in a sea of self-pity. Call.

ASH   Call.

CARL   Call.

SWEENEY   Come on, Frankie, let's go . . .

FRANKIE (*standing*)   I'd better get him home.

STEPHEN   It's your bet, Frankie.

Pause.

FRANKIE (to SWEENEY)   You OK? I mean . . .

Pause.

SWEENEY   No, you stay.

FRANKIE   Cheers ... I'm doing my money here, mate, sorry.

FRANKIE sits down.

SWEENEY   See you, guys.

MUGSY   See you, Sween.

CARL   Night, Sween.

SWEENEY   Nice to meet you, Ash, I hope you win the fucking lot. I'll see you, Stephen.

STEPHEN   Sweeney, do you think you and Louise will manage to find somewhere with no entrance fees tomorrow? You could try the Tate gallery ... is she fond of Giacometti?

Beat.

I'll see you first thing, Tuesday, lunch. Sweeney?

SWEENEY (*in tears*)   Yeah.

STEPHEN   Here you are ... fifty quid ... overtime.

He holds up a fifty-pound note.

SWEENEY (*taking the note*)   Cheers.

FRANKIE   Sween ...

SWEENEY   No.

SWEENEY exits.

Beat.

ASH   Your bet.

FRANKIE   Yep.

CARL   Eights or better?

FRANKIE   Yep.

MUGSY   The wheel goes?

FRANKIE   Uh-huh.

STEPHEN   With declarations?

FRANKIE   Cards speak. I raise.

STRAIGHT FLUSH

BY

W. SOMERSET MAUGHAM

"The fact is that if you are a storyteller," wrote Somerset
Maugham in his preface to his *Complete Short Stories*, **"any
curious person you meet has a way of suggesting a story."**
Forever taking notes, Maugham lacked no shortage for
material on his steamship voyages across the Pacific—good
stories seemed to seek him out. "Straight Flush" is one
such transcript from his travels in the 1920s: a late night,
rough-seas, smoking-room encounter with two curious
individuals, resulting in two curious tales.

I am not a bad sailor and when under stress of weather the game
broke up I did not go below. We were in the habit of playing poker
into the small hours, a mild game that could hurt nobody, but it had
been blowing all day and with nightfall the wind strengthened to half
a gale. One or two of our bunch admitted that they felt none too comfortable and one or two others played with unwonted detachment.
But even if you are not sick dirty weather at sea is an unpleasant
thing. I hate the fool who tells you he loves a storm and tramping the
deck lustily vows that it can never be too rough for him. When the
woodwork groans and creaks, glasses crash to the floor and you lurch
in your chair as the ship heels over, when the wind howls and the
waves thunder against the side, I very much prefer dry land. I think no

one was sorry when one of the players said he had had enough, and the last round of jackpots was agreed to without demur. I remained alone in the smoking-room, for I knew I should not easily get to sleep in that racket and I could not read in bed with any comfort when the North Pacific kept dashing itself against my portholes. I shuffled together the two packs we had been playing with and set out a complicated patience.

I had been playing about ten minutes when the door was opened with a blast of wind that sent my cards flying, and two passengers, rather breathless, slipped into the smoking-room. We were not a full ship and we were ten days out from Hong Kong, so that I had had time to become acquainted with pretty well everyone on board. I had spoken on several occasions to the pair who now entered, and seeing me by myself they came over to my table.

They were very old men, both of them. That was perhaps what had brought them together, for they had first met when they got on board at Hong Kong, and now you saw them sitting together in the smoking-room most of the day, not talking very much, but just comfortable to be side by side, with a bottle of Vichy water between them. They were very rich old men too and that was a bond between them. The rich feel at ease in one another's company. They know that money means merit. Their experience of the poor is that they always want something. It is true that the poor admire the rich and it is pleasant to be admired, but they envy them as well and this prevents their admiration from being quite candid. Mr. Rosenbaum was a little hunched-up Jew, very frail in clothes that looked too big for him, and he gave you the impression of hanging on to mortality only by a hair. His ancient, emaciated body looked as though it were already attacked by the corruption of the grave. The only expression his face ever bore was one of cunning, but it was purely habitual, the result of ever so many years astuteness; he was a kindly, friendly person, very free with his drinks and his cigars, and his charity was world-famous. The other was called Donaldson. He was a Scot, but had gone to California as a little boy and made a great deal of money mining. He was short and stout, with a red, clean-shaven, shiny face and no hair but a sickle of silver above his neck, and very gentle eyes. Whatever force he had had to make his way in the world had been worn away by the years and he was now a picture of mild beneficence.

"I thought you'd turned in long ago," I remarked.

"I should have," returned the Scot, "only Mr. Rosenbaum kept me up talking of old times."

"What's the good of going to bed when you can't sleep?" said Mr. Rosenbaum.

"Walk ten times round the deck with me tomorrow morning and you'll sleep all right."

"I've never taken any exercise in my life and I'm not going to begin now."

"That's foolishness. You'd be twice the man you are now if you'd taken exercise. Look at me. You'd never think I was seventy-nine, would you?"

Mr. Rosenbaum looked critically at Mr. Donaldson.

"No, I wouldn't. You're very well preserved. You look younger than me and I'm only seventy-six. But then I never had a chance to take care of myself."

At that moment the steward came up.

"The bar's just going to close, gentlemen. Is there anything I can get you?"

"It's a stormy night," said Mr. Rosenbaum. "Let's have a bottle of champagne."

"Small Vichy for me," said Mr. Donaldson.

"Oh, very well, small Vichy for me too."

The steward went away.

"But mind you," continued Mr. Rosenbaum testily, "I wouldn't have done without the things you've done without, not for all the money in the world."

Mr. Donaldson gave me his gentle smile.

"Mr. Rosenbaum can't get over it because I've never touched a card nor a drop of alcohol for fifty-seven years."

"Now I ask you, what sort of a life is that?"

"I was a very heavy drinker when I was a young fellow and a desperate gambler, but I had a very terrible experience. It was a lesson to me and I took it."

"Tell him about it," said Mr. Rosenbaum. "He's an author. He'll write it up and perhaps he'll be able to make his passage money."

"It's not a story I like telling very much even now. I'll make it as short as I can. Me and three others had staked out a claim, friends all of us, and the oldest wasn't twenty-five; there was me and my partner and a couple of brothers, McDermott their name was, but they were more like friends than brothers. What was one's was the other's, and one wouldn't go into town without the other went too, and they were always laughing and joking together. A fine clean pair of boys, over six feet high both of them, and handsome. We were a wild bunch and we had pretty good luck on the whole and when we made money we didn't hesitate to spend it. Well, one night we'd all been drinking very heavily and we started a poker game. I guess we were a good deal drunker than we realized. Anyhow suddenly a row started between the McDermotts. One of them accused the other of cheating. 'You take that back,' cried Jamie. 'I'll see you in hell first,' says Eddie. And before me and my partner could do anything Jamie had pulled out his gun and shot his brother dead."

The ship gave a huge roll and we all clung to our seats. In the steward's pantry there was a great clatter as bottles and glasses slid along a shelf. It was strange to hear that grim little story told by that mild old man. It was a story of another age and you could hardly believe that this fat, red-faced little fellow, with his silver fringe of hair, in a dinner jacket, two large pearls in his shirt-front, had really taken part in it.

"What happened then?" I asked.

"We sobered up pretty quick. At first Jamie couldn't believe Eddie was dead. He took him in his arms and kept calling him. 'Eddie,' he says, 'wake up, old boy, wake up.' He cried all night and next day we rode in with him to town, forty miles it was, me on one side of him and my partner on the other, and handed him over to the sheriff. I was crying too when we shook hands with him and said good-bye. I told my partner I'd never touch a card again or drink again as long as I lived, and I never have, and I never will."

Mr. Donaldson looked down, and his lips were trembling. He seemed to see again that scene of long ago. There was one thing I should have liked to ask him about, but he was evidently so much moved I did not like to. They seem not to have hesitated, his partner and himself, but delivered up this wretched boy to justice as though it were the most natural thing in the world. It suggested that even in those rough, wild men the respect for the law had somehow the force of an instinct. A little shiver ran through me. Mr. Donaldson emptied his glass of Vichy and with a curt good-night left us.

"The old fellow's getting a bit childish," said Mr. Rosenbaum. "I don't believe he was ever very bright."

"Well, apparently he was bright enough to make an awful lot of money,"

"But how? In those days in California you didn't want brains to make money, you only wanted luck. I know what I'm talking about. Johannesburg was the place where you had to have your wits about you. Joburg in the 'eighties. It was grand. We were a tough lot of guys, I can tell you. It was each for himself and the devil take the hindmost."

He took a meditative sip of his Vichy.

"You talk of your cricket and baseball, your golf and tennis and football, you can have them, they're all very well for boys; is it a reasonable thing, I ask you, for a grown man to run about and hit a ball? Poker's the only game fit for a grown man. Then your hand is against every man and every man's hand is against yours. Team-work? Who ever made a fortune by team-work? There's only one way to make a fortune and that's to down the fellow who's up against you."

"I didn't know you were a poker player," I interrupted. "Why don't you take a hand one evening?"

"I don't play any more. I've given it up too, but for the only reason a man should. I can't see myself giving it up because a friend of mind was unlucky enough to get killed. Anyway a man who's damn fool enough to get killed isn't worth having as a friend. But in the old days! If you wanted to know what poker was you ought to have been in South Africa then. It was the biggest game I've ever seen. And they were fine players; there wasn't a crooked dodge they weren't up to. It was grand.

Just to give you an example, one night I was playing with some of the biggest men in Johannesburg and I was called away. There was a couple of thousand pounds in the pot! 'Deal me a hand, I won't keep you waiting,' I said. 'All right,' they said, 'don't hurry.' Well, I wasn't gone more than a minute. When I came back I picked up my cards and saw I'd got a straight flush to the queen. I didn't say a word, I just threw in my hand. I knew my company. And do you know, I was wrong."

"What do you mean? I don't understand."

"It was a perfectly straight deal and the pot was won on three sevens. But how could I tell that? Naturally I thought someone else had a straight flush to the king. It looked to me just the sort of hand I might lose a hundred thousand pounds on."

"Too bad," I said.

"I very nearly had a stroke. And it was on account of another pat straight flush that I gave up playing poker. I've only had about five in my life."

"I believe the chances are nearly sixty-six thousand to one against."

"In San Francisco it was, the year before last. I'd been playing in poor luck all the evening. I hadn't lost much money because I never had a chance to play. I'd hardly had a pair and if I got a pair I couldn't improve. Then I got a hand just as bad as the others and I didn't come in. The man next me wasn't playing either and I showed him my hand. 'That's the kind of thing I've been getting all evening,' I said. 'How can anyone be expected to play with cards like that?' 'Well, I don't know what more you want,' he said, as he looked at them. 'Most of us would be prepared to come in on a straight flush.' 'What's that,' I cried. I was trembling like a leaf. I looked at the cards again. I thought I had two or three little hearts and two or three little diamonds. It was a straight flush in hearts all right and I hadn't seen it. My eyes, it was. I knew what it meant. Old age. I don't cry much. I'm not that sort of man. But I couldn't help it then. I tried to control myself, but the tears just rolled down my cheeks. Then I got up. 'I'm through, gentlemen,' I said. 'When a man's eyes are so dim that he can't see a straight flush when it's dealt him he has no business to play poker. Nature's given me a hint and I'm taking it. I'll never play poker again as long as I live.' I cashed in my chips, all but one, and I left the house. I've never played since."

Mr. Rosenbaum took a chip out of his waistcoat pocket and showed it to me.

"I kept this as a souvenir. I always carry it about with me. I'm a sentimental old fool, I know that, but, you see, poker was the only thing I cared for. Now I've only got one thing left."

"What is that?" I asked.

A smile flickered across his cunning little face and behind his thick glasses his rheumy eyes twinkled with ironic glee. He looked incredibly astute and malicious. He gave the thin, high-pitched cackle of an old man amused and answered with a single word "Philanthropy."

Shut Up and Deal

Jesse May

Poker is a ruthless game and poker rooms the world over can be desperate places. Or as Jesse May puts it: "Poker's good if you like watching people. Not if you like people because then you won't like people so much." As you might expect from a card-savvy former philosophy graduate student at the University of Chicago, there's a lot of gutshot wisdom in May's throbbing prose. His 1998 book, *Shut Up and Deal* (purportedly a novel), reels with the everyday mood swings of a high-stakes, hand-to-mouth poker existence—"to play, that's the thing," he affirms in a poetic postscript. What follows is a prologue that pretty much sets the tone for the hard-hitting action that follows. The style is engagingly simple, brutally honest, relentless.

It's all about cheating. I say cheating and people their faces drop, they get shocked. But it's not the same word I'm thinking about. Because when you're involved in the poker world, the gambling world, you spend every day thinking about that word. And because there aren't many rules, or at least there's a lot of gray areas, really it all just started as shooting angles. And you have to think about it in the context of the history of poker. The history of poker is a history of cheating, and this is not to say that the old poker players were cheaters, but many were hustlers, and they could shoot the angles.

In the sixties and seventies poker was nearly always played No-Limit, or table stakes. In No-Limit poker you can bet anything in front of you all at one time and you only need one good hand to break everyone. In No-Limit it's easier and more likely to bust a mark in one night. Because in the old days there wasn't a casino to walk into every night of the week where the games are arranged for you and the people show up and all the money is guaranteed. No, in the old days games took place all over—houses, barns, skating rinks, hotel rooms— and they went and then they broke. So you had to go in and get the money and leave town and look for the next place. There just wasn't any money in it for the house, no reason for casinos to run a game that just took place for a day or two and thousands of dollars changed hands and then everybody left town and the house didn't get any of it except maybe twelve dollars in rake. It didn't make any sense for them to spread No-Limit poker without cheating too. And a professional gambler had to thrive in that atmosphere. That's the history of poker and when I say there was a lot of shooting angles going on, it just means everybody finds their own ways to get the money.

Then came the late 1980s. A bunch of things happened round about the same time period, or all in a row. The Mirage, California, here come the Indians. And the invention of limit Texas Hold'em poker.

In 1987 there was legalized poker in Nevada and in one county of California. By 1996 poker could be legally played in casinos all over twenty-three states of the Union. And five countries in Europe.

People started playing poker. A lot of people started playing poker and there was *Card Player* magazine and tournaments and books and now instead of ten guys trying to make a living out of the same game at the Golden Nugget, there's ten thousand guys trying to make a living in one thousand poker games in casinos all over the country and at all limits and the money, the money couldn't help but be loose.

Let's make one thing clear. Limit poker was not invented by the poker players. Limit poker is the brainchild of the house and the house is who it's for and the house is who is gonna get the money. Along with a few other people, maybe.

Someone said what if, instead of being able to bet whatever you want at any time, there's a set limit—so people can't win or lose too much per hand. This will make them play longer, and make the games last longer. It also increases the luck factor and lessens the skill. So now if the house is charging players by the hour or taking a nominal amount from each pot, then those nominal amounts are gonna add up. And this is how poker turned into a service industry. All the house has to do is keep people at the table, keep the games going, and their cut is guaranteed. Every pot. Every hour. Chick-chock.

Everybody starts the same way. First you think that there's no possible way to make a living at poker. Then you get involved a little deeper—you run a little lucky, quit your job, start making money and spending high. And then you think that this is the easy life and how sweet it is and the simplest thing in the world is to wake up whenever you want, go into the card room, play a little, and win.

But then you run bad. There's no possible way for you to win—you could be playing head up with a blind man. And then you think that you must be the unluckiest guy in the world and then you go broke and then you borrow some money and then you go really broke and then you decide that there's no possible way to make a living at poker and anyone who says he is is either lying or just has a horseshoe stuck up his ass and hasn't been around long enough to see it turn. Or both.

Everybody wants to know about skill. Who's the best and who's got it and who ain't and what we've got here, and all I can say is that the answer is never that easy. Like for example there's this guy, call him Ace, and he plays well, I mean he plays really well, better than me, like if we were ever to get involved in a heads-up match, Ace would clean me up. And he has. Nothing to it. But one night maybe Ace and I are in a Hold 'em game together, and we both have bad luck and we both lose five thousand dollars. Now Ace, what does he do? He gets so mad at losing that five thousand that he stalks off into the pit to try and get even and blow off some steam and he ends up losing twenty thousand more playing craps. Meanwhile, I get so mad at losing my five dimes that I go home, get in my closet, stuff a pillow in my face, and scream until I lose my voice. What's the difference? Twenty thousand dollars. Now who's the better poker player? It ain't that easy.

Or, Ace feels good because he's generally considered the best poker player in the room and in the town, and so when the games are real good and the money is fast and loose, then Ace he won more than a bunch of money. Meanwhile me, the plodder, I'm considered one of the worst and I'm just there showing up every day. After a while the money dries up, lots and lots of people go broke, and the games start getting pretty tough. Sometimes real tough. But Ace, he's still the best Hold'em player in the game, in the room, in the town. So he's still there every day. But now his edge it ain't so big, and now when he wins it ain't so much, and when he runs a little unlucky he's going off big time. Meanwhile, what do I do? When the games start getting tight and the money ain't flowing, I pack up and head off to Austria, where they just opened a new card room and everybody's rich and nine out of ten of 'em are still dumb as a stump. Now does that make me a better poker player? The answer's not so easy.

One more example about Ace. He's a Hold'em player, a Hold'em specialist, Hold'em is his game, and that's all he plays because he don't want to play anything else. And he's just so good at Hold'em, I guess. I'm a Hold'em player too. That's what I started at, that's what I know, and that's where I made my bones. But in Atlantic City in the Taj Mahal something began to happen. Look in the poker room and look who the good players are and nine out of ten of 'em are Hold'em players, that's what they like to play. So all these pros are packing the Hold'em games. Meanwhile, there ain't a fuckin' Stud player in the town and all the live ones, all the marks and the drunks and the guys who are dripping with dead money, when they come into town they're playing Stud. Why? No reason, they just maybe like it better. I start playing Stud. I force myself to learn it, and hell, I may not be that good but I'm gonna play with the idiots. But Ace, he ain't gonna learn no new game. He figures he don't have to because he's so good at Hold'em and he's been playing it for years and years, and for him to get that good at Stud would take so much time it ain't even worth it. He figures. The answer is never so easy. But some people are still here and others have left town in a bus. That's what happens in the poker world. And that's what I mean by shooting angles.

See, poker didn't just start as a hustler's game. I mean it always was and always will be. But what I mean by hustling, well, maybe it's just shooting the angles. Shooting all the angles. Because when you want it bad enough you'll do anything to get the money. People just do what they have to do to survive. To survive. I've seen so many world champions on the rail, and why, because they figure they're so good that there's an angle that they don't have to shoot, something they can let get away. When they're broke they're still the best player, ain't no one gonna argue about that. But there ain't no corporate sponsorships for the top guys. Not yet at least. And when you're down and out, man, who the fuck cares how big your dick is. I mean, I really don't. It's just talk.

Now don't go thinking about who the better poker player is, because I could just as easily tell a hundred stories that make Ace look good and me look like a chump. And what's the moral? What I'm saying is this—there is no reality, it all depends on how I present what is and how I cloud it. And the answer doesn't matter. No, the answer only matters if you're trying to make a judgment, if someone else is making a judgment. It only matters if you got something to prove. But if you're trying to prove something to someone besides yourself, then I say you're in a whole other kind of trouble. That's gonna hurt you too.

In poker, skill ain't a marketable commodity. Skill ain't marketable to no one but yourself. That's it. And that's important.

Poker is a combination of luck and skill. People think mastering the skill part is hard, but they're wrong. The trick to poker is mastering the luck. That's philosophy. Understanding luck is philosophy, and there are some people who aren't ever gonna fade it. That's what sets poker apart. And that's what keeps everyone coming back for more.

EVERYTHING IS WILD

BY
JAMES THURBER

Constant bickering between the sexes was a popular theme with James Thurber, the cynical genius who wrote *The Secret Life of Walter Mitty*. In this selection (originally published in *The New Yorker* in 1932), he serves up a delightful grump who loathes any variations of a "fine old game." (Thurber himself couldn't have been too fond of frilly, wild-card poker.) In the end, as the dour Mr. Brush takes his revenge on his wife and her good-natured friends, one can almost sense the author mirthfully chuckling away at his typewriter.

In the first place it was a cold and rainy night and the Cortrights lived eighteen miles away, in Bronxville. "Eighteen hundred miles," Mr. Brush put it, bitterly. He got the car out of the Gramercy Lane garage, snarling savagely at the garage man, an amiable and loquacious fellow who spoke with an accent and who kept talking about winter oil and summer oil, and grinning, and repeating himself. As they drove out, Mrs. Brush told her husband that he didn't have to be so mean, the man hadn't done anything to him. "He kept yelling about oil, didn't he?" demanded Mr. Brush. "I know about oil. Nobody has to tell me about oil." Mrs. Brush kept her voice abnormally low, the way she always did when he was on the verge of a tantrum. "He wasn't yelling," she said. "He'll probably ruin the car some night, the way you acted."

The drive to Bronxville was as bad as Mr. Brush expected it would be. He got lost, and couldn't find Bronxville. When he did find Bronxville, he couldn't find the Woodmere Apartments. "You'll have to ask somebody where it is," said Mrs. Brush. He didn't want to ask anybody anything, but he stopped in front of a bright little barbershop, got out, and went inside. The barber he encountered turned out to be a garrulous foreigner. Sure, he knew where eez these Woodmare Apartamen. "Down is street has a concrete breech," he said. "It go under but no up to the first raid light. Quick, like this, before turn!" The barber made swift darting angles in the air with his hand. He also turned completely around. "So not down these light, hah?" he finished up. Mr. Brush snarled at him and went outside.

"Well?" asked Mrs. Brush. She knew by his silence that he hadn't found out anything. "*I'll* go in and ask next time," she said. Mr. Brush drove on. "The guy didn't know what he was talking about," he said. "He's crazy." Finally, after many twists and turns, most of them wrong, they drove up in front of the Woodmere. "Hell of an apartment building," said Mr. Brush. Mrs. Brush didn't answer him.

The dinner, fortunately, was quite nice. Mr. Brush had expected, indeed he had predicted, that there would be a lot of awful people, but the Brushes were the only guests. The Cortrights were charming, there wasn't a radio, and nobody talked about business or baseball. Also there was, after dinner, Mr. Brush's favorite liqueur, and he was just settling comfortably into a soft chair, glass in hand, when the doorbell rang. A man and a woman were brought into the room and introduced—a Mr. and Mrs. Spreef, as Brush got it. The name turned out to be Spear. Mr. Brush didn't like them. They were quite nice, but he never liked anybody he hadn't met before.

After a flurry of trivial talk, during which Spear told a story about a fellow who had been courting a girl for fifteen years, at which everybody laughed but Brush, who grinned fixedly, the hostess wanted to know if people would like to play poker. There were pleased murmurs, a grunt from Brush, and in a twinkling a card table was pulled out from behind something and set up. Mrs. Cortright brightly explained that one leg of the table was broken, but she thought it would hold up all right. Mr. Brush didn't actually say that he thought it wouldn't, but he looked as if he did.

Mr. Spear won the deal. "This is dealer's choice, Harry," his hostess told him. "Change on each deal." Harry squealed. "O.K." he said. "How about a little old Duck-in-the-Pond?" The ladies giggled with pleasure. "Whazzat?" grumbled Brush. He hated any silly variation of the fine old game of poker. He instantly dropped out of the hand, and sat staring at Mr. Spear. Mr. Spear, it came to him, looked like Chevalier. Mr. Brush hated Chevalier.

The next deal fell to Brush and he immediately named straight poker as his game. Mrs. Spear said she was just crazy about Duck-in-the-Pond and why didn't they just keep on playing that? "Straight poker," said Mr. Brush, gruffly. "Oh," said Mrs. Spear, her smile vanishing. Mr. Brush won the straight-poker hand with three of a kind.

Mrs. Spear was the next dealer. "Seven-card stud," she said, "with the twos and threes wild." The women all gave little excited screams. Mrs. Cortright said she was crazy about seven-card stud with something wild. Mrs. Spear said she was, too. Mr. Brush said yah. Mrs. Spear won the hand with four kings—that is, two kings, a deuce, and a trey. Mr. Cortright, the next dealer, announced that they would now play Poison Ivy. This was a nuisance Mr. Brush had never heard of. It proved to be a variation of poker in which each player gets four cards, and five others are placed face down on the table to be turned up one at a time. The lowest card, when all are turned up, becomes the wild card. Mr. Brush rolled his cigar from one corner of his mouth to the other, and narrowed his eyes. He scowled at Chevalier, because Chevalier kept repeating that Poison Ivy was the nuts. Brush folded up his hand and sat stiffly in his chair, rolling his cigar and grunting. Four aces won that hand, and in doing so had to beat four other aces (there were two fours in the hand on the table, and they were low).

So the game went wildly on, with much exclaiming and giggling, until it came Mr. Brush's time to deal again. He sat up very straight in his chair and glared around the table. "We'll play Soap-in-Your-Eye this time," he said, grimly. Mrs. Spear screeched. "Oh, I don't know that," she cried. Brush rolled his cigar at her. "Out West they call it Kick-in-the-Pants," he said. Mrs. Brush suggested that they better play Duck-in-the-Pond again, or Poison Ivy. "Soap-in-Your-Eye," said Brush, without looking at her. "How does it go?" asked Cortright.

"The red queens, the fours, fives, sixes, and eights are wild," said Mr. Brush. "I'll show you." He dealt one card to each person. Then he dealt another one around, face up this time. "Ah," he exclaimed, "Mrs. Spear draws a red queen on the second round, so it becomes forfeit. It can be reinstated, however, if on the next round she gets a black four. I'll show you." Mr. Brush was adroit with cards and he contrived it so that Mrs. Spear did get a black four on the next round. "Ho," said Brush, "that makes it interesting. Having foured your queen, you can now choose a card, any card, from the deck." He held up the deck and she selected a card. "Now, if you don't want that card," continued Brush, "you can say 'Back' or 'Right' or 'Left' depending on whether you want to put it back in the deck or pass it to the person at your right or the person at your left. If you decide to keep it, you say 'Hold.' The game, by the way, is sometimes called Hold Back or Right and Left. Get it?"

"I don't think so," said Mrs. Spear. She looked vaguely at the card she had drawn, "Hold, I guess," she said.

"Good," said Brush. "Now everybody else draws a card." Everybody did, Mrs. Brush trying to catch her husband's eye, but failing. "Now," said Brush, "we each have four cards, two of which everybody has seen, and two of which they haven't. Mrs. Spreef, however, has a Hold. That is, having black-foured her red queen, she is privileged to call a jack a queen or a trey a four or any other card just one point under a wild card, a wild card. See?" Nobody, apparently, saw.

"Why don't we just play Poison Ivy again?" asked Mrs. Brush. "Or a round of straight poker?"

"I want to try this," said Brush. "I'm crazy about it." He dealt two more cards around, face down. "We all have six cards now," he went on, "but you can't look at the last two—even after the game is over. All you can look at is the four cards in your hand and this one." He put a card face down in the middle of the table. "That card is called Splinter-Under-Your-Thumb, and is also wild, whatever it is," he explained. "All right, bet." Everyone was silent for several seconds, and then they all checked to him. Brush bet five chips. Mrs. Spear, encouraged in a dim way by the fact that she had black-foured her red queen, thus reinstating it after forfeit, stayed, and so did Mrs. Cortright (who always stayed), but the others dropped out. The two ladies put in five chips each, and called Mr. Brush. He turned up the card in the middle of the table—the queen of diamonds. "Hah!" said Brush. "Well, I got a royal flush in spades!" He laid down the four of diamonds, the eight of hearts, and a pair of sixes. "I don't see how you have," said Mrs. Spear, dubiously. "Sure," said Brush. "The queen of diamonds is a wild card, so I call it the ace of spades. All my other cards are wild, so I call them king, queen, jack, ten of spades." The women laid their hands down and looked at Brush. "Well, you both got royal flushes, too," he said, "but mine is spades, and is high. You called me, and that gave me the right to name my suit. I win." He took in the chips.

The Brushes said good night and left shortly after that. They went out to the elevator in silence, and in silence they went out to the car, and in silence they drove off. Mr. Brush at last began to chortle. "Darn good game, Soap-in-Your-Eye," he said. Mrs. Brush stared at him, evilly, for a full minute. "You terrible person," she said. Mr. Brush broke into loud and hearty laughter. He ho-hoed all the way down the Grand Concourse. He had had a swell time after all.

A Game, Gentlemen, a Game . . .

by

Barbara Tuchman

Written for *Esquire* in 1966, this piece is a most ingenious, curmudgeonly (and immensely readable) defense of sloppy poker play—from no less than one of the twentieth century's greatest historians. "I play poker by instinct, not as a science," writes Tuchman, professing a total ignorance of the relative odds of improving hands. She goes on to criticize various experts of the day (for all their strategizing and killjoy "nevers"), as well as regulars from her own game (for their lack of imaginative play).

Today's professionals have a term for Tuchman's style: "calling station," as in—never met a hand she didn't like. But if the Pulitzer Prize–winning author of *The Guns of August* really did manage "over the years to more or less break even," she surely must have faced her share of like-minded non-folders across the table. History can be rewritten, but poker odds are intractable.

Poker is not a science any more than is history. To say this is to fling a gauntlet in the face of all the experts who write the treatises on how to play poker and how to explain history and who, along with their fellow experts in other fields, dominate our age. Nevertheless, let me make my small rebellion. I am tired both of experts and of science whose supreme achievement, in this second half of the twentieth century, has been the underground shelter—and the need for it. Since the best that science could do has been to bring man, who thought himself a little lower than the angels, to the proud condition of an earthworm, I think we might reserve a small area free of its influence. I have a longing for the spirit of an older, happier time, for something unscientific, undisciplined, free and ebullient, and if we cannot have it in the real world around us, at least let us have it in poker.

The experts in the stern prefaces to their books invariably admonish us to approach poker as a "scientific study," to play with uncompromising regard for the "immutable" law of averages, to memorize the mathematical odds, never to stay on a short pair, never to stay in a jackpot with less than a pair of aces or kings (what is the matter with queens?), plus a whole string of other killjoy "nevers." In return for faithful and unflinching obedience to the odds, they promise that one will always come out ahead of the game and presumably never enjoy oneself for a minute. It is economics, I believe, that has been called the dismal science, but compared to poker rigidly played according to the law of averages economics must be positively exhilarating. Let those who have been bullied into attempting it take heart from the memory of Dr. Johnson's friend, Oliver Edwards, who confessed, "I have tried too in my time to be a philosopher; but I don't know how, cheerfulness was always breaking in."

Indubitably, if a person plays poker solely to make money as a means of, let us say, putting himself through Princeton, in preference to washing dishes, as a young friend of mine did, then I grant he must play strictly and coldly in the spirit of a laboratory science. He will measure the hands as if they were solids and gases and make his bets as if balancing a chemical equation. He will never allow himself a play that is uncalculated or prompted by emotion or just for the hell of it. Secure and superior in the assurance that four out of five play in careless if happy disregard of the odds, he will certainly succeed in putting himself through Princeton—or even Yale. This type of player, however, belongs to a rare and restricted category that need not concern us. Poker, on the whole, is played for sociable reasons, not because people need the money but because they enjoy the game.

What joy is there in playing at a science? What surprise? What unexpected triumph? What delicious thrill of suspense? One is even precluded by the experts from paying to fill a four flush or double-ended straight unless four players have entered the pot ahead of one. Is there a man with sense of pleasure so benumbed that he can bear to throw away a four flush and forego the prickly, tingling sensation of drawing that one card merely because the pot does not promise a return equal to the odds against filling? Does a golf pro advise his pupils to stay out of the game and brood on the clubhouse terrace merely because the other members of his foursome for that day have lower handicaps? If he stayed on the terrace all day, how would he ever hit a hole in one—which, I understand from hearsay, is the lovely dream that every golfer carries, like the marshal's baton of Napoleon's soldiers, in among his clubs.

A straight flush is the poker player's hole in one. Yet no challenge of the odds evokes such high-pitched scorn from the experts as to draw two cards to a three-card open-ended straight flush. They positively bleat in sarcasm over the benighted player who lets himself be tempted into this idiocy. Personally, rather than wait supinely until fate deposits the longed-for gift in my lap, I like to knock on fate's door every now and then to show that I deserve it. Without shame I confess that whenever fortune deals me three to a straight flush, I *always* pay to draw to them. And oddly enough, on my wall at home hang three signed and framed straight flushes filled in the course of my poker career. Haughtily the experts will retort that I have lost more money paying to draw to the ones I never filled than ever I won by the successes. True. But what price do they pay on the excitement of those occasions when I watched the two exactly right cards slowly appear in their miraculous black—or pink—perfection?

I do not for a moment suggest the outcome was anything but the result of purest chance. I believe in chance. It is certainly more game-some than spending an evening of poker immersed in arithmetic. Moreover, one is disallowed from taking any pride in skill, for Archibald Crofton, the classic authority, says, "There is no such thing as a skillful player," any more than there is a skillful bookie. "Both simply play within the mathematical odds of chance and let the general public pound itself to pieces against the invincible laws of average." Those iron laws . . . they are always "invincible," "immutable," "infallible," as if they were British battle cruisers. They are the very core of the experts' case, yet if they are indeed so scientific, how does it happen that they seem to have whims? Irwin Steig, for instance, says the odds against improving a double-ended three-card straight flush are 22 and 23 to 1 for a straight and flush respectively; Crofton says they are a flat 12 to 1. Is that science? Oswald Jacoby says the chances of improving a pair by a three-card draw are 2 in 7, or 3.5 to 1; Steig puts them at 2.5 to 1. Is that immutable?

If these omnipotent laws of average are not scientific after all, what then becomes of the experts' claim that obedience to them will ensure long-run winning? To me it would seem to ensure only a very dull evening. The blurb on the jacket of a recent book on poker proudly proclaims that the author "explains the logical procedure in every situation." What could be more deadly? The charm of poker, or so it seems to me, is that it permits one to play the *illogical* procedure and, every once in a while, to get away with it.

Nine times out of ten the "logical" play advised by the experts is to drop. They are lavish with this dreary injunction. They detail carefully all the situations in which you should check and all the combinations that should cause you to fold, but none in which they are really happy to have you open. They appear not to *want* you to open. The horrid necessity of making the opening bet they airily assume will be undertaken by that amiable and uninstructed fellow on your left who has *not* read Jacoby. The question inevitably comes to mind, what happens when everyone at the table has read the experts? No one opens, no one bets, no one raises, thereby achieving the ultimate perfection: no play. The game comes to a dead stop. When I read books on poker I always hear a faint echo from my childhood:

Mother, may I go in to swim?
Yes, my darling daughter,

Hang your clothes on the mulberry bush
And don't go near the water.

I have never had the opportunity to meet any of the poker pros in person but in my mind's eye they all look like Jonathan Edwards in a Puritan hat preaching certain hellfire for the sin of deviating from the mathematical odds. The most severely cautionary of the lot is Herbert O. Yardley (*The Education of a Poker Player*, New York, 1957) who on page after page takes a fierce joy in laying out every possible kind of hand you should stay out of. After several chapters of this you feel it is unwise to enter any pot unless you hold a pat hand, everyone else has dropped and two F.B.I. men stand behind you with pistols pointed through the pockets of their trench coats. One cannot help wondering if Major Yardley wants to be *that* safe, would he not be better off in bed with his head under the covers?

This suggests a further thought. To extrapolate: suppose the poker men wrote the marriage manuals? Would they advise no activity except under the scientifically favorable odds of a full moon, a Bahamian island, a room temperature of 68 degrees and a background recording of the love duet from *Tristan und Isolde*? This raises the possibility of the race ceasing to reproduce itself altogether. To such ends could science bring us.

I play poker by instinct, not as a science. There will be those who will snort that they expect nothing else of a woman and I will not dispute them. Many men would like to keep poker an inviolate masculine preserve like the Yale Club where a lady who is invited to lunch is hurriedly shunted into a screened-off antechamber as soon as she comes inside the front door. Actually this procedure is rather more enjoyable than otherwise. It gives one a pleasantly illicit feeling as if one were smuggled goods.

I would not attempt to persuade to the contrary those men who refuse utterly to play with a woman, although I have never found them very articulate as to their reasons. They generally mutter something grumpy and vague about "talking too much," yet I doubt if this can be the real reason because in all the games in which I have played the men talk more than the women. They tell funny stories—occasionally funny—and they indulge in prolonged and mysterious argument, renewed every time they meet, which has something to do with betting into or on an open pair and on which they claim there is one "right" play, although I have yet to discover what it is because they have yet to settle the argument. Most deplorable of all, they rehash the last hand and tell each other how it should have been played. This interrupts the game and takes time away from playing; besides, rehashing is for bridge players. The peculiar, the essential charm of poker is that it is *not* bridge.

For one thing it has no partners. Each player is blissfully on his own and if he makes a foolish move or misjudges a situation it harms no one else and should concern no one else. In this attribute poker is like skiing, a sport for individuals, a blessed escape from this age of teams when everything, even thinking, is considered to be done twice as well if engaged in by two or more people at once. Even in company, skiing has a lovely singleness, the one sport from which one can get full pleasure without having to score points or beat an opponent or worry about a partner. Poker has the same attraction. It is less combative and disputatious than bridge and more sociable than solitaire. It is an exercise of wits without ill will; light-hearted, not grim. Above all it is non-authoritarian, a quality I have come up against in my ceaseless quest for an evening, or just an hour, oh well, even just a *round* of straight draw *without* variations. I think this is really a very sensible proposal that would allow one to settle into the rhythm of the game, but no one seems prepared to accept it; someone always wants stud or dealer's choice and, as it is impossible to lay down the law to poker players, my yearning for an hour of straight draw is still unsatisfied.

Arthur, one of the group with whom I play, also suffers from chronic frustration of a cherished aim. Every time we play he proposes that the dealer should ante for everyone to obviate the tiresome business of counting the kitty and exchanging charges and counter-charges about whose ante is missing. Although most of us agree that Arthur's plan makes sense, there is something vaguely authoritarian about it that provokes resistance, as if we were holding onto states' rights against any increase in central government. No matter how urgently Arthur returns to the attack, as he does each time we set up a table, we somehow always continue to ante erratically in the old way with all the old disputes as to which of us is light.

I suspect that the reason why the group instinctively closes ranks against both Arthur's and my really very reasonable proposals is because they smack of the dictatorial while the nature of poker is libertarian. I cannot imagine a Nazi or Communist Party member in good standing ever enjoying himself at poker; it is too fluid and flexible. Unable to obey or lay down a law, he would soon become desperately uneasy and end up screaming.

To return to the question of why some men will not play poker with women. Is it because we are less scientific and, by not paying attention to the odds, thereby upset their calculations? If so, their refusal is a sound defensive instinct which must excite our respect, if also our sorrow. I believe it is probably true that women on the whole are not inclined to discipline their playing according to a scientific law of averages. Speaking only for myself, I find that the incomparable advantage of playing by instinct is that no one has the slightest idea what I am likely to do or why. Neither have I, of course, and the regulars with whom I play realize this but the knowledge is scant help to them. They cannot carry out an artful maneuver—keeping the fifth card, for example, to make two pair look like a pat hand—in a just expectation that I will react with proper respect for the odds. These would require me either to fold or, by staying, to indicate that I have possibilities for a five-card hand that could beat the pat hand. I don't have anything of the kind, as it happens; I have three little threes, but I stay anyway and draw two to them, flouting Hubert's pat hand with unruffled insouciance.

Hubert looks at me speculatively from under a pair of imposing eyebrows. "Now what is that girl up to? Why does she draw two cards against my pat hand? Doesn't she know the odds against improving three of a kind are 15.5 to 1 against a full house and 22.5 to 1 against four of a kind? She must think I'm bluffing, and so I am, but a good raise should knock her out. With only three of us in the pot the amount she could win if she called me wouldn't be worth the amount she would have to put up." Firmly Hubert raises.

But, confuting all his careful reasoning, instead of dropping, I call. I have not, needless to say, the slightest idea what the odds are against filling a full or four of a kind, nor have I paused to consider whether the value of the pot is worth the bet. I call simply because I hold three little threes and I *like* three threes. There is something appealing about them. One would as soon deprive them of their brief moment of life as snuff out a butterfly's single day. Who knows—their fourth little brother just might be waiting there at the top of the pack, on tiptoe, to join them. How mean not to give him his chance. It is this sort of thing that is going through my head while all the scientific players are figuring the odds. So I call his raise, the third player drops, and my three little threes beat Hubert's aces up. My play may not have been the "logical" one called for in that situation, but it has a certain efficacy.

It might be called the Unenlightened or Reverse Self-Interest gambit. In war it frequently operates with disturbing effect. Nothing so discomfits an army launched on a planned offensive than the refusal of the enemy to deploy as expected in his own best interest. The attacking army may find itself in the position of a prizefighter who punches the air and falls over from the force of his unmet blow.

To play poker in obedience to mathematical odds requires one thing often overlooked: a knowledge of, or understanding of, or at the very least a reasonably friendly acquaintance with mathematics. I, for one, lack this altogether. I failed math in college (a required freshman course in those days); I have not been able to help my children with their homework in this subject beyond the third grade; and I have yet to balance a checkbook. To memorize tables of odds, much less to figure in my head the chances of my hand in a given pot, is beyond the most generous stretch of my capacity. I see an image of Messrs. Jacoby, Yardley, Crofton and Steig rise up in accusing phalanx and sneer in chorus, "And *you* presume to play poker!" Well, gentlemen, it *is* possible for a mathematical moron to play poker and, if not to win consistently, at least, over the years, more or less to break even and—what is after all the main object—to enjoy the game.

Let me illustrate. It was possible for me, totally ignorant of military theory, strategy, tactics and weapons when I began, to write a book about war that evoked a letter from a colonel in the United States Army congratulating me on "not having made a single military mistake, not even the layman's usual mistake of mistaking wing with flank." I was particularly pleased by this bouquet because technically I am not sure I could explain the difference between wing and flank, but instinctively I understood it through a feeling for the meaning of words. Likewise I met cryptography head on in my earlier book, *The Zimmermann Telegram*. Only accountants, wizards and mathematical geniuses understand cryptography, in none of which categories I qualify, yet I made no noticeable boners and indeed spent a genial evening after publication as the guest of the New York Cipher Society. The point is, I managed by instinct and by concentrating on the human drama rather than on science, whether of gun calibers or codes and ciphers, so why should I not in poker?

Wars are fought and history made and poker played by individuals, not IBM machines. The big thinkers in the field of history, known to the trade as historiographers, generally fail to notice this because they are too occupied in constructing systems and elaborating cycles into which they can squeeze the past—not to mention the future. When history, never amenable to such treatment, bursts the seams of the systems and pops up in the wrong places, the historiographers hurriedly explain it by the climate. They need not reach so far. It is a matter of people. And people, if one may call to witness Dostoevski, let us say, or Shakespeare or the Book of Genesis, or the person you know best, are likely to be complex. They suffer from ambition, headaches, a sense of inferiority, a sense of humor. They fall in love, they have bad days at the office, they daydream, they compete, they drink, they write poetry, they fight. They cannot be trusted to behave scientifically like bees and ants. Their behavior is said by psychologists to conform to patterns and be predictable—which is what the poker pros say—but if history is any guide, the pattern is never foolproof.

There is always the odd chance, the unexpected friction, the horse-shoe nail, Cleopatra's nose, a prime minister's ulcer, in short the accident that gives a twist to the course of events and causes it to take a direction other than expected.

If cards were dealt to six or seven IBM machines sitting around a poker table, no doubt they would play the odds flawlessly and even, if prompted by the right electrical impulse, exhibit those infallible "give-away" reactions so astutely noticed and described by Mr. Jacoby. He asserts that in stud a player who has a high hole card—ace, king or half of a pair back to back—will invariably place his chips on top of his hole card in an instinctive gesture of concealment. It is all very well to rely on this Jacoby syndrome if one is playing with IBM machines, but in the more customary case of the players being human, there always exists the possibility that a person placing his chips on top of his hole card may simply be moving them away from the wet ring made by his glass of beer. He may be acting, not according to science or the laws of probability, but from that unique, that glorious and special possession of a human being—his private reasons. This eccentric attribute is what makes people more interesting than, say, seventeen-year locusts who unfailingly appear at that predictable if peculiar interval.

It is also what makes poker a game.

THE PROFESSOR'S YARN

FROM *Life on the Mississippi*

BY

MARK TWAIN

Who better to expose the nasty ways of shipboard card hustlers than the master storyteller himself? In his matchless style, Twain brings a wide-eyed innocence to the proceedings—not as participant or victim, but as a wary spectator and humble observer. Twain, who also touched on riverboat card sharps in other writings (*Fables of Man*), doesn't appear too fond of what was back then a wide-open, cutthroat game.

The climax hand, four aces over four kings, would seem obvious, save for the fact that straights and flushes had yet to enter poker play at the time of the author's travels as a young man in the 1860s (the short story was actually written in 1882). The final twist, however, is timeless.

It was in the early days. I was not a college professor then. I was a humble-minded young land surveyor, with the world before me—to survey, in case anybody wanted it done. I had a contract to survey a route for a great mining ditch in California, and I was on my way thither, by sea—a three or four weeks' voyage. There were a good many passengers, but I had very little to say to them; reading and dreaming were my passions, and I avoided conversation in order to indulge these appetites. There were three professional gamblers on board—rough, repulsive fellows. I never had any talk with them, yet I could not help seeing them with some frequency, for they gambled in an upper-deck stateroom every day and night, and in my promenades I often had glimpses of them through their door, which stood a little ajar to let out the surplus tobacco smoke and profanity. They were an evil and hateful presence, but I had to put up with it, of course.

There was one passenger who fell under my eye a good deal, for he seemed determined to be friendly with me, and I could not have gotten rid of him without running some chance of hurting his feelings, and I was far from wishing to do that. Besides, there was something engaging in his countrified simplicity and his beaming good nature. The first time I saw this Mr. John Backus, I guessed, from his clothes and looks, that he was a grazier or farmer from the back woods of some western state—doubtless Ohio—and afterward when he dropped into his personal history and I discovered that he *was* a cattle-raiser from interior Ohio, I was so pleased with my own penetration that I warmed toward him for verifying my instinct.

He got to dropping alongside me every day, after breakfast, to help me make my promenade; and so, in the course of time, his easy-working jaw had told me everything about his business, his prospects, his family, his relatives, his politics—in fact everything that concerned a Backus, living or dead. And meantime I think he had managed to get out of me everything I knew about my trade, my tribe, my purposes, my prospects, and myself. He was a gentle and persuasive genius, and this thing showed it; for I was not given to talking about my matters. I said something about triangulation, once; the stately word pleased his ear; he inquired what it meant; I explained; after that he quietly and inoffensively ignored my name, and always called me Triangle.

What an enthusiast he was in cattle! At the bare name of a bull or a cow, his eye would light and his eloquent tongue would turn itself loose. As long as I would walk and listen, he would walk and talk; he knew all breeds, he loved all breeds, he caressed them all with his affectionate tongue. I tramped along in voiceless misery whilst the cattle question was up; when I could endure it no longer, I used to deftly insert a scientific topic into the conversation; then my eye fired and his faded; my tongue fluttered, his stopped; life was a joy to me, and a sadness to him.

One day he said, a little hesitatingly, and with somewhat of diffidence:

"Triangle, would you mind coming down to my stateroom a minute, and have a little talk on a certain matter?"

I went with him at once. Arrived there, he put his head out, glanced up and down the saloon warily, then closed the door and locked it. We sat down on the sofa, and he said:

"I'm a-going to make a little proposition to you, and if it strikes you favorable, it'll be a middling good thing for both of us. You ain't a-going out to Californy for fun, nuther am I—it's *business*, ain't that so? Well, you can do me a good turn, and so can I you, if we see fit. I've raked and scraped and saved, a considerable many years, and I've got it all here." He unlocked an old hair trunk, tumbled a chaos of shabby clothes aside, and drew a short stout bag into view for a moment, then buried it again and relocked the trunk. Dropping his voice to a cautious low tone, he continued, "She's all there—a round ten thousand dollars in yellow boys; now this is my little idea: What I don't know about raising cattle, ain't worth knowing. There's mints of money in it, in Californy. Well, I know, and you know, that all along a line that's being surveyed, there's little dabs of land that they call 'gores,' that fall to the surveyor free gratis for nothing. All you've got to do, on your side, is to survey in such a way that the 'gores' will fall on good fat land, then you turn 'em over to me, I stock 'em with cattle, *in* rolls the cash, I plank out your share of the dollars regular, right along and—"

I was sorry to wither his blooming enthusiasm, but it could not be helped. I interrupted, and said severely—

"I am not that kind of a surveyor. Let us change the subject, Mr. Backus."

It was pitiful to see his confusion and hear his awkward and shamefaced apologies. I was as much distressed as he was—especially as he seemed so far from having suspected that there was anything improper in his proposition. So I hastened to console him and lead him on to forget his mishap in a conversational orgy about cattle and butchery. We were lying at Acapulco; and as we went on deck, it happened luckily that the crew were just beginning to hoist some beeves aboard in slings. Backus's melancholy vanished instantly, and with it the memory of his late mistake.

"Now only look at that!" cried he; "My goodness, Triangle, what *would* they say to it in *Ohio*? Wouldn't their eyes bug out, to see 'em handled like that?—wouldn't they, though?"

All the passengers were on deck to look—even the gamblers—and Backus knew them all, and had afflicted them all with his pet topic. As I moved away, I saw one of the gamblers approach and accost him; then another of them; then the third. I halted; waited; watched; the conversation continued between the four men; it grew earnest; Backus drew gradually away; the gamblers followed, and kept at his elbow. I was uncomfortable. However, as they passed me presently, I heard Backus say, with a tone of persecuted annoyance:

"But it ain't any use, gentlemen; I tell you again, as I've told you a half dozen times before, I warn't raised to it, and I ain't a-going to resk it."

I felt relieved. "His level head will be his sufficient protection," I said to myself.

During the fortnight's run from Acapulco to San Francisco I several times saw the gamblers talking earnestly with Backus, and once I threw out a gentle warning to him. He chuckled comfortably and said—

"Oh, yes! They tag around me considerable—want me to play a little, just for amusement, they say—but laws-a-me, if my folks have told me once to look out for that sort of livestock, they've told me a thousand times, I reckon."

By and by, in due course, we were approaching San Francisco. It was an ugly black night, with a strong wind blowing, but there was not much sea. I was on deck, alone. Toward ten I started below. A figure issued from the gamblers' den, and disappeared in the darkness. I experienced a shock, for I was sure it was Backus. I flew down the companionway, looked about for him, could not find him, then returned to the deck just in time to catch a glimpse of him as he re-entered that confounded nest of rascality. Had he yielded at last? I feared it. What has he gone below for? His bag of coin? Possibly. I drew near the door, full of bodings. It was a-crack, and I glanced in and saw a sight that made me bitterly wish I had given my attention to saving my poor cattle friend, instead of reading and dreaming my foolish time away. He was gambling. Worse still, he was being plied with champagne, and was already showing some effect from it. He praised the "cider," as he called it, and said now that he had got a taste of it he almost believed he would drink it if it was spirits, it was so good and so ahead of anything he had ever run across before. Surreptitious smiles, at this, passed from one rascal to another, and they filled all the glasses, and whilst Backus honestly drained his to the bottom they pretended to do the same, but threw the wine over their shoulders.

I could not bear the scene, so I wandered forward and tried to interest myself in the sea and the voices of the wind. But no, my uneasy spirit kept dragging me back at quarter-hour intervals; and always I saw Backus drinking his wine—fairly and squarely, and the others throwing theirs away. It was the painfulest night I ever spent.

The only hope I had was that we might reach our anchorage with speed—that would break up the game. I helped the ship along all I could with my prayers. At last we were booming through the Golden Gate, and my pulses leaped for joy. I hurried back to that door and glanced in. Alas, there was small room for hope—Backus's eyes were heavy and bloodshot, his sweaty face was crimson, his speech maudlin and thick, his body swayed drunkenly about with the weaving motion of the ship. He drained another glass to the dregs, whilst the cards were being dealt. He took his hand, glanced at it, and his dull eyes lit up for a moment. The gamblers observed it, and showed their gratification by hardly perceptible signs.

"How many cards?"

"None!" said Backus.

One villain—named Hank Wiley—discarded one card, the others three each. The betting began. Heretofore the bets had been trifling—a dollar or two; but Backus started off with an eagle now, Wiley hesitated a moment, then "saw it" and "went ten dollars better." The other two threw up their hands.

Backus went twenty better. Wiley said—

"I see that, and go you a *hundred* better!" then smiled and reached for the money.

"Let it alone," said Backus, with drunken gravity.

"What! you mean to say you're going to cover it?"

"Cover it? Well I reckon I am—and lay another hundred on top of it, too."

He reached down inside his overcoat and produced the required sum.

"Oh, that's your little game, is it? I see your raise, and raise it five hundred!" said Wiley.

"Five hundred *better*!" said the foolish bull-driver, and pulled out the amount and showered it on the pile. The three conspirators hardly tried to conceal their exultation.

All diplomacy and pretense were dropped now, and the sharp exclamations came thick and fast, and the yellow pyramid grew higher and higher. At last ten thousand dollars lay in view. Wiley cast a bag of coin on the table, and said with mocking gentleness—

"Five thousand dollars better, my friend from the rural districts—what do you say *now*?"

"I *call* you!" said Backus, heaving his golden shot bag on the pile. "What have you got?"

"Four kings, you d—d fool!" and Wiley threw down his cards and surrounded the stakes with his arms.

"Four *aces*, you ass!" thundered Backus, covering his man with a cocked revolver. *"I'm a professional gambler myself, and I've been laying for you duffers all this voyage!"*

Down went the anchor, rumbledy-dum-dum! And the long trip was ended.

Well—well, it is a sad world. One of the three gamblers was

Backus's "pal." It was he that dealt the fateful hands. According to an understanding with the two victims, he was to have given Backus four queens, but alas, he didn't.

A week later, I stumbled upon Backus—arrayed in the height of fashion—in Montgomery Street. He said, cheerily, as we were parting—

"Ah, by the way, you needn't mind about those gores. I don't really know anything about cattle, except what I was able to pick up in a week's apprenticeship over in Jersey just before we sailed. My cattle culture and cattle enthusiasm have served their turn—I shan't need them any more."

POKER NIGHT

BY

JOHN UPDIKE

There are few subjects that the prolific John Updike hasn't touched on. In this story from the 1987 collection *Trust Me*, the narrator is hammered by an ominous doctor's report, allowing him new perspective on his longtime regular poker game. By the author's telling, there *is* such a thing as friendly poker, especially in such darkly introspective moments. "The crazy thought came to me," muses Updike's protagonist between hands, "that people wouldn't mind which it was so much, heaven or hell, as long as their friends went with them."

The plant has been working late, with the retailers hustling to get their inventories up for Christmas even though this is only August, so I grabbed a bite on the way to the doctor's and planned to go straight from there to poker. The wife in fact likes my not coming home now and then; it gives her a chance to skip dinner and give her weight problem a little knock.

The doctor has moved from his old office over on Poplar to one of these new medical centers, located right behind the mall, where for years when I was a kid there was a field where I can remember the Italians growing runner beans on miles and miles of this heavy brown string. The new center is all recessed ceiling lighting and there's wall-to-wall carpet everywhere and Muzak piped into the waiting room, but if you look at their doors you could put a fist through them easily and can hear the other doctors and patients through the walls, everything they say, including the breathing.

What mine said to me wasn't good. In fact, every time I tried to get a better grip on it it seemed to get worse.

He provided a lot of cheerful energetic talk about the treatments they have now, the chemotherapy and then cobalt and even something they can do with platinum, but at my age I've seen enough people die to know there's no real stopping it, just a lot of torment on the way. If it wasn't for company insurance and Medicaid you wonder how many of these expensive hospitals would still be in business.

I said at least I was glad it hadn't been just my imagination. I asked if he thought it could have been anything to do with any of the chemicals they have to use over at the plant, and he said with this prim mouth how he really couldn't venture any opinion about that.

He was thinking lawsuit, but I had been just curious. Me, I've always figured if it isn't going to be one thing it'll be another; in this day and age you can stand out on a street corner waiting for the light to change and inhale enough poison to snuff out a rat.

We made our future appointments and he gave me a wad of prescriptions to get filled. Closing the door, I felt somebody could have put a fist through me pretty easily, too.

But drugstores are bright places, and while waiting I had a Milky Way and leafed through a *People*, and by the time the girl behind the counter had the medicine ready you could tell from her smile and the way the yellow Bic-click stuck out of her smock pocket that nothing too bad was going to happen to me, ever. At least at a certain level of my mind this seemed the case.

Moths were thick as gnats under the streetlights and there was that old sound of summer happiness in the swish of the car tires on sticky tar and the teen-agers inside the cars calling out even to people they didn't know. I got into my own car and after thinking about it drove in the Heights direction to poker.

I wanted to be sharing this with the wife but then they were count-ing on me to be the sixth and a few hours couldn't make much differ-ence. Bad news keeps: isn't that what the old people used to say?

The group has been meeting every other Wednesday for thirty years, with some comings and goings, people moving away and com-ing back. We've even had some deaths, but up to now none of the reg-ulars, just substitutes—brother-in-laws or neighbors called in to round out the table for just that one night.

It was at Bob's tonight. Bob's a framer, in his own shop downtown: it's amazing what those guys get now, maybe forty, fifty bucks for just some little watercolor somebody's aunt did as a hobby, or some kid's high-school diploma.

Jerry does mechanical engineering for an outfit beyond the new mall, Ted's a partner in a downtown fruit store, Greg manages the plumbing business his father founded way back, Rick's a high-school guidance counsellor believe it or not, and Arthur's in sales for Doerner's Paints and Stains. Arthur had to be on the road tonight, which is why they needed me to make six.

It all began when we were newlyweds more or less starting up our families in the neighborhood between Poplar and Forrest, on the side of the avenue away from what used to be the great old Agawam Wall-paper factory, before they broke it up into little commercial rental units. One April night I got this call from Greg, a guy I hardly knew except everybody knew his old man's truck.

I thought Alma would make resistance: both Jimmy and Grace must have been under two at the time and she was still trying to give piano lessons in the evenings. But she said go ahead, I'd been working pretty hard and she thought I could use the relaxation.

Now none of us live in the neighborhood except me and Ted, and he talks about moving to a condo now that the kids are out of the house, except he hates the idea of fighting the traffic into town every day. From where he is now he can walk to the fruit store in a blizzard if he has to, and that crazy Josie of his never did learn how to drive.

For years Arthur has been over on the Heights too, about three of these curving streets away from Bob's place, and Rick is over on the other side of town toward the lake, and Jerry has gone and bought himself some run-down dairy farm south of the mall; he's fixing up the barn as a rental property, doing most of the work himself on weekends. Also over the years there have been a few changes as to wives and business situations.

But the stakes haven't changed, and with inflation and our moving more or less up in the world the dimes and quarters and even the dollar bills look like chips, flipping back and forth. It really *is* pretty much relaxation now, with winning more a matter of feeling good than the actual profit.

I arrived maybe ten minutes late because of the wait in the drugstore. The little paper bags in the pocket rattled when I threw my jacket on the sofa and the sound scraped in my stomach, reminding me.

Did you ever have the strong feeling that something *has* to be a dream, and that tomorrow you'll wake up safe? It used to come to me as a kid, whenever I'd be in real trouble, like the time Lynn Pechilis said she was pregnant or when they caught us stealing the comic books from Woolworth's.

I got a beer and settled in at the table between Ted and Rick. The five faces, all lit up already with beer and the flow of the cards, looked like balloons, bright pink balloons in that overhead light Bob has rigged up in his den, a naked 100-watt bulb on an extension cord propped up there among the exposed two-by-eights.

He's been working on his den for years, bringing the ceiling down and the walls in for better insulation. But the framing business keeps him downtown Saturdays as well as evenings, and the plasterboard sheets and lumber and rolls of insulation have been leaning around so long in this den it always gives us something to rib him about.

I thought, *I'll never see this room finished*. The thought hit me like lead in the gut; but I figured if I sat perfectly quiet and drank the first beer fast the balloons of their faces would slowly take me up with them, to where I could forget my insides.

And it worked, pretty well. The cards began to come to me, under the naked bulb, the aces and deuces and the queens with their beautiful cold faces, and I really only made two mistakes that night.

The one was, I hung on with two pair, jacks and eights, all the way into the dollar-raise stage of a game of seven-card high-low when Jerry had four cards of a straight showing and only two of the nines, the card he needed, were accounted for. But I figured he would *have* to bet as if he had it whether he did or not; as it turned out, he *did* have it, and I wasn't even second best, since Greg had been sitting there sand-bagging with three kings.

The other was, in the last round, when what with the beer the pots really build, I folded a little full house, fives and treys, in a game of Twin Beds, because so many pairs were already out there on the board I figured somebody had to have me beat. I was wrong: Rick won it with an ace-high heart flush.

Can you imagine, winning Twin Beds with a flush? It's in my character to feel worse about folding a winner than betting a loser; it seems less of a sin against God or Nature or whatever.

Maybe my concentration was off; it did seem silly, at moments, sitting here with these beered-up guys (it gets pretty loud toward the end) playing a game like kids killing a rainy Sunday afternoon when I'd just been told my number was up. The cards at these moments when I thought about it seemed incredibly thin: a kind of silver foil beaten to just enough of a thickness to hide the numb reality that was under everything.

My cards as it happened were generally pretty dull, so I had time to look around. The guys' faces looked like pink balloons but their hands as they reached on the table were another story altogether: they were old guys' hands, withered long wrinkled white claws with spots and gray hair and stand-up veins.

We had grown old together. We were all drawing near to death, and I guess that was the comfort of it, the rising up with them.

Ted spilled his beer as he tends to do as the evening wears on, reaching for some cards or the popcorn basket or his bifocals (it's an awkward length: you can see your own cards fine with the short vision but the cards in the middle tend to blur, and vice versa) and everybody howled and kidded him as they always do, and my throat began to go rough, they were all so damn sweet, and I'd known them so damn long, without ever saying much of anything except this clowning around and whose deal was it; maybe that was the sweetness. Their faces blurred and came up in starry points like that out-of-focus thing they do with television cameras now—the false teeth and glasses and the shiny high foreheads where hair had been—and the crazy thought came to me that people wouldn't mind which it was so much, heaven or hell, as long as their friends went with them.

Ted has these slightly swollen-looking hands, nicked around the fingers and fat at the sides of the palms, from handling the crates I suppose, and you would think, deft as he must have to be every day in the fruit store, picking out plums and tomatoes for the lady customers, he would be the last one of us to be knocking his beer glass over. But he's always the one, just like Rick is the one to hang in there with junk and Jerry the one to catch that one card in the deck he needs.

I wound up about five dollars down. If I'd had the guts to stay with that little full house I might have been five dollars ahead.

I put on my jacket and the rustling in the pocket reminded me of the prescriptions and the doctor. Woolworth's didn't prosecute, and it turned out Lynn just wanted to give me a scare.

The wife wasn't up. I didn't expect her to be, at quarter to twelve.

But she wasn't asleep, either. She asked me from the bed in the dark how I did.

I said I broke about even. She asked me what the doctor had said.

I asked her if she'd like to come down to the kitchen and talk. I don't know exactly why I didn't want anything said in the bedroom, but I didn't.

She said she'd love to, she had skipped dinner tonight and was starving. There was some leftover lasagna in the fridge she could warm in the microwave in a minute; she'd been lying there in the dark thinking about it.

Alma isn't fat exactly; solid is more how I think of it. When you're with her in bed, you can feel she still has a waist.

We went downstairs and turned on the light and she in her bathrobe heated the Pyrex dish half full of lasagna and I thought about one more beer and decided against it. Then the lasagna was so hot—amazing, how those microwaves do it; from the inside out, they say, vibrating the molecules—I went and got the beer just to soothe my mouth.

I told her everything as much like the doctor had told me as I could. His exact words, his tone of voice as if it wasn't him saying this but a kind of pre-recorded announcement; the look of the recessed lights about his examining table and his steel desk and of his fake hardboard wood-grained wainscoting all revived in me as if I'd just come from there, as if I hadn't been to poker at all.

Alma did and said all the right things, of course. She cried but not so much I'd panic and came up with a lot of sensible talk about second opinions and mysterious remissions and modern medicine and how we'd take it a day at a time and had to have faith.

But she wasn't me. I was me.

While we were talking across the kitchen table there was a barrier suddenly that I was on one side of and she was on the other, over-weight and over fifty as she was, a middle-aged tired woman up after midnight in a powder-blue bathrobe but with these terribly alive dark eyes, suddenly. I had handed her this terrible edge.

You could see it in her face, her mind working. She was considering what she had been dealt; she was thinking how to play her cards.

FROM

POKER, HOW TO PLAY IT

BY

CHARLES WELSH

Anthony Holden unearthed the following epigraph (from an 1882 text) while thumbing through odd poker books at the U.S. Card Company Museum in Cincinnati. As Holden (a Shakespearean scholar as well as a pokerist) wrote in *Big Deal*, "the pained parody of Hamlet's famous dilemma capped all my efforts to drag the Bard to the green baize." Once again, with all due apologies to the Bard:

> *To draw or not to draw, that is the question.*
> *Whether 'tis safer in the player to take*
> *The awful risk of skinning for a straight,*
> *Or, standing pat, to raise 'em all the limit,*
> *And thus, by bluffing, get it. To draw—to skin*
> *No more—and by that skin to get a full*
> *Or two pair, the fattest bouncin' kings*
> *That luck is heir to— 'tis a consummation*
> *Devoutly to be wished. To draw, to skin:*
> *To skin! perchance to bust—aye, there's the rub!*
> *For what in that draw of three cards may come,*
> *When we have shuffled off this uncertain pack,*
> *Must give us pause. There's the respect*
> *Which makes a calamity of a bobtailed flush;*

For who would bear the overwhelming blind,
The reckless straddle, the wait on the edge,
The insolence of pat hands, and the lifts
That the patient of the bluffer takes,
When he himself might be much better off
By simply passing? Who would trays uphold,
And go out on a small progressive raise,
But that the dread of something after call,
The undiscovered ace-full, to whose strength
Such hands must bow, puzzles the will
And makes us rather keep the chips we have
Than be curious about hands we know not of!
Thus bluffing doth make cowards of us all,
And thus the native hue of a four-heart flush
Is sickled o'er with some dark and cussed club,
And speculators in a jack-pot's wealth,
With this regard, their interests turn awry,
And lose the right to open.

FROM

THE EDUCATION OF A POKER PLAYER

BY

HERBERT O. YARDLEY

Ever since it was first published in 1957, Yardley's classic has endured as a bible of instructional texts. The author, a cryptographer and spy, wrote the book in the form of remembrances from his Midwestern adolescence and later travels abroad—all interspersed with technical poker advice drawn from experience. The lessons are at times tryingly conservative; the tales from a poker youth well spent (under the predatory tutelage of Monty the local poker king) are sheer delights.

Upon first reading Yardley in the late '50s, A. Alvarez wrote (in his introduction to *The Biggest Game in Town*): "It was the beginning of my real education and I sometimes wonder if that was what Yardley, too, was implying in his title. In the end, what he is describing is not so much a game of cards as a style of life."

I was eating prairie chicken at ten cents a chicken at Monty's bar when Jack came in to tell me that he wanted relief and that he had left a vacant seat.

"Is Monty playing?"

"Yes. It's eight o'clock now. I'll be back at 2 A.M."

I went in and sat down in the chair vacated by Jack. There were two new faces. I had seen the two hanging around the tent show where they featured such plays as *Ten Nights in a Barroom, Uncle Tom's Cabin, Dr. Jekyll and Mr. Hyde,* and the like.

"Kid, you know Tom Lawrence and Pete Hunter, leading man and producer," Monty said with a sweep of his hand.

I nodded the introduction. The handsome chap sitting at Monty's left I judged to be the leading man; the other, sitting next to the actor, looked for all the world like a producer. He was chewing at a dry cigar and he grinned constantly, showing yellow teeth filled with gold inlays which glistened in the lamplight.

I sat next, then Chic the chicken picker, Doc and then Bones Alverson, the farmer, his leatherlike face beaten from exposure. I knew he had lost most of his farm at poker. Rumor had it that he had hocked everything to Bert Willis, the land speculator, known to be a ruthless and shrewd operator.

I turned to Chic. He had several stacks in front of him. "You must have sold some more dead chickens," I said in a low voice. Chic was a notoriously poor poker player and when he wasn't taking live chickens to New York he picked them dry at the poultry house for three cents a head.

He gave me a sour look. "Keep your mouth shut, you little shrimp," he warned.

The game progressed as usual—some winning, some losing. I was trying to remember all that Monty had told me, and played carefully.

Monty looked bored. Doc Prittle nodded in his seat between deals, his head resting on his double chin. Bones Alverson was getting some good hands and was winning consistently. The actor and his backer seemed alert and were holding their own.

The game droned on. I got up and stretched my legs to relieve my nervousness. I don't know what it was but I had a feeling of impending tragedy. And it wasn't long in coming.

Doc Prittle was fumbling with the deck. He had put in the joker preparatory to dealing deuces wild and was awkwardly reshuffling the cards.

Monty watched him in disgust. "Deal, goddammit, Doc."

Startled, Doc yelled back, "Hold your horses," then, after taking his time, began to deal five-card draw deuces wild.

Bones, the farmer, skinned back his cards in his gnarled hands. I imagined I saw a flicker in his eyes. Anyway he made an unusual opening bet. He bet $50 right under the gun.

Monty, sitting next, studied Bones for a fleeting moment, then folded. He later told me he held a jack full.

The actor tossed his hand in the discards in disgust.

But his producer was grinning impishly. "I raise one hundred," he said and tossed in the chips.

I threw my hand in the discards, as did also Chic and Doc, the dealer. Looks like those two had all the wild cards, I reflected.

Bones pretended to study a moment, then counted out a big stack of chips, for he had been winning. "I up you five hundred," he said, his voice quivering.

Bones had a mouthful of tobacco juice and was watching the producer intently. I could see he was afraid to turn his head to spit. He made the motion to do so, but changed his mind and swallowed tobacco cud, juice and all. He choked a bit, and pulled out a red handkerchief and wiped his mouth.

Monty, seeing the play, cried the usual "I'll be a son-of-a-bitch."

Bones choked again. "Well," he said to the grinning producer, "what the hell are you going to do?"

The producer took out a sheaf of hundred-dollar bills. "I'm just going to raise you five hundred."

"Raise you five hundred more," Bones quivered, "you city prick." He turned to Monty. "Put in one thousand, Monty," he said. Monty demurred. "You've never seen me welch on a bet," Bones pleaded.

"No, I never did," said Monty thoughtfully. "But you used to have a farm. Do you have one now?"

"I'll tell you the God's own truth, Monty," he said. "I've got the farm, stock and implements plastered to Bert Wills for fifteen thousand. Bert offered me twenty thousand. So I have five thousand equity."

Monty shook his head sadly. "Bones, let me give you some friendly advice. Just call him. I'll lend you money for that."

"Call, hell!" exclaimed Bones. "This is a chance of a lifetime. Loan me the thousand. I want to raise the bastard."

"I can't understand you, Bones. You've lost three-fourths of your farm and now you want to bet the last fourth."

"Goddammit, yes. I might just as well be broke as to try to pay ten percent interest on fifteen thousand to that goddamned blood-sucker."

"Jesus," said Monty, "I don't mind risking the thousand but—"

"You ain't risking nothing, goddammit. I've got him beat."

"All right. But just give me first chance to buy the farm if you do lose." Monty tossed two five-hundred-dollar bills in the pot and took Bones's IOU.

The producer had lost his grin. Even the unlighted cigar had disappeared somehow. He reached for his purse and spread five hundred-dollar bills and pushed them in the pot.

He said in a subdued voice, "There's my five hundred and I raise two thousand. I'll have to give you an IOU."

"You will in a pig's ass. Go get it."

"How can I? The banks are closed."

"You ain't got no two thousand in the bank. Put up or shut up," said Bones.

"Monty, will you take my IOU?" asked the producer.

"Let me tell you bastards something," Monty replied. "I'm not financing this poker game. I'm just playing in it. If I'd wanted to stay I'd have stayed and financed myself if I got in trouble. And another thing. You bastards slow up a game. I only get fifty cents cut. This one I should cut five hundred."

No one offered to agree to this but I had a sneaking feeling that Monty was going to profit in this transaction somehow.

The producer placed some chips on his cards resting on the table and got up and pulled along the actor with him. They went in the other end of the room and I couldn't hear what they said, but the actor was protesting and the producer was really telling it to him. Finally, they both sat down.

The producer addressed Monty. "You know my reputation. You

know I own three other tent shows and I can tell you I don't owe a dime on them. My leading man here owns one-third of this show. I'd like to own that farm even if it is mortgaged."

"Well," said Monty, "what's your proposition?"

"This farmer gave you an IOU for one thousand. Put it in the pot and take out one thousand in cash. That makes you square. I'll make out a bill of sale for my show for two thousand, if this farmer will make out a bill of sale for his farm for three thousand. The extra thousand covers the money you take from the pot."

"Bones, do you understand the deal?" asked Monty.

"Is the show worth two thousand?"

"I'd like to own it for that."

"But I'm pledging three thousand and my equity is five thousand."

"You'll get the difference if you lose."

"Goddammit, I'm not going to lose. I'd like to own a show. More money in it than following a plow around a field, I reckon."

"It's your funeral," said Monty prophetically, and directed Runt to bring in bills of sale, pen and ink. When Monty looked over the papers he pointed out that the producer's bill of sale needed the actor's signature because of a one-third interest. He put Bones's IOU in the pot and took out a thousand according to the agreement.

"Just a minute, Monty. I didn't pledge my prize bull. Nobody's going to plaster him with a mortgage."

"He'll get plastered if you fill your hand." Monty laughed. "How many cards you want, Bones? You take cards first."

"I want one," Bones said and tossed his discard toward Doc.

Doc was so nervous he could scarcely get a card off the top of the deck. Monty didn't help much by yelling at him. Doc finally flicked a card face down toward Bones. It touched Bones's hand, bounced; then turned over, exposed. I looked at it horror-stricken, for I had said a little prayer for Bones.

It was the joker.

"I'm sorry, Bones," said Doc.

Bones opened his mouth as if to protest, but no sound came. He just sat there fascinated and stared at the joker who, I thought, stared impishly back at him. Then a deep pallor began to creep slowly over Bones's weather-beaten face.

"What'll I do, Monty? Can't Bones take the joker?"

"No. If you'd read the rules you'd know he can't. They're all printed and framed on the wall behind you. You deal whatever cards the producer wants to him, then Bones gets the next card. Tough luck, Bones."

The pallor had spread over Bones's face. His eyes looked glazed. Suddenly he fell over the table, clutching the cards in his heavy fist.

At this Doc jumped up, handing me the deck. He examined Bones for several seconds. At last he said, "He's dead, boys."

An air of disbelief settled over the players. Even Monty was speechless for the moment, then, "You're sure, Doc?" he asked.

"Yes, I'm sure. His heart stopped. Too much excitement. I guess I killed him."

The producer made a pass at the pot, starting to rake it in. Monty's fist reached out and nearly broke the showman's wrist. "Hands off!" Monty snarled.

"It's mine," protested the producer.

"Not yet, my friend," Monty said softly. "I think he had you beat. He didn't need the joker."

"Well, I don't think so, and I demand to draw my hand," said the producer.

"Kid," asked Monty, "has the deck been disturbed?"

"No. Doc handed it to me."

"Well, I'm going to write a new rule that Hoyle didn't cover. If you fellows agree, I'll rule we let our producer draw to his hand, then take Bones's cards from his fist and add the next card to it." They all nodded agreement except for the producer, who protested feebly.

"How many cards you want?" asked Monty.

"One," said the producer.

"Kid, give him a card."

The producer threw me the discard and I gave him one, face down.

By that time Doc had pried Bones's cards from his huge fist, so I slipped Doc a card to fill out the hand.

"Now wait a minute, boys," said Monty. "Who wants to bet on the winning hand?"

The actor was the only one to answer. "I've got five hundred that says my producer wins."

"Covered," said Monty, tossing the money on the table. The producer spread his hand. He held Q K K K 2. "Four kings," said Monty.

Doc turned over Bones's cards one at a time, calling them out as he did so. "Ace, ace, ace, jack, deuce—four aces."

"You ran second," Monty said to the producer. "That's irony for you. A man dies holding the wining hand—" and he picked up the actor's bet. Then he began to rake in the pot. "I'll take this to Bones's widow. She'll probably grieve a couple of days, then be relieved that he's dead. At least he can't gamble the farm away now."

The producer said, "I'll redeem that bill of sale, Monty, when the banks open."

"You will like hell," said Monty. "I'll redeem it myself if the widow consents. I've always wanted to go in show business."

PERMISSIONS